MISTER

For Bob Brandt

A brief glimpse of
historic times and how they
affected our lives.

With Best Wishes.

Eugene Fletcher

MISTER

The Training of an Aviation Cadet in World War II

Eugene Fletcher

Foreword by Robert S. Johnson

UNIVERSITY OF WASHINGTON PRESS

Seattle and London

Library of Congress Cataloging-in-Publication Data
Fletcher, Eugene.
    Mister : the training of an aviation cadet in World War II /
Eugene Fletcher.
        p.   cm.
    ISBN 0-295-97181-9 (alk. paper)
    1. World War, 1939-1945—Aerial operations, American.   2. World War,
1939–1945—Personal narratives, American.   3. Air pilots, Military—
Training of—United States—History.   4. Flight training—United States—
History.   5. Fletcher, Eugene.   I. Title.
D790.F55   1992
940.54'4973—dc20   91-46781
                                                                                        CIP

The paper used in this publication meets the minimum requirements of
American National Standard for Information Sciences—Permanence of Paper
for Printed Library Materials, ANSI Z39.48-1984.

I respectfully dedicate this book to all the fine young men and women who have aspired, and will aspire, to soar as eagles, and especially to those who heeded the call of our nation's military to become aviation cadets. Whether fate willed you to become navigators, bombardiers, pilots, or aircrew members, this is a portion of your story.

In order to preserve a small but specific segment of our nation's history **Mister** *is written for David, Gary, James, and Sherry Lee.*

Contents

Foreword

Mister by Eugene Fletcher stirs up many memories—rough but fond memories of growing up in the depression days of the 1930s—jobs at $4.00 per week—the overrunning of Europe by Hitler's Germany—the breaking up of the football team as we went into the Army, Navy, Air Corps, and Marines—early marriages without thought, or doubt, about the future.

As individuals, we reflected all the indecisions, the complacencies even, of a nation reluctant to go to war. Reluctant, that is, until Pearl Harbor jolted us right into the middle of World War II. In this vigorous recounting of his cadet experience, in training to become an Army pilot, Fletcher captures singular voices and telling details. He brings to life a pivotal moment in American history.

Cadet training was right on target. There was no lack of grit and courage—that was a given. What we acquired were focus, skill, discipline, and resoluteness—honed through relentless hazing, toughened through basic and advanced training—creating the teamwork necessary for actual combat missions.

Fletcher takes us there from day one. His account is authentic and accurate. Arriving in civilian clothes at their first base, his reporting class had no idea that the caustic barrage—the belted commands: *Hit a brace, mister!*—were but the sniffles of a minor cold. Ahead lay a regular plague of hazing—chills and fever, flu and pneumonia!

Hazing during pre-flight training was delivered by the newly commissioned second lieutenants. Believe me, there was no ogre worse! In primary and basic, the upper classmen outdid one another in ways to degrade a person. In advanced flight training, hazing was still a threat, but it dropped off considerably as the upper classmen concentrated their efforts on winning those silver wings. Its point, of course, was to ensure battle-ready discipline— unquestioning, unquitting.

Fletcher tells of the many courses in preparation for combat flying. Instructors were both civilian and military, each dedicated to imparting knowledge essential to survival. They knew their subjects, and they knew how to cram a lot of information into a minimum of time.

Like Fletcher, I had previous flight experience and my private license. Unlike Fletcher, I flew the open cockpit PT-18 Stearmans in primary training at Sikeston, Missouri, in 20-degree December weather. At Randolph Field for basic training we flew night and day, formation, short cross-country, and instrument flights in the BT-9. At Kelly Field for advanced training we were assigned the AT-6 and the BC-1.

Finally, upon graduation, we received our wings. Although we had flown only single-engine aircraft, we had completed our training as bomber pilots. We were told to request where we would like to be stationed. I requested: first, the A-20 attack bomber at Oklahoma City; second, the A-20 school at Seattle, Washington; and third, A-20 flight training at Orlando, Florida. I received orders to report to the 56th Fighter Group at Bridgeport, Connecticut, to fly the Thunderbolt, the new P-47 fighter.

That's the military way. Hurry up and wait! Spin your wheels until they need bodies, and *then* you know. Fletcher does an excellent job of conveying the frustrations and quandaries of training and assignment as well as the indomitable spirit of flyers whose sights were set on being part of an Allied victory.

Rivalry existed among all pilots, especially between fighter and bomber pilots. This rivalry extended as we progressed to the combat theater, but on mission day it ceased to exist. A comradeship was forged as the "little friends," flying cover over the bomber stream, rallied to protect and escort home the crippled "big friends."

As we performed in the various theaters of World War II, in diverse aircraft and on multiple missions, the cadet experience was a vital link among us, a common bond. Fletcher recaptures those years of remarkable happiness, disappointment, courage—and the humor that sustained us all. *Mister* delivers a fitting and memorable salute to the cadets—a group of proud, eager, and determined young men. And, as a cadet of that period, I would say, in a loud and clear voice:

Aviation Cadet
Robert S. Johnson,
0661217, SIR!

[Publisher's note: Colonel Robert S. Johnson was the first American ace to exceed Eddie Rickenbacker's World War I record of twenty-six victories. When Johnson returned from the European Theater in 1944, he was the highest-scoring American ace of World War II, with twenty-eight confirmed aerial victories against the fighter pilots of the Luftwaffe.]

Author's Note

It is now June 1991. The undulating hills are green with the young growing wheat plants while the cattle patiently graze under the trees in the valley below. The tranquil sky overhead is a brilliant blue broken only by an occasional hawk or crow riding the thermals while watching the ground for prey.

Many years ago, as a boy, I watched this same picture unfold. One might have the impression that this pastoral, pacific scene had always been my way of life. But, like many others, I experienced an interruption of several tumultuous years during World War II, the greatest conflict ever waged. This was a war which required a countless number of machines on the ground, in the air, and on the seas. Millions of men and women were needed to build and operate these machines of destruction.

Because of changes in the concepts and the actual weapons of war, never again will we see this tremendous build-up of men and machines or the magnitude of training involved to provide crew members to all branches of the service. I will address, generally, only one phase of this build-up: the training of the aerial crew members needed for the U.S. Army Air Force and, in particular, the pilots needed to man these weapons.

Air power was gaining recognition as a viable weapon in conflict when our country launched a massive crash program to provide the thousands of pilots needed to fill this gap in our nation's human arsenal. This specialized training was not easy nor could it be accomplished in a matter of weeks.

This is the chronological story of the training of one pilot who enlisted as an aviation cadet. All of the incidents are true and I

xiii

hope every cadet, service person, flyer, or reader can identify with some of the occurrences in this story.

Take a glimpse at the end product in the Introduction, then, keeping in mind the ultimate goal, travel with me from beginning to end through the process which molded the bulk of the pilots of the U.S. Army Air Force.

Acknowledgments

I would like to acknowledge and express sincere thanks and gratitude to Professors Maclyn Burg and Tom Pressly of the University of Washington History Department for their critique of the manuscript. May they know that their support and input were truly appreciated. A warm thank you to my good friends Ruth and Louis Kirk for their encouragement and suggestions after reading a very rough composition. And especially to Lane Morgan, who spent many hours skillfully preparing the manuscript for publication, my deep appreciation and heartfelt thanks.

MISTER

Introduction

The B-17 was battered and war weary. The camouflage paint was blistered and peeling, the fuselage and wings held together by an assortment of patches of all shapes and sizes attesting to the accuracy of the German fighters and flak gunners. But the old queen was flying smoothly. The four Wright-Cyclone engines were purring in perfect synchronization, a tribute to the constant loving care she had received from the ground crew who had looked after her since her first combat mission and baptism of fire on March 27, 1944.

It was July 6, and again she was headed for battle against the Third Reich. While four months doesn't seem long, in combat it can be an eternity and, in this case, it would be the midpoint in her lifetime because she would not live to see the end of the year. Nor would the nine-man crew who perished with her on December 16, 1944.

Today she was carrying a new crew who were flying their first mission and who were secretly hoping and trusting that her experience would make up for their own inexperience. She wasn't a pretty sight. Her nose bore the name *Government Issue* and above the name was the ignominious caricature of a brown roll of paper with perforations about every four inches.

Her fuselage bore the large letters "QW" which, to the knowing eye, would identify her as a member of the 412th Squadron. Her high tail fin sported the serial number 297232, indicating the year and contract number under which she had been ordered from the Boeing Aircraft Company in Seattle, Washington. Both her pilot and copilot were also Washingtonians, and one lived only a few miles from where she was built.

Beneath the serial number and near the horizontal stabilizer was the letter "O," again a squadron identifier. Then in between was a huge black "B," indicating she was a part of the Ninety-fifth Bomb Group, superimposed on a white square, which was the emblem of the Third Bomb Division of the Eighth Air Force, stationed in England. Certainly the identifiers were the most noticeable things about the plane at first glance, but upon closer inspection the eleven manned 50-caliber machine guns commanded more respect from the attacking fighters of the Luftwaffe. Loaded in her belly were twelve 500-pound bombs bound for German installations in Abbeville, France.

It was a battle-hardened rule that a new crew would not be given a new airplane. Common knowledge had it that crews were more apt to be lost on their initial mission than at any other time, so it followed that you wouldn't risk a new airplane on a crew that lacked experience. The fact that our vehicle of war was far from new did not register even though we were surrounded by many more efficient aircraft. We would gladly have flown even a bucket of bolts to get this chance to prove our worth and satisfy our curiosity.

The new crew on board was a happy but apprehensive group. We did not know what to expect, but this is what we had been training for and now was the moment of truth. What would actual combat feel like? Would we be able to perform? Would we be scared? What would a battlefield in the sky look like? We did not have any answers. All we had was the exuberance of youth, the confidence of months of training, and a desire to inflict harm on an enemy we had not yet seen.

We had been warned not to underestimate the sheer numbers, zeal, and expertise of the enemy. But listening and doing are two different perspectives and only by doing would the reality be known. We would not have long to wait as the English Channel was disappearing behind us and the land of the enemy lay 21,000 feet below.

Our formation of fifty-four aircraft was well formed into a single combat wing. Ahead and behind us at three-minute intervals were other combat wings proceeding to the targets that had been preassigned. We knew that as we reached the target, each wing would separate into eighteen-ship groups, bomb the targets as individual groups, and then re-form and head for home. We also knew that some would not return, but in our innocence we knew it would be someone else.

Combat was a term which up to now had very little meaning to any of us. It sounded romantic and glamorous. Certainly the uniform of the United States Army Air Force, which we had donned at the beginning of our training, enhanced all of our looks and turned the heads of many of the opposite sex. We were a proud crew who showed little humility, but this was the day of reckoning we had all looked forward to.

I was jolted from my reverie by an announcement from the navigator that we were now approaching the Initial Point, at which separation would take place and the bomb run begin. We were lucky the Luftwaffe had not yet appeared, but the air was filled with our own P-47 escort fighters whose mission was to protect the bombers.

My role in this aerial drama was as first pilot or aircraft commander. This was the crew that I, with the help of many fine instructors, had trained for combat against the Axis Powers.

I looked in the distance as we were turning at the Initial Point and saw the beginning of the enemy resistance. There were a few scattered aerial artillery bursts, probably from 88-millimeter guns poised to defend the target area. Small black mushroom clouds emerged from the ball of fire as the shells exploded in the air.

There was a feeling of relief as the shells burst harmlessly in the air above and below the attacking force. We could certainly survive this type of inaccurate resistance. I smiled behind my oxygen mask as I naively thought this was the best the enemy could muster.

The next four mushroom clouds moved in a little closer. There was no cause for alarm, but a pattern was developing. The guns were firing in batteries of four. As the next bursts appeared it dawned on me that some mushrooms are poisonous and that this might be one of those deadly varieties. In the next instant the whole airplane shook as the concussion waves enveloped us completely and the stench of the black smoke started coming through our masks. Several small holes appeared in the wings and then I heard the gunner call, "Tail gunner to pilot. Tail gunner to pilot. I've just been hit." There was only time to order the waist gunner to check on him when the bombardier called out, "Bombs Away!"

Immediately the radio operator reported that only half of the load had dropped. Six bombs were still hanging in the left-hand racks and the old airplane was still rolling and groaning from the initial impact. Knowing that I was asking her to respond to pressures that exceeded her original design limitations, I jammed the throttles to the fire wall.

The bombardier called again to say the bomb-bay doors would not close. The engineer called with the news that the bomb-bay motor was on fire and endangering the fuel transfer lines. Unless action was taken immediately the plane would blow apart. Was this to be the end of a gallant lady and her crew? Or was this all a nightmare that would go away on wakening?

Until this moment I had never questioned my ability to function as a pilot and crew member, and I certainly wasn't going to begin now. However, I would question my judgment and the decisions that had brought me voluntarily into a situation where we were all looking death in the face.

Where did it all start? It had to have a beginning before it could have an end.

1

Civilian Life

Walla Walla, Washington
June 2, 1942

It was approximately three o'clock in the afternoon. I had just gotten off work as an announcer for the local radio station and had returned home to rest and have dinner before going back to the station at seven-thirty to start the second session of my split shift.

Home was the apartment of my sister and brother-in-law, who had been generous enough to offer help that I might continue a college education which had started in the fall of 1940. The apartment complex was located on Park Street just across the street from the women's dormitory on the Whitman College campus.

I picked up the mail in the foyer and took it up to apartment nine. As I placed the mail on the dining room table I noticed an official-looking postcard bearing my name. It proclaimed to all who wished to read it that my 2-A (student deferment) classification would be changed to 1-A on July 1, 1942, when I would be subject to the draft and immediately inducted in order that my hometown Selective Service board might fill its quota of warm bodies for the month of July. In my own ego I had always known that I was A-1, but a rating of 1-A carried a different, ominous connotation. Though not unexpected since a war was in progress, the notice was still somewhat shocking. It was certainly a time for reflection, a time to review the events that had led to this occasion.

My mind drifted back to relive the events of my boyhood which were indelibly imprinted on my mind: the jobless facing starvation, soup lines, hobos, and extreme poverty everywhere. People would stop at our small family farm, which was off the beaten track from the town of Dayton, and ask to sleep in the barn. They would do any kind of labor for a place to stay and something to eat. These were people who knew my parents and it wasn't easy to say no, so it wasn't said. The length of the stay depended on the season and how close they were to the family. There were times when it was questionable what would be on the table, but our mother always found something. We six children were never at a loss for chores to do as we took care of the livestock, chopped wood, worked in the garden, and helped with field and housework. We weren't taught to work; we just had to.

Many people were hungry, but were too proud to ask for welfare or relief, had there been any available. Pride is a wonderful attribute. As long as you had pride you were a person who could hold your head high, who could accept almost any adverse condition and still prevail. People still cared and looked out for one another as best they could.

During this time we never thought of ourselves as poor; we just didn't have any money and no prospect of getting any. But we managed to get by from day to day.

As I entered high school the country was just starting to recover from the Great Depression. By 1938 and '39 jobs were beginning to open up and the country was starting to move ahead. But most six-day-a-week jobs, with nine- to ten-hour days, still paid under $100 a month, with many falling in the $65 range, and they were hard to come by. It was apparent that a college education would be a great plus. But how did you go to college when there was no money available and government loans were as yet unheard of?

There had to be some way. I dropped out of high school at the end of my sophomore year and went East to take a job as a jockey for a major stable. It was a career that I thought might lead to riches, but in slightly less than two years, after traveling a good portion of the U.S. and riding at America's most prestigious tracks, I returned home with a pocketful of memories and experiences, but no money.

So it was back to school and a chance to dream up new ways of getting a college education. At five feet six and 123 pounds, I had no chance at an athletic scholarship. Scholarships based on grades were few in number and very meager in support even if one could qualify as valedictorian or salutatorian. Since this was also out of my league some other solution would have to be found.

Since I was a little older than my new classmates and through my travels felt a bit more worldly wise, I sought the counsel of the superintendent of schools. He was a very kind man and sympathetic with my desires to try to improve my lot. He impressed upon

As a jockey, Detroit, 1938

me that I was attending a privately endowed public school and the first accredited high school in the state of Washington. He brought out his master's thesis and asked me to read it. The idea was to impress upon me the work and time required to be an achiever. Did I have that kind of dedication? The answer was that I would like to try. He suggested that since I had a reasonably good speaking voice and had appeared in school plays, perhaps I should enter some oratorical contests. This might be one way to grab the brass ring. I took his advice and the end result was that I was offered a partial scholarship and a work grant at a local college.

As I stood there with the draft notice in my hand the irony of my position started to sink in. My mind zeroed in on my senior year in high school as I recalled the title of a speech which I had given to the local Kiwanis Club. And, as a reporter from the local paper reported, "'Preparedness for the Safety of Democracy' was the theme and Eugene dramatically presented the case for cleaning up our internal affairs by revision of our espionage and deportation laws and preparing externally by building up our defense system":

> Through our government we enjoy more liberties than the people of any other nation and as we see bankruptcy, starvation and panic causing the abandonment of democracy in other nations we should take heed of the un-American activities in our own country. The Dies committee has found the existence of 800 un-American organizations and made a thorough study of 150 of these which are operating in the open and taking advantage of the very freedom we have built up by American democracy.
>
> We have but thirty-eight hundredths of one percent of our population protecting over ninety-nine percent, he pointed out, and rank eighteenth as a military power. In case of invasion we couldn't mobilize rapidly enough to stop a second-rate army, he declared, and with our garrisons scattered to the four winds of political expediency we would find ourselves badly handicapped. Our armies lack training in large masses as common in modern war, he stated.
>
> Further difficulties would arise from having to take the entire western fleet to the east coast to protect the heavily concentrated industries there.
>
> Preparedness then, he concluded, would be our best insurance against war and gain the respect of all nations.

The speech was generally well-received as I accepted compliments from many who attended. But later that evening my sister told me that her boss (who managed a well-known chain store) and several others had said that the speech was well presented, but the subject matter was far too mature for a high school senior.

On September 14 of that year (1940), the first peacetime draft was approved by Congress. On December 7, 1941, the Japanese attacked Pearl Harbor, and on December 8, 1941, the United States declared war on Japan. Three days later, December 11, war was declared on Germany and Italy since these two had already declared war against the United States.

Now I stood staring at a notice that I would be a part of this nation's military buildup and a part of the subject matter which two years before was deemed too mature for my consideration. But since I had considered it, I had already set in motion a plan that was supposed to keep me from being drafted and yet allow me to serve my country's needs.

Whitman College, for the past year, had been sponsoring a Civilian Pilot Training (C.P.T.) program in conjunction with the Martin School of Flying. Ground school classes were held in the evening from seven to nine. The college professors volunteered their time and it was not an easy course because the instructors took this job just as seriously as any of the regular courses they taught. The flight training was provided by the Martin School of Flying under contract with the government. We did not receive college credit for this extracurricular activity, but tuition was free and it made it possible to acquire a skill which was in demand by the U.S. Armed Forces.

When I first enrolled in the program I had serious doubts that I could learn to fly. The air seemed to be a hostile and unnatural environment, and my nervousness seemed to cloud the decision-making process. My actions and reactions were too slow for the danger involved. But I was told that this problem affected everyone. Only by spending a lot of time in the air and becoming accustomed to this environment could I feel a part of this medium which seemed so alien.

My first flying instructor was a young man named Fred Campbell, and he could make that Piper J-3 Cub do anything that was in the range of its limited capabilities. After several hours in the air the feeling of insecurity did leave. All of a sudden I felt that I was a part of the airplane and making it do what I wanted it to do instead of riding and reacting to what the plane wanted to do. But then my new confidence was shaken by the fact that every time I set up a landing procedure the instructor would start to holler and jiggle the stick or kick a rudder pedal. I would have to recover from these gyrations in the few seconds before touchdown or else open the throttle, abort the landing, and go around the pattern again and set up a new landing approach. After several hours of these antics and nervous screaming by the instructor, I began thinking about giving up the program.

I finally decided that after my next flight I would sit down with the instructor and discuss dropping out since it was apparent that I was not pleasing him. When I reached the flight line for what I thought to be my last flight, the airplane was just taxiing in from the runway to the parking ramp. I waited at the assigned spot and as the airplane came to a stop the student pilot opened the door and climbed out of the back seat. The Piper J-3 Cub had two seats in tandem in an enclosed cabin. The instructor sat in the front seat with dual controls and instruments while the student sat in the rear seat with only the controls.

The airplane had a very small tail wheel as opposed to the tricy-cle gear of modern airplanes. That meant the student, because he was lower and behind, could only see the back of the instructor while on the ground. Since he couldn't see ahead he couldn't taxi in a straight line. He had to make a series of S-turns, weaving back and forth and looking out the side window to steer clear of any ob-structions or other traffic.

As the previous student climbed out of the airplane with the en-gine still idling, the instructor gruffly shouted above the engine noise for me to get on board. Oh boy, it was obvious he was in a bad mood today. There was no friendly greeting. As soon as I had fastened my safety belt and closed the door he said that we would practice landings and would not leave the traffic pattern, so start taxiing immediately.

While I taxied to the runway he pelted me with an endless bar-rage of questions which required some concentration to answer. Meanwhile, I was also trying to locate other traffic, taxi the plane, and check the instruments. Eventually we reached the end of the runway and started the engine check. Since there were no radios in these planes and no tower for communication you waited at the end of the runway and watched until all was clear, and then taxied onto the runway and started the takeoff roll.

In the initial portion of the roll the student pilot's forward vision was blocked off, so I watched the edge of the runway for directional control. As the throttle was advanced and the speed accelerated the tail rose and I could look over the instructor's shoulder. The in-structor had a rear view mirror located so he could see what I was doing.

On this takeoff we were playing a game of cat and mouse. If I looked over his right shoulder he immediately shifted his body in that direction to block my view. And the same way to the left. At the same time he was critical of everything I was doing. But in spite of all of this, we did get airborne, around the pattern, and back to the final approach.

I had a good approach set up and was over the end of the run-way with about fifty feet of altitude when the instructor kicked full right rudder. Instantly I centered the control and applied full power for a couple of seconds to regain speed and directional control. As I pulled off the power the airplane roughly touched down onto the runway with the instructor still ranting and raving. I thought the landing was a good one in spite of everything that had taken place, but obviously my confidence was shaken as I really didn't know what I was doing wrong. Anyway, it appeared this was a good time to end the venture.

As the plane lost its speed I turned off the end of the runway and onto the taxi strip. The instructor became strangely quiet and motioned for me to head up the taxiway to the other end of the runway. As we were passing the parking area in front of the flight operations buildings he pulled the throttle back to the idle position and jammed on the brakes. The tail jumped about six inches in the air, then banged down on the ground. Immediately the door popped open and the instructor jumped out.

By now I was completely bewildered. He reached back in and fastened his safety belt across the empty seat. Then he said, "Fletcher, some day you're going to kill somebody and it's not going to be me. So take off on your own and make three landings." At this announcement I turned off the magneto switch and as the engine sputtered to a stop I crawled out too. "What do you think you're doing?" he growled.

"I've got news for you. If someone is going to be killed it's not going to be me either. I quit."

"Hey," he said, "you've got eight hours dual time, the minimum required for soloing, and you're probably the only student in my group who will solo at eight hours."

"Look, I can't be very good with all this hollering and grabbing the controls on landing. I must be doing something radically wrong; it must be time to stop."

"Fletch, you take this flying too seriously. Loosen up a bit. You've been doing too good a job on landing. I've been kidding you and kicking the airplane around to see how you would react in emergency situations, and frankly, you have come through with flying colors. Now get back in and solo."

I made one more protest and he said, "Come on, this was just a little ritual to keep you from becoming too cocky or overconfident and I wanted to see how you would react to stress. If I didn't think you could do it I wouldn't send you out alone. You don't think I would let you ruin my career and reputation as a flight instructor, do you?"

It seemed to make sense so I crawled into the back seat, fastened the safety belt, and closed the door. The Cub J-3 was always flown solo from the back seat in order to keep the C.G. (center of gravity) within its proper limits. I called, "Throttle cracked—switch on—brakes locked." My heels depressed the two awkward brake pedals, and immediately it was contact as Mr. Campbell swung the prop through and the hot engine sputtered to life. It was a good sound. Fred came around to the side of the airplane and with a big grin on his face gave me the thumbs up sign.

Still a little apprehensive and somewhat bewildered, I eased off the brakes, opened the throttle a little, and the plane began to move almost immediately. I was astonished how much easier it was to see without the instructor and that was a big plus. The engine was noisy and the fabric-covered aircraft vibrated incessantly, but somehow it seemed strangely quiet and maybe just a little lonesome too.

At the end of the runway I checked the magnetos, which supplied electrical current to the spark plugs, not just once as required but several times as I tried to gain confidence. It was November 4, 1941, and a cold day, but there was a drop of sweat on my forehead as I realized it was now or never.

The airspace was clear as I moved onto the runway and slowly but deliberately opened the throttle to its maximum. All sixty-five horses in the little Franklin engine were pulling together and the airplane literally leaped off the runway without the weight of the instructor on board. Before I even had time to miss the instructor's screaming it was time to pull on the carburetor heat as a precaution against icing in the carburetor, which could cut off the flow of air and gas to the engine. Then it dawned on me that in a matter of seconds I was going to have to land this craft by myself! Could I do that? I had better do it or someone was going to get hurt.

I was now passing over the airport boundary, then over the end of the runway. I kept moving the stick back, but the airplane kept floating. Would there be enough runway left? Without the instructor the airplane flew entirely differently. Finally the right wheel and tail wheel touched down—then the left wheel with a rocking motion. The crosswind correction had been kicked out too soon, allowing the left wing to rise slightly. Next time I would hold a little longer.

As the plane continued the roll-out I tried the awkward heel brakes; the airplane was under control and I was ready to try again.

Exhilarated, I felt one with the airplane again, my confidence was running high and with the completion of the third landing my head was in the clouds. I knew then that I had to fly. It would be a long haul to master the art, but I would be a pilot and I would never let another instructor get under my skin again, or so I thought that day.

As I parked the airplane and shut off the mag switch, the instructor opened the door and said, "Congratulations, you've just been initiated into the realm of those who have the flying bug. Now the real work starts." But this time a big grin was on my face.

All too soon primary was over; I had received my private pilot's license. I was now enrolled in a secondary course flying a fully aerobatic light airplane, a bi-wing Meyers with a Warner 125 horsepower engine rigged to supply fuel for inverted flight. My new instructor was Vance Call, a perfectionist in aerobatics. He taught me every aerobatic maneuver he could think of, and it was breathtaking flying in the open cockpit airplane. Helmet, scarf, goggles, and the wind in your face: every pilot's dream. It was sheer pleasure to practice the aerobatic maneuvers: spins, loops, Immelmann turns, chandelles, Cuban eights, snap rolls, slow rolls, falling leaves, and so on. But it was also work as the instructor demanded a high level of competency in precision flying. The ground school continued and the college professors demanded more than just a passing level performance in Civil Air regulations, meteorology, navigation in all its forms, theory of flight, Morse code, map reading, aircraft structures, power plants, and on through the whole range of subjects pertaining to aviation.

With the flying and ground school phases passed with good ratings, I next applied for instructor school. The school was located in Belgrade, Montana, and the graduating instructors went directly to the military primary flight schools to instruct the aviation cadets in their first phase of flying. It too could be a dangerous occupation, but it was something that I wanted to do and it would be my contribution to the war effort.

It was at this point that I stood looking at the 1-A notice and realized that I had not heard from the instructor school. However, I had mailed my application only ten days previously. There appeared to be nothing I could do but wait.

In the meantime I continued with my job as a radio announcer and kept up my flying proficiency by taking anyone for a ride, including my parents, who would pay for the rental of the airplane.

Many of my friends who were thinking of enlisting in the Army Air Force for flight training dropped by and asked me to take them for a ride so they could see if they liked flying.

Almost everyone insisted that he be given the full assortment of maneuvers that could be done in whatever plane we used. With my own experience in mind, I tried to explain that the first ride should be just a level, sight-seeing trip to get acclimated in the air. But most insisted they didn't have that much time and since they were paying the bill they wanted the whole works. Consequently, most became sick and lost interest in flying immediately. It wasn't a fair test and I knew it, although I have noted over the years that my flying seems to have that same effect on other people. Oh well, there wasn't a shortage of volunteers for air cadet training. It sounded glamorous.

By the weekend of June 20 I had received no word on my instructor application. This meant I had ten days left before induction. If I wanted to fly I had to make some decisions in a hurry because only volunteers were allowed into military flight training programs. I could already feel the weight of the backpack and the gun on my shoulder as visions of the infantry and foxholes went flashing through my mind.

On Monday, June 22, I drove to Geiger Field near Spokane, Washington, to enlist in the U.S. Army Air Force as an aviation cadet. One of the requirements at that time was two years of college. After a two-day examination including physical, mental, and psychological tests, I signed a contract specifying that if I successfully completed all of the training phases I would be commissioned a second lieutenant in the regular Army. My orders were to return to my home, which was now listed as Walla Walla, to await orders that would place me on active duty.

While at Geiger I decided to visit my cousin, Hallie Fletcher, whose outfit, the 845 Engineers Aviation Battalion, was temporarily stationed on the base. As I walked through their area looking for his tent, I became the recipient of many hoots, jeers, and catcalls from those in uniform. It seemed they didn't appreciate my civilian clothes. Even the fact that a member of my family was a part of their organization did nothing to mollify their attitude. Little did any of us realize that day that eventually I would fly off an airfield they had constructed.

I returned home the following day and on June 26 received a registered letter of acceptance for instructor training at the Civilian Flying School. The letter contained a notice that if I was now a part of any branch of the armed forces, the letter orders were without effect. The actions of the draft board and the events of the last three days had drastically altered my life. At least the uncertainty of where I would serve was gone: The military took precedence over the instructor school.

From here on I played a waiting game. True to their word the draft board ordered me to report for a preinduction physical on July 9. At this point the Army Air Force intervened by telegram stating that I was already a part of the military system, but the Dayton board could count my enlistment against their quota.

When it was late August and I still hadn't been called to active duty, I managed to talk a very lovely, vivacious young college co-ed, Evelyn (Sherry) Sherrod, into sharing a life with me, in a married status of course. I felt the knot must be tied immediately before either of us could have second thoughts. Because I was almost two months short of my twenty-first birthday it was necessary to have my father's approval in writing, a formality he was very happy to perform. Since active duty orders could arrive at any time we desired to be married that same day, so we had to find a Justice of the Peace who would waive the three-day waiting period. This accomplished, we asked our college Bible class instructor if he would perform the ceremony. So by 11 p.m. on August 25 in the presence of some family members, the ceremony was performed.

I was now a man of the world. I had a wife, a job that paid $80 a month, and a commitment to the Army Air Force. What more could one ask for? After a short honeymoon there were now four occupants in Apartment #9, all gainfully employed.

The vulnerability of our lives was brought to reality on Thanksgiving Day when my brother-in-law, Leonard Patton (Cap), received word that his younger brother, Malvern, was missing in action while flying over the Owen Stanley mountain range in New Guinea. We were in a state of shock since only six months had elapsed after his being drafted into the infantry.

Cap now felt it imperative that he enlist, although as a sole surviving son he could not be compelled to serve. But loyalty to family and the American way of life ran deep in those days. Everyone wanted to preserve this way. Even those who were physically unfit for military duty found ways they could share in this cause. Cap immediately tried to enlist in the Aviation Cadet Corps but was not accepted because of a minor eye problem. However, he was allowed to enlist in a glider training program. He too was ordered to return to Walla Walla to await the starting of his training classes.

With the exception of the family tragedy, life was beautiful for the four of us as we all had jobs and enjoyed one another's company. This happy, tranquil life came to an end on December 31 when I received a "War Department Official Air Mail Special Delivery" letter, short the required amount of postage. Apparently their franking privilege was good only for ordinary mail. It appeared that I was learning one of the first lessons of Army life—nothing is free, not even the orders to report to the recruiting station in Portland, Oregon, on Monday, January 4, 1943.

2

Preflight

Santa Ana, California

I checked into the Portland Hotel early Monday morning; the room rent was $3.50 per night and ham and eggs in the dining room $1.10. I had already spent $1.40 on taxi fare to get one-quarter mile from the train station to the hotel. At these prices I knew I had to get out of Portland quickly because I was already running over budget.

Fifty cadets reported in and when all were assembled we were given some more tests, a minor physical exam, and checked for any changes in status since our time of enlistment. In my case the only change was my marital status. It was deemed that the state of matrimony had not yet damaged my physical being so I was proclaimed fit to travel with the rest of the group by train on January 5 to the Army Air Force Classification Center at Santa Ana, California. The center was called the West Coast's "Little West Point," but any comparison to the Army's elite academy was certainly the figment of someone's warped imagination.

We arrived late in the evening on January 7. The center was a huge sprawling army air base and headquarters for the Army Air Force West Coast Training Command. It was estimated that 20,000 men were stationed here. This base combined the roles of reception center, classification center, and preflight training school for navigators, bombardiers, and pilots.

We were all overwhelmed with the size of the training facility. Everywhere you looked were two-story wooden barracks which served as housing for the cadets. There were countless other buildings whose purposes were not yet known to us. The whole base had a bleak appearance as there wasn't any grass to be seen. The area between the buildings looked like a well-pounded barnyard, but there was a huge hard-packed parade ground, larger than the south forty on many farms.

We appeared to be the only souls in civilian clothes and we certainly looked and felt out of place. In fact, we endured a few jeers and catcalls from several cadets as they sang out, "You'll be sorry." We were assigned to a holding area for the rest of the night and were told that our processing would begin the following morning.

On the morning of the eighth we were taken to a special mess hall for breakfast. We were told that we were assigned to Squadron 8 and were now in quarantine. We would be isolated for two weeks and if after that period no one had come down with a communicable disease we would be allowed to use the post exchange and other base facilities.

It was now time to receive our clothing issue and bunk assignments. Then we would assemble in uniform in front of the barracks for our official welcome from the squadron commander. Our clothing issue consisted of six pairs of olive drab (O.D.) boxer shorts and T-shirts, eleven pairs of socks, two ties, six pairs of pants, one blouse, one overcoat, one raincoat, two pairs of shoes (oxford dress and ankle top for work), six shirts, two zoot suits, one belt, four garrison caps, one service cap, several towels, a shaving kit, bedding, and other items which the military deemed necessary to our station in life.

This was more clothes than I had had at any one time in my life. Our civilian clothes were bundled up and sent home, for we would now wear a military uniform for the duration of the war. The zoot suits were really olive drab coveralls, which when issued were several sizes too large but once washed were always too small. They didn't look much like the wide-brimmed hat, broad-shouldered long coat, and key chain that inspired the name, but we felt just as ridiculous wearing them.

When it came time to assemble we stood around in front of the barracks like a band of sheep in our new uniforms. Some had perfect fits; those of us who needed alterations had to pay for them out of our own pockets. A sergeant arrived and tried desperately to get us into some semblance of formation. He was still working with us when a second lieutenant appeared and informed us that he was our squadron commander and couldn't understand why he had been chosen to receive the likes of us.

He said we weren't soldiers and it was against regulations to

Open ranks inspection

call us soldiers. We were officer material and would be spoken or referred to as *Mister* (usually in a very scornful and degrading manner). The commander impressed upon us that we were the lowest form of life standing on the earth. If we found anything lower it would probably be under a rock. We were not required to salute or to say "Sir" to the enlisted men or they to us. But to be on the safe side we had better say "Sir" or salute anything else that moved, because it would have more status than we did.

Squadron 8 had 240 men divided into four flights—A, B, C, and D—each containing 60 men. Most of us who had come down from Portland found ourselves in Flight D. We did everything by flights and always in formation. All duty details involved the whole flight. We were introduced to the world of the 3 Ws: walk, wait, and worry. In formation it was double time, "hurry up and wait." Any time three or more cadets were walking to the same destination a formation was mandatory. One cadet acted as the leader and the other two or more responded to his commands. If an officer was encountered the leader was the only one to salute. It didn't take us long to realize that being in cadets was the next (best/worst) thing to being in a nut house.

While in Squadron 8 we were introduced to a variety of tests. Although we didn't realize it at the time, this was the beginning of the winnowing process which followed us all through cadet train-

ing. First came the embarrassing physical examination which required the whole flight to line up without a stitch of clothing. Trying to hide behind a clipboard, which held our medical forms, was
next to impossible as the doctors in front paraded up and down
with stethoscopes, tongue depressors, and flashlights. The ones
behind carried rubber gloves, vaseline, and blood pressure cuffs—
each demanding the clipboard to scribble his findings. Bend over,
stand up, say ah-h-h, stand on one leg. It was probably the most
humiliating experience of our lives, but it wasn't the last.

Then came the drawing of blood and vaccinations. Some of the
cadets actually fainted at the thought and sight of needles penetrat-
ing the flesh of those ahead of them in line. For me I thought both
arms would fall off; I had the feeling I had been kicked by a mule.
The following morning I was as sick as I had ever been. I knew I
couldn't function, but I didn't want to go to sick call so I requested
that I be assigned to duty as the barracks fire guard.

Then came the psychological, mental awareness (or ability to
learn), and motor skills tests. The motor skills tests were used to
measure manual dexterity and reaction time. They were fun because it was man against the machine or the mechanical elements,
but the mental tests were a little scary. After all, who wants to tell
some sinister stranger what he sees in ink blobs. How far do you
stretch reality before you fall off the deep end? We all wanted to fly
and we surely didn't want to lose this opportunity just because an
ink blob might look like spilled ink, a naked lady, or some other
screwy imagined image or hallucination. We found ourselves giving answers to questions we didn't even understand. No one knew
how to respond to these strange people or why we had to. It was
probably just as well we didn't know what their conclusions were
because these results would follow us throughout our military career, if we were to have one.

By now we were following a regular routine. We answered a roll
call formation at 5:20 a.m. in front of the barracks. Then we were
dismissed to make our beds, sweep, mop, dust, and shine the barracks for inspection. And I do mean *shine*, for the inspecting officer
always wore white gloves and his hands found every nook and
cranny in the barracks.

The beds were tightly made. The inspecting officer would flip a
quarter on the top blanket and it was supposed to bounce high
enough for him to catch. If not, you were "gigged," given demerits.
If something was wrong in your personal area you received the gig,
but if it was something wrong in the barracks proper everyone was

gigged. Inspections could come at any time, either before or after breakfast.

The barracks were never left unattended; one cadet was designated fire guard and remained in the empty building all day. This was strange because we did not have heat in the barracks, although there was a coal burning stove. Many cadets smoked but they were allowed to smoke only in the barracks. Gallon cans which had previously held canned fruit and vegetables were obtained from the mess halls and placed strategically throughout both floors of the building. The fire guard cleaned these cans, filled them half full of water, and returned them to their assigned places. He also made sure that a five-gallon bucket of sand and fire shovel were placed by the cold stove. He then remained in the building all day to watch for unauthorized entry or to escort the inspecting officer through the building, which occasionally was three or four times a day. The fire guard missed breakfast and lunch, but someone usually stood in for him at dinner time.

Unfortunately, one of our group came down with red measles at the end of the first week and our quarantine was extended for two more weeks. We remained in Squadron 8, which was the classification unit, for three weeks. This ended our twenty-one days in quarantine and coincided with announcing the results of the tests which would tell us whether we became eligible to continue as pilots, navigators, or bombardiers. These flying specialties would lead to commissions in the Army Air Force and all would be equal in pay and rank.

Those who were not chosen but had special educational qualifications could be classified for training as a ground officer in armament, photography, meteorology, engineering, communications, or a host of other specialties. These people would be sent to technical schools outside of our training center. Some who had failed the rigid physical exam for flying but were in otherwise good health could become ground mechanics or serve in some other enlisted capacity.

The permanent personnel of this classification unit from the highest ranking officers to the lowest private were all college graduates, or so we were told. There was supposedly a preponderance of M.A.s and a heavy sprinkling of Ph.D.s. We did not doubt this assessment but we were very curious as to the institutions from which these degrees were earned. But I suspect they also had reservations about us, the safety of democracy, and the United States in general as they surveyed our motley group.

It was with mixed emotions that I waited for the day the results would be announced. I may have been a licensed civilian pilot but I wasn't sure that I would even have a chance to be a military one. The tests and treatment we had received had destroyed the confidence and hopes we all had brought with us. Now it was up to the powers that be to render judgment and point us in the direction that our military careers would lie.

January 23 was a day we could never forget. It was pouring down rain with mud six inches deep and water running freely. At the morning formation it was announced that after breakfast we would receive tetanus, smallpox, and typhoid fever inoculations and before the end of the day we would be classified.

We had already lost several of our group but we were never told why. When the names were posted approximately fifteen were listed as potential navigators, about forty were on the bombardier list, over sixty were washed out, and about one hundred were eligible for pilot training. When I found my name on the pilot list I was so relieved and excited that I ran to a phone booth and spent four dollars on a long distance call so Sherry could share in the good news.

The heavens, as if in sympathy for the cadets who were washed out, retaliated with six inches of rain in twenty-four hours. The base was a sea of mud. The only solid ground was the hardened area of the parade grounds, the outdoor basketball courts, and the streets. The cadets of Squadron 8, already stressed by the quarantine, the events leading up to classification, and knowing we were losing one-fourth of our group were a time bomb ready to explode. The tension was mounting by the hour.

On the afternoon of the twenty-fourth, after returning from a rather torturous session of physical training, clad in T-shirts and shorts, we were dismissed from formation in front of the barracks by our cadet officers. Upon dismissal one cadet slipped and fell in the mud and in one spontaneous instant all of the cadets became embroiled in a pushing, shoving mud-wrestling contest.

There wasn't any animosity, but all the pent-up feelings of frustration were let loose as we pummeled one another and rolled in the mud. The cadet cadre and the more reserved cadets were immediately pounced upon and upended in the quagmire. Two officers in a jeep stopped at the intersection and watched the melee for a few minutes. They apparently had no desire to put a damper on the unseemly conduct for they quickly drove away.

The mud battle continued for about fifteen minutes and then everyone laughingly trooped into the showers and the cleanup began.

Mud fight after a rainstorm

Within thirty minutes the barracks were shining and the cadets were all in Class A uniforms ready for the evening meal formation. At this point two officers entered the barracks and a stand-by inspection was initiated without warning.

A stand-by inspection consists of each cadet standing by his bunk at attention with his footlocker open to view. All personal belongings must be in the proper order, all shoes and brass shined, and all buttons either on the person or on display had better be buttoned.

The inspecting officers left us all standing for five minutes in a brace before starting the inspection. Then they examined the barracks and each cadet with eye-piercing scrutiny. No demerits were given and not a word was uttered as they left; however, they were grinning from ear to ear as they pulled away in their jeep. We heaved a sigh of relief and fell into formation for the march to the mess hall.

The mess halls and their procedures are worthy of note. There were three cadet mess halls on the base. Each mess hall served three breakfasts, three lunches, and three dinners and could seat over 1,000 cadets at a time.

The cadets were seated twelve to a table which was presided over, in the beginning, by an upperclassman. He decided how and

Cadet demonstrating a "brace"

in what manner you would eat, the hazing being limited only by his imagination.

The food was served family style in huge dishes and brought to the table by cadet waiters who each served three tables. The food was not placed on the table until everyone was seated so it was served piping hot. All of the dishes could be refilled with the exception of the meat dish and desserts. Milk, water, and coffee were supplied in pitchers and the waiters ran constantly between the tables and the kitchen keeping up with the demands of the table host, who was the only one allowed to summon him. Eventually, when hazing by upperclassmen was prohibited, each cadet took his turn being the table host and enforced the rule of good table manners.

January 26 our quarantine expired and we were allowed to transfer from the classification squadron to Squadron 16 where we would undergo three weeks of Pre-Preflight training. Squadron 16 was made up entirely of potential pilot trainee cadets.

Moving consisted of placing all our belongings in two barrack bags and walking to our new area. The base was still a sea of mud so it was impossible to set our bags down to rest our arms. Some cadets slipped and fell and all of their belongings were covered with mud. The rain had not let up since it started on the twenty-third and all the surrounding towns and beaches were suffering tremendous property damage, according to the newspaper headlines. But our concerns were limited only to the base where we had firsthand knowledge. By now most of us had severe head colds and bronchitis. We still did not have any heat in the barracks and our clothes and blankets were very damp.

Our squadron was the first to move and we heaved a sigh of relief as we passed the guards leaving the quarantine area. Just as we reached our new squadron area we received word that the classification unit was again sealed off under quarantine as two cases of scarlet fever and several spinal meningitis cases had been diagnosed at sick call. We had beat the quarantine by about ten minutes. We knew the other squadrons would now be delayed at least a month or more, but we weren't entirely free either as we were still restricted to the base. The post exchange and other public facilities were off limits for at least twenty-one days.

As soon as we were settled in our new squadron commander, a second lieutenant, introduced himself and we gathered that he wasn't any happier to have us under his command than we were to have him. He explained that after our partial quarantine was lifted we would be able to use the post exchange twice a week for fifteen minutes, but as a unit only. Eventually we could attend the post theater.

He explained that Pre-Preflight was a time when we would learn basic military training. We would be subjected to rigorous physical fitness training, our barracks were to be kept spotless, and he would personally make men out of us, but he certainly didn't see how any of us could expect to ever be elevated to the rank of commissioned officers. He would do his best but he held little hope for us. We would learn the manual of arms and pull guard duty. We would also learn mess management. As cadets we could not be ordered to do K.P. (Kitchen Police). But if it was called "mess management" we would be privileged to have the same opportunities to wait on tables, wash dishes, and scrub the mess hall floors and garbage cans. He felt that was enough explanation for one day as he did not want to tax our capacity to retain information by overdoing it.

By now we had him pegged as a typical tactical officer. They were called tactical officers not because they exhibited tact but only because they were assigned to carry out a small-scale action which would serve a larger purpose, namely the production of air crew officers for the Army Air Force. These men were known to us as ninety-day wonders. They were sent from civilian life to Officer Candidate School for ninety days and then commissioned second lieutenants. Some of them were so enamored with their position they felt it necessary to make life miserable for everyone else. However, for the time being we would call them "Sir" and bow to their every wish to prove we could take anything they could dish out. We had one purpose in life now and that was to get to flying school and, should we be so lucky as to endure nine months of training, win our wings and receive a commission. These people would be known to us as "ground pounders" or "gravel agitators."

The following day our partial quarantine was lifted. We could now use more of the base facilities. We were notified that it would be two days before our schedule of activities would be posted, so we were kept busy by shoveling in the ditches caused by the heavy rains. We also maintained our calisthenics and drill schedules. Since we had two free evenings, several of the fellows went to one of the post theaters. They reported that it cost fifteen cents to attend the show, which was highway robbery for the type of movie shown.

After a day of filling in ditches and generally cleaning up the area most of us were sick with colds and other ailments and about half of the squadron reported for sick call. Several heavy applications of methyl violet took care of the cases of athlete's foot caused in part by the continuous wearing of wet shoes. Cold medicines were issued, but the real relief came when the medics requested that the barracks be heated. Within hours the stoves were lighted and this gave new meaning to the term "fire guard."

What a relief to have dry clothes and bedding. Our whole outlook on life was changed by this one simple act. It had never occurred to our squadron commanders who had warm offices and quarters that our health was threatened, and they certainly didn't appreciate being told by the medics how to run their squadrons by coddling the cadets.

The schedule was finally posted and we realized we were primarily in a holding pool waiting for an opening in Preflight. A few classes were scheduled which were brush-ups on math and physics. We were assigned work details, guard duty, and mess management in addition to calisthenics and basic military training. Our days began at 5:15 a.m. and ended at 8:00 p.m. with lights out at 10:00. However, we were allowed three hours for our three meals. The exceptions were guard duty and mess management. The whole idea was to keep us busy and uncomfortable. One day we changed uniforms five times just to please the squadron commander, who felt a little harassment would do us good. It did have the effect of solidifying the friendship of the cadets, creating an esprit de corps.

We came to depend on one another and offer encouragement during the rough times. We kept repeating to one another, "Praise the Lord and pass the commission. We will not be driven out. Give us your worst treatment and we will take it." We might not smile, but inside we knew we were better men than our tormentors and someday we would prove it. This gave us all a chance to see the mettle of our classmates and we were rarely disappointed with what we saw. The cadets came from all segments of our society from big city to farm and everything in between. We had students, teachers, and many occupations represented in these cadets. They were a sharp, elite group: the cream of our youthful society. They ranged in age from a high of twenty-seven years to about eighteen. The maximum age at the time of enlistment was twenty-six years. By now the two-year college requirement had been lifted and those right out of high school could qualify on merit tests.

Our cadet officers were either graduates of private military schools or those who had transferred with previous military training. I felt very lucky to be a part of this elite group and I knew pride alone would enable me to do my best to stay with them. By now several cadets had already resigned, stating that if this was what you had to go through to fly, forget it. To me this was the challenge and simply an augmented version of the hazing my primary C.P.T. instructor had given me a year before. Taking and following orders was not new to me since I had stood many times in the paddock area of the major race tracks receiving complete instructions from the owners and trainers on how to ride a particular horse. These directions and orders were given amicably on the basis of mutual respect, but they were followed explicitly since any deviation meant a loss of job. Now the orders were given in a condescending, insulting manner. This only strengthened my resolve: Degrade me all you want, I may be thrown out or washed out but I will never resign. It was a matter of pride. I was soon to realize that this was the prevailing attitude of practically everyone in the squadron. Occasionally we could even laugh at ourselves and poke fun at one another.

At our 5:15 morning roll call we were not required to be in full uniform. This was strictly roll call. As long as our heads and bodies were covered no one cared. After roll call we would immediately return to the barracks to shower, shave, and dress for the breakfast formation. Consequently, at reveille most everyone would jump out of bed, pull on shoes and tie a bow in the laces, grab a cap, wrap his O.D. raincoat around himself, and fall out. The standing joke was that we looked like 180 flashers in flights of 60 each, just waiting for a chance to perform. Luckily there weren't any WAACs (Womens Army Auxiliary Corps) in our area of the base or the Army Air Corps would have lost 180 fine men.

We were now being introduced to a whole new vocabulary on the drill field. We soon learned that FAHOD HOOETCH (FAHOD, the preparatory command, and the command of execution, Hooetch) meant Forward March. HUT HUP HEEP HO was really a marching cadence count of One Two Three Four. ARTHRITE HOOETCH meant Column Right March. BREPP PAW meant Ready Front. This is only a sample of the many varied interpretations of the command as each individual had his own style and was not imitated by the others.

We had burly drill sergeants who dearly loved their jobs and really put us through the paces. All of this was done without a swear word being spoken. In fact, no one in command would have thought of using foul language. Sure, the cadets occasionally used raunchy language in their personal conversations, but these expressions were never used in public formation. According to *The Officers' Guide* a commander was cautioned never to swear at his troops as this would not be tolerated.

We often sang while marching in formation, or at least the others did after they realized I couldn't carry a tune. The command was "Everybody except Fletcher sing out!" The songs were *Dinah, I've Been Working on the Railroad, Count Off One Two Three Four,* and so on. This is quite a contrast to the foul-mouthed Hollywood-movie version of basic training of the 1980s.

But getting back to drill training: The drill sergeants showed us the maneuvers and led us through them, and then our cadet officers took over and drilled us until we could function as a single unit. The drill sergeants would grin or grimace as they observed our antics and offered suggestions as they were needed. But they let us know it was our show; we were the ones who would succeed or fail as they had already made their mark. The more we drilled the better we became and we made up our minds that we would be the best on the base. We were beginning to become a very close-knit, competitive unit.

Our calisthenics or physical training instructors were all either high school coaches or athletes who had been headliners on the sport pages. All were college graduates with postgraduate work in physical education plus extensive professional experience. These people knew how to get the most out of us and yet not endanger our health. They pushed us just a little more each day and when they thought we were ready they ran with us on the obstacle course. We had a lot of respect for these men because they participated in every exercise and challenged us to outdo them whenever we thought we could. At 118 pounds stripped, with strong arms developed from farm work, I could hold my own and excel at pushups and chinups, but when it came to running and many other activities I found myself in the lower echelons.

I had never played in organized sports so I stood in awe as I watched some of our group perform in basketball and baseball. I enjoyed contact sports but usually came out on the short end. However, this didn't dampen my enthusiasm. We left the physical training sessions filled with lots of aches, pains, and bruises but also with the good feeling that we were getting better each day. These instructors with their sense of humor, fair play, and dedication made a big impression on us and we forgave their "ninety-day wonder" status.

On Sunday, January 31, Captain Eddie Rickenbacker, former race-car driver and World War I flying ace credited with twenty-six kills, arrived at the base. His appearance was to coincide with the dedication of Theater 3, the newest and largest on the base. It was also the world premiere for the movie *Air Force*.

The cadets were admitted one thousand at a time with several showings. We were lined up in ranks in front of the theater. When our turn came it was dark, pouring down rain, with 999 voices singing the chorus of *Down by the Old Mill Stream*. Since there weren't any huge searchlights which were usually used in Los Angeles for a world premiere, G.I. trucks lined the streets by the theater with their headlights on bright. It was a poor substitute for the real thing but it added to the atmosphere and showed G.I. ingenuity.

At the conclusion of the movie the guest of honor was introduced. He told of his recent experience of being rescued from a life raft after drifting for twenty-two days in the Pacific Ocean when his observation plane was shot down. He also mentioned that he was envious of us because it would be our good fortune to be the ones to carry the bombs and destruction to Japan. He warned us that it would be our job "to kill, to have no pity, and to do the very best we could while here to learn this business of killing." He predicted the fall of Germany in 1944 and Japan six months to one year later.

It was all very sobering because up to this point we were only interested in flying and had not given any thought to killing anyone. In spite of this, he was given a standing ovation. The Hollywood big shots including the director of the movie and Warner Brothers executives were far overshadowed by the presence of this war hero, but they did receive attention from the newspaper reporters and photographers who were brought along to record this momentous occasion.

The following morning several measles cases were reported. If they were German measles everything would be fine. However, one case of the red variety was reported so we were restricted again for fourteen days. We were never quite able to understand why quarantine restrictions denied us all the privileges and pleasures on the base, including passes, but did not restrict our presence on work details, particularly guard duty or mess management which brought us into contact with other squadrons. Apparently we were contagious only in a social capacity.

On February 1 we were assigned to the mess management detail. We got up at 4:15 a.m., reported at 4:45, and worked until 9:30 p.m. We could volunteer for our choice of jobs: waiters, dishwashers, kitchen helpers, or garbage detail. I chose the garbage detail where there was less supervision. I felt I knew how to scrub a garbage can and did not want to run the risk of spilling a tray of food. Besides, I was running low on clean clothes as most were at the laundry. The garbage detail wore the zoot suit, or fatigues as they were later called.

The mess officer was very pleased with our performance and typed up a letter of commendation for us to give to our squadron commander. When we marched back to the barracks at 9:30 the squadron commander had just completed a tour of the living area and was waiting for us. He was given the letter from the mess officer and he proceeded to read it, with the help of a flashlight, out loud to the assembled detail. He seemed taken aback that we were praised instead of being censured. He took one long look at us and said, "If you're that good you can report for mess management again in the morning."

Our groans were suppressed until he was out of sight. Then some bright soul said, "Look at it this way, it's another day we don't have to work under the supervision of the S.O.B." This seemed to put everything in perspective. We had a good laugh and collapsed in our bunks so we could roll out again at 4:15 a.m.

None of us had any idea how many miles we had walked,

marched, or run during our first month on the base, but on February 5 my G.I. work shoes had to be resoled.

By now our routine day, excepting mess management and guard duty, consisted of two hours of classes, two hours of calisthenics or athletics, four hours marching, and three hours off for breakfast, lunch, and dinner. The rest of the time was spent marching from one place to another and changing uniforms. Our day was seventeen hours long from reveille to lights out. The C.O. said that six hours of sleep was enough for anyone and we were getting seven, but he slept until seven each morning so it didn't bother him. Maybe he was right; people have been known to die in bed and we didn't want that to happen to anyone in our squadron.

When we were assigned guard duty it was for twenty-four hours at a stretch. If we used two details it was four hours on and four hours off, but occasionally we used three details with four hours on and eight hours off. On February 6 we drew guard duty and since our twenty-four hours fell on the weekend we were divided into three details. The first detail started at 6:00 p.m. I was placed in charge of the second detail which started at 10:00 p.m. We were relieved by the third detail at 2:00 a.m. and returned to the barracks at 3:00 a.m. We jumped into bed. Those of us on the second detail of the guard protested about getting up for the 5:15 formation, after only two hours of sleep, since we had to report again at 9:00 a.m. for the rest of our shift. The squadron commander very huffily said we could sleep in till 8:00 a.m., but the barracks had better be ready for inspection before we reported for guard duty at nine. We missed breakfast, but the barracks were shining and we reported to guard duty on time. While we were relaxing before guard assignment, everyone was griping about the harassment we had received from the squadron commander. Since he knew we would be relieved from guard duty again at 2:00 p.m. he had ordered us to report in formation for the full dress parade and review which was held every Sunday at 3:00.

The sergeant of the guard overhead us and immediately disappeared into the captain of the guard's office. We knew we were going to catch the devil for griping in public. In a few minutes a grim-faced captain appeared with the grinning sergeant. We were called to attention and answered roll call. Immediately we were gruffly given the general orders of the day, the password, a lecture about how lucky we were to serve our country and how appreciative we should be of this opportunity to be able to make individual sacrifices of time and energy. After his little speech, which put us in our place, he requested the sergeant of the guard to assign the details and post the guard. He then stormed back into his office leaving a group of bewildered cadets.

After the details were assigned, four of us found ourselves as supernumeraries, which meant we wouldn't be sent out on the first shift but would wait in the guard ready room until we were needed for relief. When the old guard had been relieved and the new guards posted we extras were still lounging in the ready room reading anything we could find.

The sergeant, his duties caught up for the moment, came over to us and whispered that the captain had said that if we were really officer material we had better start reading the cadet manual, especially a certain page, and abide by the manual. He then laid a copy on the table and went about his business. We grabbed the manual and on the page mentioned it stated that a cadet called for guard duty could not be called for any other duty until his twenty-four hours were up. We were to be released at 2:00 p.m. and the parade was at 3:00, but our twenty-four hours would not be up until 6:00 p.m.

As cadets we didn't know how we were going to use this new found knowledge, but our problem was solved when we were dismissed from duty and in formation to be marched back to our barracks. The captain gave me a sealed envelope and requested that it be given to the commander of Squadron 16.

When we reached the barracks area the squadron was forming for the parade. With the guard detail still in formation and at attention, our squadron commander came over and requested that I dismiss the guard detail and fall into parade ranks. I saluted and presented the envelope to the commander. He opened it and his face grew livid as he read that we had performed well on guard duty and should be commended. It also stated that we were not relieved from duty and were to remain on stand-by status until 6:00 p.m., February 7, signed by the captain of the guard.

The 2nd Looey, a typical shavetail, was beside himself with rage and if looks could kill we would have all been dead. He looked at us with scorn and said, *"Misters,* thank your lucky stars that you are being transferred in the morning or I would make life hell for you." We thought he had done pretty well already. "Mister, dismiss your troops and get out of my sight." I was so weak I could barely mumble "dismissed." The mental depression set in as I realized how many more weeks were to come.

We heard that one squadron was summoned for a duty detail where the squadron commander asked all college graduates to step out and line up. Then he called for all who had two or three years of college to step forward. He requested that all the graduates take canvas bags and pick up the papers and cigarette butts in the squadron area. Those with some college time, but without a degree, were to start raking the area. Then he stated that the rest of the dumb clucks could stand around and watch those who were working and learn something.

We knew then that we were not the only ones who were being hazed. We just wished our squadron commander could have had an equally good sense of humor. By now we all had the impression that second lieutenant was a condition, not a rank.

On Monday, February 8, we moved to a new squadron which was just four barracks away. Here we joined another group of cadets to bring our pilot squadron up to a strength of 180 men. We brought our quarantine status with us so, consequently, the others were not overjoyed to see us since they had been released from quarantine only two days before. We had been on the base for a month with only three days out of quarantine. While in quarantine we could not leave the squadron area. This meant we could not go to the cleaners to get our clothes and couldn't go to the P.X. We could leave our barracks area only to go to class, drill, athletics, the mess hall, and work details.

Our moving day is best described by an excerpt from a letter I wrote to Sherry immediately after moving in:

> Today was the day of our big move. This is the last time we will move until Primary Flight School. That is, if I don't wash out in the meantime, which could happen. But I don't think so. Preflight is going to be okay. We now have upperclassmen on the top floor and we neophytes occupy the ground floor. Each of us has been assigned to an upperclassman, consequently we will experience some hazing.
>
> We will do mess management here every eighth day which isn't too bad. There are other work details plus guard duty. But I think we'll have a little time to study for a change, although as soon as we moved in I was appointed fire guard and will remain on duty for twenty-four hours. As fire guard you do not fall out for any formations, although they made an exception and allowed me a chance to pick up my books, sixteen of them in all, even though I will miss the start of our first four classes. We will progress through these books in six or nine weeks, depending on the time we spend here. It hasn't been definitely settled yet, but I expect it will be nine weeks in Preflight. That's all right if it is because after you've

been here so long you don't care when you're leaving or where you're going or what you're doing. It's just the old army spirit beginning to grow on us.

We had a swell day to move. For the past three or four days we've been enjoying California sunshine, then last night it started raining. So this morning we had to move in a sea of mud with more rain coming down and a cold wind blowing just to help matters along. Boy, this is the life. If you don't get the flu and die it will make a man out of you.

We have plenty of pet peeves and gripes too numerous to write about, but when we get together I'll explain army regulations and the reasons for many of them. Oh yes, another thing, our new squadron is also without heat. After everyone recovered from his cold in Squadron 16 heat was again shut off. If we ever feel heat again it will probably be too much for us and make us sick, but we would like to find out.

Classes begin in the morning at eight. This squadron is really on the ball.

While the squadron was in classes, as fire guard I was present for three inspections and watched demerits being handed out rather generously. But luckily my upperclassmate mentor and I were not recipients. Since I had free time I had given extra polish to our respective areas. We were allowed eight demerits per week. If you received more you had to forfeit your weekend pass and march a one-hour tour for every demerit over eight. Anyone receiving a total of over 100 demerits before commissioning would be automatically washed out. These records would follow us all through our cadet career.

After I was relieved from fire guard duty it was too late to participate in the activities of the squadron, which were mainly classes. Since I couldn't check in late I studied in the barracks until 4:30, at which time another cadet, Hunter by name, a former schoolteacher from southern Idaho, came by and suggested we go to the post office to purchase some airmail stamps. All cadets had franking privileges for regular mail, but for faster delivery most of us used the six-cent airmail. We knew if we hurried we would have time to get our stamps and still be back by five o'clock for our formal retreat formation. However, in our hurry we forgot to sign out, a procedure which was required when leaving the wing area.

Upon our return, when we were about four blocks from the barracks, we saw the squadron falling out the front door ten minutes early for the retreat formation. We started running but when we reached the rear door of the barracks the squadron was already in formation and being reviewed by a lieutenant. We couldn't break into the formation late and admit to being AWOL because we hadn't signed out, so we hid inside the back door and listened to roll call. Five cadets failed to answer, including us.

The lieutenant and first sergeant came in the front door looking for the absentees, but they made one mistake. They stopped to look at the sign-out sheet before proceeding into the barracks proper. This gave Hunter and me the opportunity to run out the back door and hide behind some other buildings. The other three cadets, who hadn't seen us, were caught in the stairway leading to the second floor which was occupied by our upperclassmen. They were tried and sentenced on the spot to three hours of marching every Sunday morning for the next three weekends. Since we were now AWOL for sure and didn't want to be caught in the squadron area, we took off for Squadron 16 which was still in the quarantine area. We rationalized the pretext that we would pick up the mail which had been delivered in the last two days for anyone who had mail in Squadron 58. We sorted the mail and picked it up for everyone we knew.

By then we figured it was safe to return to our area, but we also knew we would have to face the squadron commander in the morning to explain our absence. We were hoping to use the excuse that we had gone after the mail but had neglected to sign out. It was a flimsy story and we knew it wasn't an acceptable excuse, but we desperately needed something to enhance our story.

When we got back to the barracks with the mail we had some happy friends because letters were always the highlight of the day. We very innocently asked if we had been missed. The cadet flight commander said, "Fletch, because of the way you handled the guard detail last Sunday and took the chewing out, we tried to cover for you guys. I told the lieutenant that Hunter and you were on a work detail. I think he bought the story. However, if he has suspicions and checks up, 'Katie, bar the door' because all hell will break loose and we'll all be walking tours." Such is the bond that forms when everyone faces adversity.

Nothing was mentioned the following morning when everyone responded to roll call and we realized we were home free. After dismissal the cadet flight commander whispered, "Fletch, never again." The warning wasn't needed because I wanted to fly and wouldn't make those stupid little mistakes again.

In Squadron 16 we used double bunk beds. I had the lower and the upper was assigned to Larry Luzader from Centralia, Washington. He was a good buddy and we became close friends. When we moved from Squadron 16 to Squadron 58 our unit was split between Squadrons 58 and 59. Larry was assigned to 59. Their barracks were adjacent to ours but by some strange reasoning our unit was in quarantine, yet 59 was not. However, this worked to my advantage in that Larry knew that I smoked and he also knew I was broke since I had only budgeted enough money for one month. I assumed we would be paid on the last day of January or the first day of February, but this did not happen. It was my first lesson on assuming anything in the Army.

After several days in the squadron one evening after dinner a cadet called and said that someone was waiting for me in front of the barracks. As I walked out of the door there was Larry standing in the middle of the street. He had just been to the P.X. He was carrying a small box which he placed on the ground and with a pleasant "Here's a present for you, Buddy," he hurried on. In the box were four packs of cigarettes and a ten-dollar bill. I thought this was very thoughtful for a new friend who didn't smoke and had known me for only a few weeks. He must have been psychic because I was out of cigarettes and about to have a nicotine fit.

This spontaneous action started a real trend as others in the squadron started contacting their friends in Squadron 59 requesting favors of such nature. This practice was short-lived as measles broke out in Squadron 59 and they too went into quarantine. However, these acts merely reinforced a bond that was rapidly drawing everyone together. There were a few personality conflicts among the cadets and several know-it-alls, but given the number of people in these units the individual conflicts were very few and we lived in a climate of mutual respect.

The welcome speech we received from our new squadron commander was in marked contrast to any we had received up to now. The C.O. was a second lieutenant, whom we again met with skepticism. He bade us welcome to the squadron and stated that he expected the very best from every man and if we gave our best we would find him fair and willing to help. If we were prone to goof off or disobey regulations we could expect no quarter and would be washed out immediately. There would be no second chances for disobedience and willful disregard of the rules. His job was to produce and bring out the best in us so we might be a credit to the Air Force, and to that end his career was dedicated.

He explained that the Air Force needed all the pilots it could get, but they had to be the best. From now on until we were commissioned probably 40 to 50 percent of us would fail. But he wanted us to realize that we were not in competition with one another. "Help one another if you can; encourage one another. If any of you have special skills use them to tutor those who need it. If you help one another you will be helping the military." Help, however, did not mean cheating. That would be grounds for immediate dismissal. He encouraged us to set up study groups and work as a unit.

He explained that Flights A, B, and C made up Squadron 58-J of the Third Wing on the base. The J, the tenth letter of the alphabet, corresponded to the tenth month. Those of us who survived all the training phases would be commissioned the last of October 1943. He wished that it could be all of us but knew it would not. Recognizing that most of us had spent all our time in quarantine, he said he would intervene to help us if it were to continue.

According to the C.O., Squadron 58 had been the top squadron on the base in the past and it was his job to make sure it remained that way. There was only one excuse for missing a scheduled formation and that was death. If we goofed and missed we had better have the certificate in hand. He also praised us for having the fortitude to enlist as cadets. Ours would not be an easy task but the goal, if attained, would certainly be worth our effort and any sacrifice we had to make. This was a man we could understand. It was the first time anyone had expressed confidence in us. We would give our all and hope for the best.

Our new routine was now established as we embarked on a highly intensive course of study in ground school. Our academic classes included such courses as: Army Organization, Customs and Etiquette, Naval and Aerial Recognition of Both Surface Vessels and Army and Navy Aircraft, Physics, Mathematics, Psychology, Radio Code, Photography, Meteorology, Theory of Flight, and Identification of Poison Gases. This constitutes a fair sampling but is not a complete list. The instructors for these classes were both civilians and military officers. They were outstanding in their field, the best the nation could offer. The military instructors were high school and college educators who were offered a commission upon completion of Officer Candidate School. They were in stark contrast to the ones we referred to as "ninety-day wonders." These were very dedicated, sincere men. Their job was to teach and they were not into hazing.

Classes were primarily lectures and demonstrations. Classroom participation was at a minimum and then only to ask a question. The cadets could respond every Saturday when the weekly tests were given. The cadets' grades were posted publicly on Monday starting with the highest down to the lowest. This provided additional incentive to do well, as no one wanted to be at the bottom.

In our unit we used the time from 8:00 in the evening to lights out at 10:00 studying or conducting study groups for those who felt they needed help. Our aim was to become the top academic squadron on the base as well as the top military unit. The latter we were quick to achieve.

Every Sunday all cadets on leave had to be back on the base at 2:00 for the 3:00 p.m. parade. Only those who were physically unable or on duty details were exempt. The units formed in their squadron areas in Class A uniform to be marched to the parade grounds where all units participated in the presentation of the colors and the grand review. During all of this the base military band played stirring marches. Each squadron marched past the reviewing stand, which usually contained all the visiting dignitaries and the highest ranking officers on the base. The base and wing commanders graded each unit on a variety of qualities all pertaining to military bearing. Each unit was formed with the tall men in the front ranks and working back to the shortest bringing up the rear.

After the judging, the top squadron in each of the bombardier, navigator, and pilot units was awarded a flag indicating they were tops in these specialties. Also a grand champion flag was awarded to the top unit on the base. This was a large blue flag with a red "E" for excellence inset in its center.

On Sunday, February 14, Squadron 58 was awarded not only the top pilot training flag but also the grand champion E flag. Our reputation was established, but we would have to work hard to keep these flags since they were re-awarded every week. All the other squadrons would now be out to beat us. Our upperclassmen and squadron commander were elated that we had not become the embarrassment they thought we might be. However, most of the credit should go to our cadet officers. These cadets had exemplary military training and were true leaders, well-liked by all of us.

On Monday four cadets, former Army men (two sergeants and two corporals), asked to be transferred back to their original infantry unit and reinstated with their original rank. They said that a commission was not worth all the grind and hassle that they had been subjected to. Their request was granted.

After our first week of classes the grades were posted and I heaved a big sigh of relief when I found my name listed in the top five. The squadron composite grade was very high and we were even more determined to become the top academic squadron in J-class.

While we were all under constant strain and knew we were over-worked, it was quite a surprise to find we were all gaining weight. In my case thirteen pounds had been added. I found it hard to rec-oncile this with the letters I had been writing home detailing all of the hardships and deprivations we were forced to endure.

February 17 the Army and Navy conducted a mock dogfight over the base, the Navy using Grumman Avengers and the Air Force P-38s. The cadet corps was really pumped up as we cheered the 38s on. This was an inspiration as we imagined ourselves in the pilot seats. It was positive proof of the goal we hoped to achieve. I re-ceived further encouragement when the next set of grades was posted. With a composite score of 97.5 percent my name was listed at the top of the academic list.

On the twentieth, after we had completed our ground school ex-ams, we were ordered to remain in the barracks because the wing commander wanted to address the squadron. When the order came to fall into formation in front of the barracks we were pleasantly surprised to see our squadron commander wearing the silver bars of a first lieutenant. He introduced the Third Wing commander, who was a major. The major proceeded to tell us that he was very proud to have the grand champion red E flag and the top pilot train-ing flag in his wing. He was also very pleased with the academic showing of both the upper and lowerclassmen. He noted that our quarantine would expire on Sunday, but since no new cases of measles had broken out they were lifting the quarantine immedi-ately. Also as a reward for our good showing, arrangements had been made for us to attend The Camel Caravan show, a nationally known radio show troupe with twenty singing and dancing stars. They would present two one-hour shows on the base at Theater #3, and we were scheduled for the 8:30 performance.

The major also told our upperclassmen that if our group could win the Big Red E again they could have their pick of any Primary flying field in California. This could range from the country club of the air at Oxnard to the dust bowl of Blythe. We were also informed that passes would be issued so we could leave the base Sunday morning, but we had to return by 2:00 p.m. for the parade. For our group this would be our first time off the base.

Before the passes were issued we had to pass personal inspec-tion. The ranks were opened and the inspection party started down the ranks. At the end of the inspection 100 of us had failed. We needed haircuts so the lieutenant ordered the cadet officers to put us in formation and march us to the barber shop. He personally intervened and cleared the barber shop for us, using the quarantine clause. There were nine barbers on duty and in just fifty-five minutes the last cadet was sheared. Our hair was about one inch long, standing up on top and shaved on the sides. In formation we looked like 100 breathing scrub brushes.

The Camel Caravan show was a rousing success as the star-quality performers included comedians, singers, and dancers. Each cadet was given a pack of cigarettes. The smokers did okay as the nonsmokers handed over their packs. We all enjoyed the show and the cigarette company got their advertising.

As soon as the show was over at 9:30 we were hurriedly marched back to the barracks in order to beat the 10:00 p.m. lights out deadline. When we entered the barracks it was three minutes until ten. On Saturday we were required to strip our beds so the thin mattresses were folded in half and placed at the head of the bed. There was, of course, a certain procedure for folding the blankets, sheets, and mattress covers. The slip was removed from the pillow and all these items were displayed in neat piles in proper order on the end of the bunks. This process was not only designed to air the bed, which was certainly needed, but also to provide the inspecting officer with another chance to find something out of order and to give demerits.

Needless to say, lights out occurred before anyone had a chance to make his bed, so most gave up trying to put the mattress covers on in the dark. Sunday morning found most had simply crawled into the mattress covers and pulled the blankets over them. It was probably the funniest sight many of us had seen. Laughter broke out as each surveyed his own predicament as well as his neighbor's. An aura of irresponsibility pervaded the area and provided the first moment of complete abandonment of responsibility since the mud fight.

The following morning we caught the bus for the ten-minute ride to Santa Ana, a town with a population of about fifty thousand. Almost immediately the married men separated from the singles as we were concerned primarily with the availability of rooms or apartments just in case we could talk our wives into coming to join us.

The Army had written all wives that housing was critical and their presence would be frowned upon by the military, a policy which was in force all through cadet training. In the few hours available to us we sadly came to the conclusion that short-term housing was practically nonexistent and it was a poor place for a wife whose husband could only be there one night per week. A single bedroom was priced at five dollars a week. A room with eating facilities was about eight dollars, and some places had room and board for forty or forty-five dollars per month. Housing wasn't impossible but it wasn't desirable to bring a wife into this uncertain environment. For the present we knew they were safe at home with relatives, which eased some of the worry.

In our case my brother-in-law, Cap, had been called to active duty January 17. After reporting to a personnel pool at Hondo, Texas, he received his uniforms and orders to report to Okmulgee, Oklahoma, for the first phase of glider training. Sherry and my sister, Leora, were now war widows still occupying the apartment in Walla Walla. They both had jobs and there were relatives and friends near for help or visiting. Their biggest problem came when the landlord, realizing their husbands were gone, thought it would be a good time to raise the rent. Rents were frozen at this time but he apparently thought they weren't aware of this. He had underestimated these young women as his actions were reported to the rent control board. The raise was refunded immediately along with an apology stating he did not understand the rules.

I was amazed at the number of married men in our unit, almost 50 percent. Of course our biggest gripe and source of unhappiness was the separation from our loved ones. We lived for the letters and boxes of goodies which they sent although we knew they were using their sugar rations to make the candy and cookies to boost our morale. Without their support I don't believe we would have endured the separation. Perhaps the time of my worst loneliness came during the rainy weather when I received a package which contained an olive drab wool sweater knitted for me by Sherry. At the same time it was also a proud moment when I showed it off to the other cadets.

When we arrived back at the base at 2:00 it was pouring down rain and this time even the parade ground was a quagmire. The base commander called off the parade and we were allowed to retain possession of the honor flags for another week.

Tuesday brought the news that we were back in quarantine. Red measles was the culprit again. The upperclassmen were fit to be tied as they had just two weeks left before Primary and they didn't know what would happen if the quarantine wasn't lifted.

Our academic load continued to increase; the instructors were really pushing. We knew if we dropped our pencils that by the time we could pick them up we had just lost half a college semester in the course. Two cadets flunked out due to a poor showing on the exams and two others asked for voluntary relief. We finished a course in military hygiene and now knew how and where to dig latrine trenches. We just thought we were going to spend our time in the air; we had no idea that this would be a pilot's duty. We were also surprised to find out that the FBI wanted to know everything about our personal lives as well as our parents and ancestors. Some of them would have rolled over in their graves had they seen the questionnaire. All of this just to determine if we would be eligible to receive a commission.

Saturday night the wing commanding officer had one of the theaters cleared out so all of the quarantined squadrons in the Third Wing could see a movie. Squadron 59 was now back in quarantine so all the old buddies were able to see the movie together. It was a typical propaganda movie called *Hitler's Children*, designed to bring out anger in all of us and make us feel that it was our personal responsibility to exterminate all Nazis.

When we left the movie Squadron 59 collected ten cents from each of its members for a total of eighteen dollars. They wanted to bet that they would beat us out in the parade on Sunday and take possession of the prized flags. We couldn't let the opportunity pass so the bet was called and the squadron C.O. held the stakes. They also challenged us to a football and basketball game Sunday morning.

With all these challenges we felt we needed some divine guidance. With the quarantine we couldn't go to church so the C.O. notified the chaplain. Early Sunday morning church came to us. The chaplain packed up a portable organ and lectern and we had an outdoor service in front of the barracks. Squadron 59, sensing that we might be trying to gain the edge spiritually, immediately formed in front of their barracks where they could participate in the service and nullify any gain we might receive.

I cannot say enough about the quality of military chaplains. They are very sincere, dedicated men, good speakers who know what they're talking about. The chaplains know what they want to say and when it is said they quit. I've seen too many ministers in civilian life pass up many good opportunities to end their services.

With the close of the church service the football and basketball games started simultaneously. I was not a participant. Both squadrons claimed victory since no time limit or rules had been decided ahead of time and certainly no one was going to officiate at either contest. The competitors decided to finish the duel on the parade ground where impartial judges could render the decision.

We had just enough time for dinner, and then it was time to shine shoes, polish brass, break out the guidon and the winning flags, and march to the parade ground. We placed our three tallest men with impeccable military bearing in front of the squadron as flag bearers and guidon. It is impossible to describe the feeling of marching in a unit 180 strong with thousands of cadets participating, each hoping his unit will be chosen as the best. There was a lump in the throat as we passed the reviewing stand with eyes right, marching in cadence to a Sousa march. At the command of Steady Front a feeling of pride swept over us. Each person felt himself a part of the whole. We had plenty of confidence and pride so each one stood just a little taller and the bond that strengthened us all became tighter. As grand champions we were the leading squadron and we knew we had set a high level of performance for the thousands behind us.

When the judging was over we still had the best Pilot Training Squadron flag and the Grand Champion Red E as well. The squadron commander and the wing commander were elated with back-to-back wins. Squadron 59 placed second and had given us a run for their money.

Now the squadron commander wanted to know what we were going to do with the thirty-six dollars. Since we had been in quarantine for so long everyone wanted Coca-Cola, but we couldn't go get it. The commander disappeared and after a few minutes returned with the jeep loaded with cases of Coca-Cola. At five cents apiece each cadet had four bottles. We voted whether or not to share with 59. The vote was an overwhelming "no," so we went on a real Coke binge, drinking them as fast as we could and putting the empties in the jeep to be returned.

While we were enjoying our cold drink I started wondering how many cadets were in the parade. The exact number was probably confidential information, but I knew it was in the thousands. Was it ten thousand, twenty thousand, or somewhere in between? Then it dawned on me that this was just the West Coast Training Center. There was also the Gulf Coast and the East Coast Training Centers which were probably as large or maybe even larger than ours. I broke out of the reverie long enough to ask my upperclass mentor how many cadets he thought we had on the drill field. He said, "Look at it this way, Fletch, you were there and I was there so logically there was more than one." Big help! But I knew within two weeks he would be gone and we would be upperclassmen. Then someone else would have to do the sweeping and mopping and take the hazing that had been handed out to us. We could hardly wait.

Midweek came to pass and two more measles cases were reported so we started another fourteen-day extension of quarantine. We felt as though we were in prison and morale started to fall somewhat. Classes were getting tougher and there were no rewards, just more mess management, guard duty, and classes. We were developing cabin, or, more precisely, squadron fever. There was more griping than ever before. We all needed toilet articles from the P.X. but we couldn't go there. Also we had not been paid. I had broken my watch crystal but could not get to the repair shop to have it fixed; I couldn't have paid for it anyway. I had received seven demerits already that week, the most I had ever received. Any more and I would be walking tours. I was in a funk.

March 5 brought some good news. It started raining so hard again that drill and athletics had to be cancelled which meant we could use the time for studying. Someone started the rumor that we would be paid, and as far as I know that was the only rumor on the base that proved to be true. We all filed through the pay line and were paid in cash, although we received some surprises as some high ranking officials on the base had decided how we were to spend our money.

Cadets were paid $105 per month gross. Since we all had been ordered to active duty January 1, 1943, we had two months' pay coming. All cadets were charged one dollar per day for room and board and eight cents a day for laundry. These two charges could not be claimed for the first six days in January since we paid our expenses while en route to Santa Ana with the exception of transportation, which was paid for by the military. Each one of us by now had figured out how much we had coming. In my case this was two month's pay, $210 plus $10 reimbursement for travel expenses from Walla Walla to Portland to Santa Ana minus $53 for room and board and $4.24 for laundry equaled $162.76. However, as we went through the pay line the finance officer gave me $159.76 without justifying the $3 discrepancy in accounting.

Going through the pay line was a very formal affair. The finance officer was seated at a table with several armed guards behind him. The cadet marched to the table, executed a left face and saluted the paymaster. Since the paymaster was not required to return the salute, the cadet sounded off "Aviation Cadet Eugene R. Fletcher, 19033417, reporting for pay, Sir." The paymaster scanned the pay list, checked off the name, reported the amount owed and counted the money out on the table.

The twenty-dollar bills were new and uncirculated with the serial numbers running in sequence. The cadet was then offered a pen, signed the payroll, picked up his money, saluted the paymaster who sort of waved his hand, did a right face, and proceeded to the next table. There he was informed that he was commanded to donate two dollars a month for grass seed for the base beautification fund, a project in which we should be happy to participate. Four dollars, please. At the next table we were told that we had to pay eight dollars for the gym suits we were issued (a pair of shorts, T-shirt, and tennis shoes). Eight dollars, please, even though they were government issue. Then on to the next table. There we were told the base commanding officer had decided that each cadet would voluntarily donate two dollars per month to the American Red Cross. Four dollars, please. Thank you.

It certainly was not going to be hard to spend our pay with this kind of help. Immediately I found the two cadets, Luzader and Hunter, and repaid the thirteen owed to them. After pay call, since we were in quarantine, the squadron commander offered to buy money orders for any of us who wanted to send money home. Most of the married men took him up on the offer and I was able to send $100 to Sherry. This left me with thirty dollars for the month. I knew I would spend $7.90 of this for a new pair of pants. After our initial issue of clothing, which was second- or third-hand, we were required to buy replacements as they wore out. The shoes issued were new, but we were expected to buy replacement shoes also as needed. We had to have a shoe ration coupon before we could buy them. These coupons were issued on an "as needed basis," but only after turning in the worn-out pair.

The next day two of our married cadets asked to be eliminated. I had a chance to talk to them before their request and they said they would rather be a part of the enlisted army and rejoin the human race where the pay was better, they could work eight hours a day and spend some time with their wives. These men had special clerical skills and felt they would not be a part of the shooting army, but would become permanent party personnel on a stateside base. They were tired of quarantine, tired of making love on paper in the form of letters to their wives, and tired of the constant hazing, put-downs, and the degrading cadet life. I knew how they felt. I, too, was lonesome but I still had dreams of silver wings and I would put up with anything to win them. We parted with mutual respect, but with each thinking the other was crazy. I hope their dreams were realized, but dreams were like rumors: not many of them came true in the army.

After we completed our weekly exams on Saturday, March 6, the squadron commander explained that more cases of measles had broken out and our quarantine was extended another fourteen days. Since we were virtual prisoners of the system he had appealed to the wing commander for one of the theaters to be cleared so all of the quarantined squadrons could have some social recreation. He knew morale was low and was doing what he could to help us, but it was an unusual situation over which no one had control. That evening we went to the movie *Amazing Mrs. Holliday* starring Deanna Durbin. It was a good try on our behalf by the lieutenant. I don't think it did much for morale, but at least we knew he was concerned about the welfare of his troops.

Sunday I again drew the fire guard detail so I was not able to participate in the parade ceremonies. When the squadron returned I learned that Squadron 61, another pilot training squadron, had taken all the honors. Squadron 58 had finished second and 59 was further down the list. Because of fire guard duties I also missed Monday classes but the fellows reported back that my cumulative grade average was back to 97.5 percent. It had fallen to 95 percent the week before. I knew this couldn't last long because one of the subjects coming up was Radio Code. This had been my poorest subject in Civilian Pilot Training where I had barely managed to pass. In high school I had problems with typing and Code required the same skill. It seemed that I was unable to acquire the rhythm necessary to do well. Maybe this all tied in with the inability to carry a tune or the rhythm for dancing.

The grade report was the only good news of the day. Our upperclassmen received the field of their choice, Dos Palos Primary Flying School, and were in the process of moving. This should have been a cause of joy for us but our squadron commander informed us that he was being transferred for duty at West Point. The policy of having upper and lowerclassmen in the same barracks was being abolished. The crowning blow came when he stated that Squadron 58 was being disbanded. Most of us would move in with our counterparts in Squadron 57 located three barracks away. Everyone felt a little sick when he realized that our squadron identity as well as the academic and military records we had established were now gone.

Squadron 57, which had been released from quarantine for two weeks, was not happy to receive us in our quarantine status and we weren't happy to be there so that placed us on equal footing. We didn't mind not having underclassmen as we didn't feel like hazing anyone. Besides, with our experience we could sweep, scrub, and polish better than any underclassmen. At least we were in charge of our own demerits when we did the work.

Our Radio Code class started. At the first session the instructor told us that anyone failing to make a grade of 70 would have to forfeit his weekend pass. The class erupted in a roar of laughter and the instructor was caught off guard. He was not used to anyone making a laughing matter out of his instructions. Before he could chastise us some brave cadet explained that we were in quarantine. We had been off the base only six hours since we arrived the first week of January. Once the instructor realized we were not laughing at him but only at our own misfortune he registered disbelief. Upon reassurance that this was true he smiled and said, "Don't worry, I'll find another method of punishment," and we knew he would.

He also explained that we would be required to have a cumulative average of 85 percent in order to go to Primary. However, we could not fall below 70 in any one course. If that happened we would not be washed out but would be held back one class and allowed to go through Preflight again. By now they felt that they had such an investment in us that both we and the service could benefit. This was a relief to me because I now knew that if I failed Code I still would have another chance.

Another problem was that we wanted to let our wives and families know as quickly as possible that we had moved and changed addresses. This way our mail would be delivered directly to our squadron rather than coming to the old squadron and being rerouted, a procedure which took several days. There were pay phones in our quarantine area but they took only nickels, dimes, and quarters. We had just recently been paid and everyone had money, but it was paper money and no one had any change and we did not have access to any place where we could get change. Also the schedule called for us to pull mess management on the eleventh and guard duty on the twelfth. This meant missing two days of classes, then reporting for exams on Saturday.

These conditions did not make for a happy squadron. Everyone wore a long face and griped constantly. In fact, by now we could outgripe a five-stripe (five hitches) enlisted man in spite of his experience and longevity. We were quick learners.

Mess management went without incident, but guard duty was a little different. Up to now we had only learned the manual of arms and had not fired live ammo. Guard duty had been only an exercise. We were given guns without ammunition, posted at our stations of patrol, and told if we had problems with anyone who did not know the password or did not heed our commands after hearing the clicking of the rifle bolt to call out "Corporal of the Guard" for assistance. Most of the time was spent challenging members of the permanent guard who were constantly trying to catch us off guard and figuring out ways to get our weapons away from us. It was nerve-racking but also fun. It tended to break up a very boring job and was a learning situation in that you matched wits with some unidentified person or persons.

On earlier guard duty sessions we asked why we were not given ammunition. The answer was that earlier classes had been given ammo and several incidents of accidental discharge of weapons plus several close calls by challenging teams had led to an order to stop issuing live ammo.

I was placed on the detail that had the 10:00 p.m. to 2:00 a.m. shift. When we reported to the guard station it was a beehive of activity and we sensed an air of tension and urgency. We were immediately issued our weapons and flashlights and given live ammunition. The sergeant of the guard appeared to be nervous and explained this was not a drill. We would not be challenged by any of the permanent guard. This was for real; the base was under a red alert. We didn't even know what he was talking about but we understood that no one without the proper password and identification was to pass our position.

We were loaded into trucks and transported to our guard posts. I was stationed on foot patrol in a large warehouse unit. My surveillance area was about the length of a city block and how it was patrolled was left up to me. I was let out of the truck at the center point of my beat and admonished that if I had to fire my weapon the first shot was to be in the air unless my life was threatened. It sounded very romantic and intriguing until the truck pulled away. Suddenly it was pitch black and very lonely. I couldn't even see the ends of my patrol in the dark and it was cold. I tried to walk the beat, then realized my back was exposed. It didn't take long to discover that you can't walk in one direction and still protect your rear. The problem was: How do you protect your front, rear, and both flanks at the same time? No wonder they gave me that responsibility. Obviously they didn't know either.

I didn't have any idea where the other guards were stationed in relation to my location, so I tried side-stepping and walking in circles as it was too cold to stand still. Eventually my eyes adjusted somewhat to the darkness and that made it worse as the shadows took on shapes and my imagination willed them to move occasionally in synchronization with the night noises.

We didn't know if the base or the coast was being invaded, if saboteurs were reported in the vicinity, or whether the whole thing was a sham. It was the longest four hours I had ever spent in my life wandering around with a bullet in the chamber of my gun with the safety on. At one strange sound I wheeled around with the rifle at ready only to see the blinking blackout lights of the truck bringing my replacement. It was still terribly cold but my palms were sweaty. However, I suddenly became very brave as I crawled into the back of the truck. It was a quiet bunch of cadets who were transported back to the warmth of the guard headquarters. I knew then that I wasn't cut out for the infantry. I had to get to flying school.

Several days later rumors circulated that there had been submarine sightings off the coast and this had triggered our state of alert. All I knew was I had been asked to serve in a field which did not appeal to me.

With guard duty over and exams completed on Saturday we felt brave enough to ask our new squadron commander, Captain Wright, if there was any way we could have our money changed so we could use the telephones. Also, we all needed personal items from the Post Exchange. Our message fell on sympathetic ears. He went to the Third Wing commander and explained the problems of the men who had transferred in from Squadron 58. The wing commander, having a soft spot in his heart for us, requested that the P.X. be cleared and we were allowed thirty minutes to attend to our personal needs.

Once we were back in the squadron area we really burned up the telephone lines as we lined up at the booths. By limiting our calls to three minutes we could let everyone who wanted to call home. The change in morale was immediate. We were again civil to one another and the squadron commander's stock rose 100 percent. We knew we would never approach the esprit de corps of Squadron 58; we would still be a good unit but not a superior one.

Saturday night after Taps four cadets from the original Squadron 57 decided to sneak out of the barracks and go to town. Several of their friends tried to reason with them to forget it, but they were determined to go regardless of the consequences. They were tired of being cooped up in quarantine. We didn't know whether they got off of the base or not, but suspected they were apprehended at the gate. About 11:00 p.m. the O.D. (officer of the day) came to the barracks supposedly for inspection. The lights were turned on. He found the four empty bunks and left without saying a word to us. It was the first time the O.D. had ever come to our unit. We never saw the cadets again and their personal effects were picked up Sunday morning by the M.P.s.

Another strange thing about the Army was that the officer of the day always served at night. He was the stand-in for the base commander at night when he was home or off duty. The O.D. had many duties and carried a manual of duties and instructions, but his main duty was to relieve the commander after hours. He could solve all minor problems on his own and he kept a log of his activities. However, in an emergency he could call the base commander for instructions on major decisions.

Sunday afternoon I was one of the last to fall out of the barracks for the big parade. I fell into the last rank since this was where the shorter men were. Since there were only four of us in the last rank we were excused so the squadron would be uniform. They were a good looking group as they marched off but they didn't bring back any award flags. Our time in the limelight had passed, but this didn't mean we were giving up. Time was against us with two or three weeks left in Preflight. At this point survival was our main concern.

On Saturday, March 20, after exams we were told that our quarantine had been lifted. Captain Wright inspected the ranks and gave us all passes good until 2:00 p.m. Sunday. His order was to get off the base, loosen up, and have some fun. He noted we had been in quarantine so long that if we needed help finding the main gate he would be happy to escort us. Before he could dismiss us the whole squadron broke into the chorus "For He's a Jolly Good Fellow." He just smiled and said, "Don't forget, Misters, I'll be waiting when you return."

The cadets from Los Angeles and the surrounding area headed

for home. The rest of us didn't really know what to do, but finally four of us decided to go to Long Beach. When we arrived there about seven in the evening we found the town packed with soldiers, sailors, and marines. It took us over an hour to find a hotel room for two so we flipped coins. Cadet Hunter and I won the tosses and took the room while the other two kept looking. The room was six dollars for the night. We felt the price was inflated because of the influx of service people and the shortage of rooms, but at three dollars apiece we splurged.

We wandered along the streets which were literally jammed with young sailors, more than I had seen in my life. Here a surprising thing happened which boosted our morale and made us feel like human beings. The cadet uniforms were very similar to the army officer uniform. We wore the round blue cadet shoulder patch with gold wings and prop on the left shoulder. We also wore the U.S. brass insignia and the combination brass propeller and wings on our blouses. The visored cap had the wings and propeller insignia in place of the American Eagle on the officer's cap.

The young seamen and army privates looked somewhat perplexed when they saw us, but immediately saluted. The first several times this happened we looked behind us to see who they were saluting. Finally it dawned on us we were being accorded the honor. We immediately returned the salutes until we felt our arms would fall off. It is impossible to describe the feeling of rising from the lowest thing on earth to a position of respect in one hour. It didn't matter that it was a case of mistaken identity.

We found the huge Long Beach amusement pier and tried all of the rides including the roller coaster. There was also a small lake so we rented electric powered boats and drifted in the moonlight dreaming dreams of home and our loved ones until 2:00 a.m. closing time. It was interesting to note that practically all the young ladies, who were few in number, were always escorted by a group of sailors. It must have been the white bell-bottomed trousers.

We piled into bed at 3:00 a.m. dog-tired but with a feeling of satisfaction that would last a lifetime. By the time we got up for breakfast it was time to catch the bus back to Santa Ana. Our little escapade had cost fifteen dollars apiece, but never again would therapy be so cheap.

When we arrived back at the base the single cadets were talking and bragging about their evening on the town. One said he met a young lady who accused him of being AWOL. There was no doubt in my mind that he was a wolf on the loose and my sympathy was with the young lady. After hearing all sorts of amorous tales we felt there couldn't be a virtuous female left in Southern California, but we knew it was mostly hot air designed for the benefit of the married cadets. Squadron 57 was a sorry lot at the Sunday review, but luckily we placed higher than I thought we deserved.

When classes started on Monday I checked the grade list. My Code grade was 70 percent, barely passing, and it had pulled my aggregate down to 95 percent. However, good news came when the Code instructor announced that he would gladly donate his time for an evening class for any of us who wanted to participate. All we had to do was sign the sheet and show up at 8:00. My name headed the list because I could surely use the practice.

The rest of the week passed very quickly; every spare minute was spent studying. Several of us spent our evening hour in remedial Code classes. The instructor and several sharp cadets were doing all they could to help us. We were concentrating on receiving. The code messages were on tape and we used headsets to receive the sound. The tape was played at a speed which would enable the slower of us to copy. Someone finally experimented with speeding up the tape to a point where we were pushed and didn't have time to think but only record our first impression. Then things started to fall in place. The instructor seemed pleased with our progress and stated he would give us three final tests over a three-day period, then take the highest grade of the three. This gave me cause for renewed hope that I would depart for Primary with J-class.

During the week we were informed that no longer would top squadrons be allowed to choose their Primary field. In fact, we would leave the base under classified orders without any advance notice. This seemed to dispel all the rumors we had heard, but it was also a cause for more griping and complaining since this would mean another lengthy interruption of our mail service.

After the exams on Saturday we picked up our passes and seven of us went to Long Beach again. This time hotel rooms were readily available. The four of us who were married spent most of the evening trying to call our wives. Everyone was successful except myself. Since we did not have a telephone at home it was necessary to reach Sherry at work, but by the time I was able to get a circuit she had gone home.

We wandered around the streets for a while looking for someone to visit with but saw only two other cadets from the squadron and they had other things on their minds rather than visiting with us. Next we found a photo booth and for ten cents had our pictures tak-

First picture in cadet uniform.
The photo-booth camera
reversed the U.S. insignia on
the uniform, but what could
you expect for ten cents?

en to send home since this was the first time in uniform. We found an all-night movie house and watched movies until 2:00 a.m., then found an all-night restaurant and had breakfast. We turned in and didn't get up until time to return to the base the next day.

When we reached the barracks everyone was upset. It seemed that another case of red measles was reported Saturday and the unit immediately went back into quarantine and the passes were revoked. The guards at the gate were notified to refuse exit and pick up the passes of any Squadron 57 cadets. Apparently about twenty of us had beaten the order by twenty minutes. It was a great homecoming: just like old times, back in the slammer. We had very little hope of getting off the base again before we left for Primary.

We grudgingly participated in the parade and our attitude was reflected in our placement which I do not care to reveal, but it wasn't good.

On Wednesday, the last day of March, Captain Wright, the squadron C.O., gave us a real pep talk. He knew we were disgruntled, especially the guys who had not been able to get off the base on Saturday. Captain Wright, in our eyes, was the perfect example of an Army officer. His very presence commanded respect. He was a handsome man whose military bearing and uniform were impec-

A segment of Squadron 57. (Front row center) Captain Wright; (second row standing, third from left) Cadet Fletcher

cable. He let us know he was disappointed with our showing and felt that we were now underachievers. He knew we had fallen from the best to the mediocre. Our morale was low and he knew why, but what we were experiencing now was probably child's play compared to what we would face when we were commissioned and reached combat. It was imperative that we shape up and he was willing to help. He knew that the original members of Squadron 57 were in quarantine and had not seen the movie *Air Force,* which had premiered on the base in conjunction with the appearance of Captain Eddie Rickenbacker, so he felt that now was a good time to see the movie and reevaluate our goals in the light of what we would see in the movie. Perhaps we would show more dedication to a greater cause. He cancelled our drill and calisthenics classes for the afternoon and we were marched to one of the theaters for a special matinee showing. The movie made more of an impression on me this time since I could now see what we were training for and view it in that context.

This was our last week of classes and his lecture couldn't have come at a better time. We didn't need sympathy, we just thought we did. We needed the boot applied to where it would do the most good.

By the week's end our classes and exams were over and the scores posted Saturday morning. I had finally managed to get an 80 in Code and my final average or aggregate was 95 percent out of a possible 100. It wasn't the top but it was a long ways from the bottom. At Sunday's parade we made a decent showing but certainly were not contenders for the big E flag.

The new week started with our old nemesis drill, calisthenics, and instructional training films. All of our academic classes were over and we knew we were now going to Primary. The attitude of the unit was one of relief. There should have been cause for joy, but the strain and hustle of the last three months had taken its toll. It was just one big let-down. We had a little more free time but quarantine was still in effect so we couldn't use the time for anything constructive. What it meant was that we had more time to gripe. The C.O. felt we had reached a point where we would still gripe even if we knew we were going to be hung with a new rope. His theory was everything had a bright side and we should find it. Stress the positive.

This sounded good but at our first calisthenics session after Preflight we were informed that we still had to participate in a calisthenics physical test. It seems that on our first session after arriving on the base someone had recorded all our performance statistics: number of chinups, pushups, time over the obstacle course, and on through every exercise. We were now put through these tests again. Then these scores were compared with our beginning ones to measure our performance improvements. Everyone did compete to his limit but only to work off the feelings of frustration. When it was over we were so tired and sore we couldn't even gripe.

The following day we were introduced to the world of chemical warfare. We had studied this in the classroom, but we now experienced it in the field under actual conditions. We were placed in shacks where tear gas was released so we had to immediately don our masks and get out of the building. There were enlisted personnel standing by to help if anyone should experience trouble or panic. Then in the open field we were exposed to all of the poisonous gases we had studied about including lewisite, phosgene, mustard, and chloropicrin. As each one was released we opened our masks, took a quick short breath, closed the mask and identified by smell which gas had been released. I was glad to see this day end as the only way you could flunk this test was to croak. That evening some of the cadets had slight headaches, but that was the worst that happened.

Wednesday morning dawned hot and cloudless. The squadron commander announced that we would be going to the gunnery range. Since we would no longer be drawing guard duty the Army in its infinite wisdom had decided to teach us how to fire our weapons. The commander stated that we might want to bring our shorts and T-shirts and perhaps make a small contribution to the squadron fund. Each cadet put in fifty cents and wondered if we were buying our own ammunition. We loaded into army 6×6 trucks and were transported to the firing range which was located near the beach. We spent three hours of fun shooting 30-caliber machine guns at moving targets, firing shotguns on the skeet range, and then firing at fixed targets with 45-caliber Thompson machine guns.

My scores were terrible. The gunnery sergeant had a little talk with me but I told him he had no reason to complain since I had not ruined any of his targets. He should be getting after the cadets who were blowing them full of holes. His final statement was, "Let's you and I both hope you or no one else has to rely on your shooting for survival. I certainly wouldn't recommend you for infantry training." It proved to me there were some very bright enlisted men on the base. There was one ray of light. I did qualify with the 45-caliber handgun, which was the only score that mattered.

When we left the firing range the truck drivers took a very poor road on down the beach to a secluded cove right on the ocean. When we unloaded we were met by Captain Wright who explained that the cove was a safe place for swimming. We could have a swim if we wanted, and then we should gather driftwood for a fire. His vehicle was loaded down with soft drinks, a keg of beer, wieners, and buns. Our squadron fund had been transformed into a picnic. We didn't know how he was able to get the wieners since meat was rationed but he said that was his secret, to forget it and have a good time. We did and it was my first chance to ride the breast of a WAVE (Women Accepted for Volunteer Emergency Service—a woman serving in the Navy). Taking no chances, I explained this joke to Sherry in my next letter.

It was a tired but happy squadron that returned to the base. We knew we would miss the captain. He had taught us a very valuable lesson in the humanities: be tough, be demanding, be fair, be concerned, be interested in the welfare of the people in your command. It was a lesson I would never forget.

At noon Saturday our quarantine ended and since this was our last weekend here everyone except the fire guard was given a twenty-four hour pass. I polished my shoes and shined my brass. I didn't know where I was going but I was getting off the base. The fellow who drew the fire guard detail was a married cadet from the Los Angeles area. He tried desperately to get someone to take his place so he could visit his wife and family before we shipped out. All of his close friends turned him down even though he offered several twenty dollars to trade places. They were sorry but it was the luck of the draw. I was secretly hoping he would have some luck, but when it was apparent that he was stuck I told him I would trade places with him. He immediately opened his billfold. I said, "No, I won't take your place for money." As his face fell I explained that I knew how he felt as I would like to see my wife too, but since that was impossible I certainly wouldn't be the one to ignore his entreaty. It was with very misty eyes that he thanked me and said maybe some day he could repay the favor. "Let's hope you don't have to. Get moving, Buddy. Time's a-wasting." I settled down to twenty-four hours of peace and quiet with a good feeling.

I wrote a long letter to Sherry explaining what a nut she had married, but I suspect she was secretly happy that I had been confined for most of my stay at Santa Ana. That was one sure way to resist temptation. This was also the last letter that I was allowed to write from Santa Ana. Orders to leave were in the mill. Troop movements, times, and placements were classified. We would be able to write again when we reached our new base.

Several days earlier I had received a letter from Cap informing me that the glider training program had folded. With his flying experience documented he was immediately transferred into cadet class 43-J. Apparently his eye problem had improved over the last few months, or else the brass had now come to the conclusion that anyone who could fly a glider could fly an airplane. He was now at Muskogee, Oklahoma, a Gulf Coast Flying Training Command base for Primary training. Soon he would be flying a Fairchild PT-19 Cornell, a low-wing monoplane. Cap had managed to escape all of the Pre-Preflight hassle we had to endure and Sis would be able to join him before long.

On Friday, April 16, about ten of us stood around and watched the rest of Squadron 57 move out. We were confused and were not told anything. I looked around and realized I was in good company regardless of what happened because included in the ten were the top academic cadets. We were placed in a convoy for some destination wholly unspecified, but obviously to the north. Of the ten most of us were acquainted but not close friends. However, in this new group there was a cadet named Gene Jones, who was a classmate and friend at Pietrzyski High School in Dayton, Washington. I didn't even know he was on the base at Santa Ana. While there I had met two college classmates and one fraternity brother, but these were only chance meetings. This was different: two cadets from a small town in Eastern Washington headed for the same flying school.

3

Primary Flying School
Oxnard, California

The Primary Flying Schools were all civilian contract schools direct-ed by a small cadre of military officers and enlisted men. The flying training was conducted by civilian flight instructors, whose ranks I might have joined had the draft board not forced my enlistment. All of the ground school classes also were taught by civilian instructors. Classes in military discipline were conducted by the officers, but their primary function was administration. They must have been overstaffed, for we soon learned they had plenty of free time to make life miserable for the cadet corps.

As the convoy rumbled along it was a quiet group in the truck in which I was riding. Occasionally someone would mention the name of the town we were passing through. Because of the canvas covering which enveloped the bed of the truck, only the cadets on the side benches at the rear could get a glimpse of the countryside. Now and then someone would speculate on our destination only to be greeted with dead silence. We were happy to be out of Santa Ana and on our way to Primary, but as yet we were practically a group of strangers.

The convoy eventually ground to a halt and we were ordered out of the truck by a group of cadets who referred to us as "dodos." As such we were ordered into formation complete with barrack bags containing our extra clothes and toilet articles which were slung over our shoulders. As we were forming according to their commands I could see a sign over the main gate which read Mira Loma Flight Academy, Oxnard, California.

We were marched onto the field parade ground and here were drilled with our packs until I thought we would drop. The cadet

Flagpole in center of courtyard, Mira Loma Flight Academy

cadre from Class 43-I finally wearied of their ignoble hazing and we were ordered to remove all wing and propeller combinations from our caps and uniforms. As dodos instead of cadets we were ordered to stow the brass and only when we had soloed would we be allowed to restore the combination wings to our uniform. We were informed that our military unit consisted of sixteen officers, six of whom were rated pilots, and thirteen enlisted men. The Base Commanding Officer was Major J. S. Fouche, Jr. The director of training and adjutant were both captains, the rest were lieutenants. Lt. W. S. Powell was introduced as the commandant of cadets. He explained that the Class of 43-I, the upperclassmen, was divided into four squadrons numbered 1, 2, 5, and 6. Our hazing by I-class was now over. They were allowed to welcome us but that was the end.

The upperclassmen occupied one half of the housing area which was arranged in three concentric circles separated at one end by the headquarters building and the other by an entry arch. The round parade ground with the flag pole in the center constituted the inner open circle. We would occupy the other half of the housing area. The two classes would have very little contact since our schedules were designed so that only one class would be on the flight line at a time. We would alternate between morning and afternoon flying.

Class 43-J, Squadron 8, Flight 1. (Front row, left to right) *DuMont, House, Durnal, Clay;* (second row) *Algranti, Bostford, Riggs, Hornbeck, Boldi, Pulaski;* (third row) *Pollack, Emery, Powell, Hammond, Bell;* (rear row) *Wilson, Bride, Turner, Fletcher, Kelly* (Flight 2 not shown)

J-class would be divided into two groups of two squadrons each. Group 1 contained squadrons 3 and 4, Group 2 received squadrons 7 and 8.

He now demonstrated how we would be picked for squadron assignment. In the past we were assigned alphabetically, but here we saw something different as we lined up according to height. Squadron 3 became the big gun group since their average height was six feet two inches. Squadron 4 had an average height of five feet ten inches and soon became known as the raunchiest squadron. Squadron 7 became the odd-ball squadron since these people didn't fit anywhere. Squadron 8 was tagged the 8-ball outfit, the short end of 43-J, because we were all under five feet nine inches. I thought it an odd way to make assignments, but since we were all strangers and no one asked my opinion that was the way it was.

We were ordered into formations by squadrons, each squadron with approximately fifty men. We opened ranks and Lieutenant Powell and the first sergeant started down the line. The first three cadets were asked their names and the first sergeant wrote down the names and gave them a cottage assignment. This continued until everyone was assigned. This is how our roommates were decided. After our room assignments we were given a smattering of do's and don'ts including an admonition that we were in quarantine for fourteen days, a procedure that would be followed after every move. So what else is new? In the sixteen weeks I had been in the military service I had received only one twelve-hour and two twenty-four-hour passes.

My reaction to our new base can best be described in an excerpt from a letter sent to Sherry dated April 18, 1943, two days after our arrival:

> At long last we've finally reached Primary. We are now at Mira Loma Flight Academy, Oxnard, California. The day for which all of us here have been waiting has finally arrived. We will now be *flying*, believe me it is really a happy day because we've been building up to this for quite some time.
>
> The type of ship we will fly here is called a Stearman and looks very much like the Meyers I used to fly in Secondary Civilian Pilot Training except this one is quite a bit bigger as it has a 220 horsepower engine.
>
> This is one of the best Primary fields in the country and known as the Country Club of the Air. It is run by civilians. I was really fortunate to be sent up here as my old squadron at Santa Ana was either sent to Blythe or Hemet which is just as bad. About ten of us were picked out and we joined a convoy and were sent here. Maybe our Preflight grades had something to do with it.
>
> This place is really beautiful and for once we're living like civilians again. Instead of barracks we live in little cottages with private bathrooms, three men to the cottage. All the woodwork is done in pine paneling and believe me we keep the place shining. Another thing, we sleep in real beds with inner spring mattresses, none of this G.I. issue army cots and iron bunks like Santa Ana.
>
> K.P. and guard duty are things of the past. We are now going to be flyers so all our work will be in that direction. This is really a dream place and I know I'm going to like it. I feel very lucky to be here.

On the morning of the seventeenth we marched to the flight line and were introduced to the civilian flight instructors. These men wore the uniforms and A-2 jackets of commissioned officers, but lacking military insignia. They wore a set of wings on their caps. Before the assignments were made Herman Asmus (pronounced *Ace Mus*), who was the squadron commander, asked for all men with previous flying time to drop out of the formation and wait in his office. Two of us from Squadron 8 entered the office. Asmus asked the first cadet how many flying hours he had and the cadet

Flight instructors, Class 43-J, Squadron 8. (Front row, left to right)
J. E. McLean (Laughing Boy), W. L. Martin, H. A. Asmus, E. H. Busch,
A. W. Soare, M. J. Mabry (dispatcher); (rear row) I. Miller, P. A. West,
L. Pulici, A. A. Gabardi, P. E. Reed

replied, "Five hours, Sir." He was then told to rejoin the squadron where assignments were being made. Then he turned to me and asked what my qualifications were. I said I was a licensed single-engine civilian pilot rated to fly aircraft from 0 to 330 horsepower. After I recounted my flying experience a big smile lit up his face and he stated that he would be my instructor. As squadron commander he had many duties, so he took two or three students and chose only those with considerable flying experience. We would begin flying together Monday.

Ordinarily an instructor had five students, but since there was a shortage of instructors on the base some had six. These men were really overloaded. I knew then that only the quickest to learn would pass and the instructor load would be brought back to normal.

After the assignments we were welcomed to the academy by Major C. C. Moseley, who owned the flying school. It turned out that he also owned Cal-Aero at Ontario and Polaris Flight Academy at Lancaster. We were given this background information before his speech:

Major Moseley was a World War I veteran who had been a pursuit pilot with the Twenty-seventh Squadron of the First Pursuit Group and was credited with the destruction of enemy aircraft. After the war he was a test pilot for the Air Corps Engineering Division at Dayton, Ohio, and won the first Pulitzer Prize for the High Speed Trophy Race in the International Air Races in 1920. From then until his retirement from the Army he was involved in a number of Air Corps training programs and also organized, commanded, and trained the California National Guard Air Forces. In civilian life he was a director for several commercial airlines.

As novices we were quite impressed with Major Moseley. He spoke to us as though we were pilots. He did not mention his administrative accomplishments but gave us a hearty welcome and then reminisced about his flying experiences. He made us feel that we had to succeed, not only for ourselves but for the Air Force and for our country. He left us pumped up and ready to emulate his accomplishments and ideals. But perhaps most important, he left us with a sense of pride in ourselves and a feeling that we could control our destiny.

Monday morning the nineteenth we again met our instructors in the ready room at the flight line. Each instructor took his students to a private area where the first half hour was spent visiting. I suspect they wanted to learn a little more about our personalities and goals before risking their lives in the cockpit with strangers. I am not sure what our instructor learned from us, but we found out that he had been a Navy carrier pilot before becoming an instructor. In addition to being the squadron commander he was also one of the senior pilots on the field, and because of his many ratings, he wasn't sure how much longer he would continue to be an instructor.

Since all of the instructors were civilians they were referred to as Mister. By now most of the cadets were sick of this title. Because it had been used in a derogatory manner most of the time we felt it didn't convey the measure of respect to which he was entitled. He was a thin-faced man with very sharp, piercing eyes. He fixed us in a frozen gaze for a moment, then after ascertaining we were sincere, gave a tight smile and stated we could call him Captain Asmus. We immediately came to attention and saluted. This rather embarrassed him and he reminded us that it was not necessary to salute the civilian instructors. We told him we were aware of this,

Stearman PT-13Bs

but since we had to salute the military officers, it would be good training for us. He conceded that it would be okay to salute at our first and last meeting of the day. He would cheerfully return the salute as a matter of courtesy and recognition.

Next we proceeded to the flight line where there were about 150 primary trainers, all Stearman PT-13Bs, biplanes produced by the Boeing Company under Stearman patents. We were given a thorough briefing on the physical characteristics and instrumentation of the aircraft. The wingspan was approximately thirty-two feet and the length about twenty-five feet with a height of a little more than nine feet. The instructor sat in the front cockpit and the dodo in the rear.

I was impressed with the size and the 220-horsepower engine, but two features caught my attention. One was the engine starting device. In all the aircraft I had flown the engine was started by pulling the propeller through by hand, but here we had an inertia starter which consisted of a geared flywheel and counterbalanced weights. Two cadets would crawl up on the lower wing, insert an iron crank into an opening in the engine compartment, and then turn the crank until the flywheel reached a howling speed. There wasn't a tachometer to measure the speed so the two cadets cranked until it sounded right, which was usually when they were sweating and out of breath. Then they stowed the crank, crawled down from the wing, and moved clear of the plane. The pilot then called Contact, turned on the ignition switch, engaged the weight-ed flywheel to the engine, and hoped the inertia was great enough to spin the engine and propeller fast enough to start. Occasionally the engine fired on the first cranking, but more often not. The ca-dets cheerfully performed this act when an instructor was around, but woe be to the solo cadet whose engine wouldn't start on the first try. He was subject to ridicule and verbal abuse as though he alone were responsible for the extra work of cranking.

The other system was a method of communication. In the past my instructor had always used hand signals and dirty looks to con-vey what he wanted done, a crude but effective method which thor-oughly intimidated a student. But this airplane was equipped with a more confusing system. It was called the gosport system by the more respectable persons. However, it had many more less reputa-ble names applied to it by cadets who had just been chewed out by a screaming instructor.

The device was very simple. The instructor spoke into a funnel which was attached to a rubber hose that ran to the rear cockpit. The hose was divided by a metal fitting into a "Y" of two smaller hoses; these hoses were then slipped over a metal tube which pro-truded from the ears of the cadet's flying helmet. This system worked well on the ground before the engine was started, but in the air the engine noise and howling wind of the slipstream ren-dered communication almost impossible. It didn't take the cadets long to appreciate the noise, however, as it partially and sometimes completely drowned out the invectives directed at them by the in-structor. This was strictly a one-way system, instructor to cadet. It worked the best for the first two cadets who flew with the instruc-tor. By the time the last three or four students had their turn the in-structor was so hoarse he could barely whisper. He would stick the funnel out in the slipstream and let the cold blast of air and engine noise be directed to the cadet's ears to get his attention. At this point he reverted back to hand signals. The result of all this was that by the day's end the instructor had lost his voice and could only whisper while the cadet was stone deaf and couldn't hear.

In the beginning two factors had to be considered before deter-mining whether this was a plus or a minus. First, the mood of the instructor, and secondly, the type of ride the cadet had given the instructor. Later a third factor entered in, the condition of the air-plane on completion of the landing roll. The instructors' job was not an easy one and I'm sure they questioned their own sanity for applying for the job on more than one occasion.

After our briefing and familiarization session Captain Asmus asked who wanted to receive the first lesson. I immediately volunteered and crawled into the rear cockpit. My motivation to be first stemmed more from the fact that I did not want to crank the engine than from the genuine desire to fly. However, the good captain interpreted it to think I was an eager beaver. My first dual flight lasted forty-two minutes; I was almost overwhelmed. I had been idle for so long that it appeared I was starting from the beginning. I had lost the feel that goes with good piloting, but the desire was still there. I was bewildered by all of the aircraft in the air, in the landing pattern, and on the ground. Previously a half dozen airplanes in the air seemed like a lot, but here there were over a hundred. We had three runways side by side, and consequently there were three aircraft landing or taking off simultaneously. I was so busy watching out for the other planes I hardly had time to concentrate on flying. When the forty-two minutes were up I was in a daze. The instructor was not displeased with my efforts, but I knew enough about flying to know that it was far from a stellar performance and I had a lot of work cut out for me if I were to graduate.

We were able to fly for three consecutive days: another forty-minute session plus a sixty-five-minute one. Then we were grounded for two days because of morning fog. In between classes we all engaged in hangar flying, which amounted to everyone telling tall stories. This is a ritual in which most pilots perform their best flying feats. We never tired of boring one another, but occasionally the truth came out and we could profit by someone else's mistake. Certainly we couldn't learn from our own.

It became apparent that I would have to learn to fly all over again. Most of the maneuvers were performed differently in the military than I had been taught in civilian flying. The changeover was not that great, but I had to be careful not to revert back to my old ways. While my mind should have been concentrating on my problem, here I was usually thinking of home and trying to figure out how to get Sherry from Walla Walla to Oxnard. I wasn't overjoyed with my two roommates. They were good fellows but hard to get acquainted with.

After five flights with Captain Asmus, which amounted to just under four hours of flying time, I was summoned into his office where he explained that I was being assigned to another instructor who had just arrived at the base. When he saw my crestfallen look he was quick to explain that it had nothing to do with my flying. On the contrary, it was just the opposite. He would no longer be an instructor but would be a check pilot and ride with the students as they progressed through the various stages. He would decide who was passed through the stages and he would also give the final check flights for the cadets of Squadron 8 and some of the other squadrons to determine who went on to Basic.

I was immediately relieved and my morale soared. Every cadet hated and feared check rides because these determined your future in flying. Now I knew that I had started with the best and had pleased him, so every check ride from now on would be just the same as taking my instructor for a ride. There would be anxiety to do well, but not the fear and uncertainty of riding with a stranger.

The incident gave me even greater reason to be happy as I described the aftermath in a letter to Sherry:

> Changing instructors is never pleasant, but this change appears to have a plus side. One of the cadets told me that he overheard Captain Asmus' conversation with my new instructor and this was his version of what took place. It seems that he really built me up to the new instructor, not only because of my flying ability but because of personality and military bearing. He gave compliments like I've never heard in the army. While this has bolstered my morale and makes me feel good it has also caused a lot of ribbing from the other cadets and brought forth hot pilot innuendos all of which are done in the spirit of fun.
>
> Now that I've started off on the right foot I only hope I can stay that way. The first impression means a lot here and I know if I can just keep improving on my flying I'm going to stay here because it looks like the big boy is on my side.
>
> When I heard this it made me feel good because I was just about disgusted with flying, the army and everything that goes with it. But this made it different. It let me see that I was getting someplace and that all my time here and at Santa Ana wasn't being wasted. . . . It makes little difference whether the cadet was pulling my leg or actually telling the truth. . . .
>
> By now we've settled into a regular routine. Our first call is at 6 a.m., reveille at 6:15. Then we begin cleaning the cottages until 6:45 breakfast time. Immediately after breakfast we finish cleaning our rooms and living area for a white glove inspection. These inspections are just as thorough as those at Santa Ana, but here our college campus-style semi-private living quarters give us greater incentive. We are proud of our units and this provides the motivation to keep them spotless. It is also possible that this short poem posted on the bulletin board provides some stimulus:
>
>> One drop of water, one grain of dust,
>> Makes inspecting officers raise an awful fuss.
>> One fuss a day, seven days a week,
>> Gad, how those ramp hours wear upon my feet.

Seven-forty finds us marching to the flight line where we remain until 1:10 p.m. The time on the line is spent flying, receiving ground instruction, studying or flying a no-name static monstrosity, a contraption which is a modified version of the Link trainer. At 1:15 we change from flight clothes to the uniform of the day for dinner at 1:30. At 2:00 we go to classes which last until 4:00. At that time we change clothes again and go to physical training where a lieutenant tries to whip us into shape. A better name would probably be physical torture. This lasts until 5:10, then we shower and change to our olive drab uniforms and are ready for drill at 5:30. We drill for an hour and then stand in formation for the retreat ceremonies which take place at 6:35. From there we are marched directly to the mess hall which is now called the restaurant since we are on a civilian field. Evening chow is over by 7:15 when we proceed back to the living area. If we don't have evening classes we're free from then on until 9:30. But at least two or three nights a week we have classes from 7:30 to 9:30.

But if we don't have classes then we have exactly two hours and fifteen minutes to do our studying for the next day, shave, write letters, shine shoes, carry out missions assigned to us, look out for the rest of our personal things and then possibly ten whole minutes with absolutely nothing to do but loaf before lights out at 10:00.

I'm not overdoing this a bit for that is our actual schedule and it is followed to the letter. If you're more than 45 seconds late for any one of these formations it is a gigable offense and the usual sentence is three demerits. Again the rules are the same as at Santa Ana; eight demerits and you start walking tours. So you see we spend most of the day double-timing. People say that idle hands create trouble, but we cadets are living proof that even the busiest of people can also get into trouble.

What I wouldn't give just to sit down once in the middle of the day for ten minutes with absolutely nothing to do. It must be a wonderful feeling.

The food here is good but I believe I'm losing weight. My clothes are beginning to fit loose again so that's a good indication. This running all day is taking all the fat off that I put on in Santa Ana.

My new instructor was just out of flying school and a swell guy. We immediately developed a good rapport. He did not have the flying experience of Captain Asmus, but he was determined to prove that he was a good instructor, just as I was trying to prove that I could be a good student. On our first flight together we flew out to an auxiliary flying field where we practiced landings, then finally up into the blue where I had to demonstrate all of the maneuvers that were required for soloing. He was attempting to determine my level of competence.

When the flight was over he stated that I was capable of soloing immediately. However, there was a rule that a cadet could not solo

Instrument training class

before receiving six hours of dual instruction regardless of how much previous time he had. (My first solo under civilian flight rules required a minimum of eight hours dual instruction.) That was all right with me for I was still scaring myself to death on landings even though they were good. At least the instructor hadn't detected a lack of confidence, for which I was very grateful. I knew my flying was improving and that in another few days I probably wouldn't even mind riding with myself. These feelings were transmitted to Sherry in my letter for the day. I hate to admit it but there was more truth than humor in the letter.

That evening the base went on blue alert at about 10:30 p.m. The entire cadet corps was routed out of bed in a blackout and rushed to the flight line to manually disperse 150 aircraft. It was almost daylight when we finished and a short time later the alert was lifted.

This was a regular occurrence at Santa Ana, too, but there we did not have aircraft to push around. Here at the flying field it meant a lot of hard work. These alerts were prompted any time a coastal aircraft strayed off course and remained in effect until the plane was identified either by radio or aerial interception. All of the towns in the coastal western states had organized a twenty-four-hour-a-day sky watch under the auspices of the Ground Observation Corps, an agency of the Office of Civil Defense. People volunteered their time to man these lookout points and they called in every aircraft sighting they could not identify in the daytime. At night every aircraft was reported to a central point where flight plans were matched with the reported sightings. Thus an aircraft off course or unidentified was reported immediately to the military, triggering an alert.

While those of us who were pushing airplanes around were not overjoyed with these reports, we certainly appreciated the fact that people were volunteering their time to help protect us. In fact my father-in-law, a farmer near the little town of Tekoa, Washington, gave generously of his time even during his heavy work season. Apparently most of the people involved gave a minimum of three hours one day a week, and all they received for this vital contribution was a pair of silver wings. In the center of these wings was a large letter "O" (U.S. Air Observer). In the center of the "O" were the letters GOC (Ground Observation Corps). They were well trained in aircraft identification and knew what they saw in the skies. This was a group that never lacked for volunteers since everyone in the communities had friends or relatives who were actively involved in the military service. This was just another way they could show their loyalty and support.

It was a sleepy group that reported to the flight line on the morning of the twenty-sixth, but at least the instructors were wide awake. Since they lived away from the base their sleep was not interrupted. Because it was impossible for Oxnard to handle all of the air traffic, several auxiliary fields were set up. These were just grass fields without any accommodations. As the dispatcher assigned the airplane to the instructor he was also told which auxiliary field the squadron would operate from. The instructor and one cadet would board the aircraft and fly to the auxiliary field, receiving his lesson on the way out. The rest of the students, along with the dispatcher, went by bus to the same auxiliary field. By the time the first student had completed his lesson the rest were already waiting.

The first student crawled out of the cockpit and the second student climbed aboard for his lesson. While this was going on the idle students were studying their ground school textbooks. All students received sixty-five hours of flying time, including dual and solo time, in the Primary School. These figures were not estimates but accurate right to the minute.

Another purpose of the auxiliary field was to provide a place with less traffic for the student's initial solo flight. This was pressure cooker time and the cadet did not need the distraction of having the whole field watching as he performed his maiden flight. A pilot never forgets his first solo flight. He can always recall his feeling of uncertainty before and during as well as the joy of a successful conclusion. It is the major event in a lifetime of flying.

On Friday, April 30, the instructor said I would receive the first lesson so I was to check in with the dispatcher, get our aircraft number, and find out which auxiliary field Squadron 8 was using. On our way to the airplane he explained that he had checked my log book and I had exactly six hours; today would be my big day. So far no one from our four squadrons of 43-J had soloed. I was excited and could hardly wait to get to the auxiliary field. We climbed into the plane and two cadets performed the starting ritual. The engine fired on the first go-round and while the engine was warming up at idle speed the instructor quietly stated into the gosport, "Mr. Fletcher, I want you to take off on the left-hand runway and make three full-stop landings. On the third, come back to the ramp and pick me up, then we will go to the auxiliary field. By the way, don't make me regret my decision." He slowly crawled out of the cockpit and when he cleared the wing he turned, grinned, and gave me a thumbs-up gesture.

The two cadets who had cranked the plane were bug-eyed and in a state of shock, but I knew they weren't any more surprised than I was. As soon as the initial shock of being told to solo on the home field had worn off a feeling of exhilaration swept over me. I slowly started taxiing toward the end of the runway. I pulled over, ran the engine check and, satisfied that everything was okay, inched toward the runway. Suddenly I was almost blinded as the green light from the tower operator's Aldis lamp hit me in the face. I was now cleared for takeoff. Go man, go. I slowly opened the throttle, gently applying rudder pressure to counteract engine torque. Then I was suddenly in the air. I made the left-hand turn as I passed the end of the runway onto the crosswind leg, another left-hand turn and I was on the downwind leg at traffic altitude. Two-thirds of the way down the downwind leg I retarded the throttle and set up my landing pattern. One more descending left turn and I was on the base leg. Starting the descending left turn of the final approach leg I was hit again with the green light which meant I was cleared to land. Without having to apply any more power the plane settled on the end of the runway and I turned off at the first taxi strip to repeat the same procedure again. On the third landing, turning final, I got the red light which meant pull up and go around. The runway was occupied with a ship on takeoff. I immediately cut across to the downwind leg while climbing to pattern altitude and resumed the same procedure. This time the green light was forthcoming and again I settled onto the runway and taxied to the ramp to pick up my instructor. He was grinning from ear to ear, but he wasn't nearly as happy as I was. I had spent my first thirty-four minutes of solo military time in the air. The instructor and I spent another hour and twenty minutes practicing maneuvers before we landed at the auxiliary field.

The news of my solo flight had already been reported to the waiting cadets by the two who had cranked the engine. I was hazed and kidded as the cadets of Squadron 8 realized that one of their members was the first on the flight line to solo and had beaten out the other squadrons. It was with great humility that I explained to them what it was like to pilot an airplane without an instructor on board and that I was reasonably sure that some of them would be able to follow in my footsteps. I'm positive it was only the presence of the dispatcher and the bus driver that allowed me to return to the base unharmed.

As we marched to the restaurant for dinner I was on cloud nine for I now had all the brass back on my uniform, which placed me in the same category as the upperclassmen. I was no longer a dodo.

The afternoon brought another surprise. Since this was the last day of the month we were informed that it was payday. The flight school issued the following explanation about our pay. It was a different procedure and did not create the controversy and surprises which happened at Santa Ana.

About Pay Day...
So that you will understand "what it's all about" when pay day comes around, the following explains Army practice in this regard.

When Army personnel live on an Army post, they receive their regular rate of pay and the Army supplies housing facilities and food.

When, for any reason, Army personnel such as yourself must live off the post for either a temporary or an extended period, they are given an additional allowance to cover housing and food...a total of $64.50 for "room and board."

Therefore on pay day, Army paymasters will give you a total of $139.50—your $75 salary plus the $64.50 explained above—and representatives of the commissary and housing organizations will, in turn, collect from you for these costs, leaving you the full $75 pay of your rank.

So—when you draw $139.50 on pay day instead of the $75 you were promised, don't think you've had a raise in pay! When you live on an Army post, the expenses of food and housing are taken care of by the government "behind the scenes." But when you're on detached service, as you now are, you do this yourself and the government supplies you the additional funds with which to do it.

On Saturday, May 1, I received forty-five minutes of dual instruction. It was a case of the instructor trying to out-fly the cadet. We had a ball. The session ended with the instructor flying over the fair-weather cumulus clouds floating in from the ocean. He dropped down into the valley of a cloud and we flew below the peaks, banking the plane very steeply to remain in the valley and, on occasion, applying full power and maximum climb to retain visual contact and stay out of the cloud proper. Finally the instructor said we had better stop before we met two other nuts who might be coming in our direction and doing the same thing. We pulled up over the top and found a large hole between clouds to make a let-down for landing. The instructor said we had had our fun, but if I ever attempted to do this on a solo flight and he heard about it I would be washed out immediately. It was a bumpy, fun ride that I'll never forget, but I took his warning seriously and never attempted it on my own, at least not where there was any chance of being seen.

When we returned from the flight line we were told quarantine had been lifted and we would receive our first pass after supper. Since the threat of an invasion was always present, all coastal bases were required to have 50 percent of their personnel on the base at all times. Thus leave time had to be scheduled between the two classes. During the time we were in quarantine the upperclassmen were allowed longer passes, a privilege which would be granted us when our time came. My pass was good from 7:00 p.m. Saturday until noon Sunday.

Sherry and I had discussed the possibility of her joining me at Oxnard. Up to now everything had been based on speculation. The feasibility of her coming now depended on the conditions I would find in the local area. As soon as I got back from my first visit I wrote to her:

> Here it is Sunday and I've just returned to the post after enjoying a few hours of liberty. I was quite surprised by the town of Oxnard. It's much smaller than I had imagined. Most of the buildings are wood-frame structures and quite old. But then again I guess a town of 8,000 wouldn't be very large or too modern.
>
> The town is divided into two sections. One part is very run down and its population consists almost entirely of people of Mexican descent. The

Stearman PT-13

other part is much nicer and it is where the permanent residents of the
village live along with the wives of sailors and soldiers. About one-
fourth of the population is service wives. This is really a navy town as
you will see when you get here.

Last night I stayed at Oxnard's most luxurious hotel, the Hotel Oxnard. It is quite a place to say the least. It is a three-floor wooden struc-
ture built probably in the 1800s and has never been remodeled because of
its value as an antique. At least that's the way I figure it. The rooms could
be worse but only if they took the beds out. It reminded me of the hotel at
Tekoa, but Tekoa has the edge I think. The hotel is inhabited with mostly
wives whose husbands are in the service.

The lady who runs the hotel said her husband was in the South Pacific
so she was interested when I told her I was expecting my wife here and
would be interested in obtaining a room for a while until we could find
an apartment. At the present all the rooms with bath were filled, but she
says she will have one for me by the time you get here. She is to call me
as soon as one is vacant and I will make a reservation and pay for the
room from then on until you get here so you will have a place when you
arrive. There are several auto courts here and if I haven't a room by next
weekend I will get you a tourist cabin there. I will make this definite by

next weekend and then wire you where to come before you leave on the 11th.

Another thing, I want you to try to plan your arrival here before evening because I don't want you to try to find your way around in a strange sailor town after dark. In the evening all coastal towns are in a partial blackout and it isn't any place to be chasing around without an escort unless you know where you're going.

Conditions here are far from being good but even at that it is much better than lots of the towns I've seen so far. Now then, you wanted to know about the work situation. Well, I don't know much about it, but I met a sailor and his wife at the hotel last night and she said finding work was no problem at all. She had been here three days and had already found a job. She also said wages were good. That's about all I know about that, but we won't worry about jobs because we know we can make everything work out okay.

I went to church this morning. By the way, I don't think there's a Christian Church in Oxnard. The one I went to was the Baptist Church. It was quite nice and they have a wonderful minister and he had a good sermon. I didn't get acquainted, nor was I able to stay for communion as my pass was almost up so I had to leave right after the sermon. I was quite impressed by the cordiality and willingness of the congregation to want to help wives and girlfriends of service men. In fact, the sermon was built around this theme and was very good. If all else fails we can probably contact the church for help in finding a place to stay.

By May 5 it was time for two-stage checks. I left the home field a little after 10:00 and flew solo to auxiliary field #3. There Captain Asmus climbed in and proceeded to give me the tests. At the conclusion he stated that he was happy with my progress, but that I should work a little harder on some of my acrobatic maneuvers and spend some time practicing forced landing approaches. He was certainly justified in criticizing my acrobatics and I was disappointed in the Stearman as an aerobatic airplane. It was heavy with a maximum gross weight of 2,700 pounds, very stable and easy to fly, but underpowered I thought for a good acrobatic plane. The little Meyers I had flown previously had less horsepower but was also considerably lighter. Consequently, all aerobatic maneuvers could be made from level flight; all that was necessary was to open the throttle and you had the power and speed to do whatever you wanted. You could also roll it upside down and fly inverted as long as you wanted. The only things you could do with the Stearman from level flight were spins, stalls, and falling leaves. In other words, anything that allowed you to lose altitude. All other maneuvers such as loops, chandelles, Immelmann turns, snap rolls, slow rolls, and the like required lowering the nose and opening the throttle to build up airspeed in order to do the maneuver. If there was any hesitation at the top of a loop or Immelmann turn the engine would cough and sputter and airspeed was lost immediately. Once the plane was back in its normal position and gas could flow to the carburetor the engine would cut in and the plane resumed flying. If the gas tank had had another outlet on top and plumbed into the fuel pump the problem could have been solved. The engine would have kept running in any position, which would have made it easier to fly, but this was a training airplane and no one wanted to make anything easier for a cadet.

I soon tired of aerial maneuvers and decided to practice forced landing approaches until I had to return to the home field at 1:00 p.m. Practicing forced landing approaches is very simple: you just retard the throttle and with the engine idling pretend you had an engine failure and pick out the best field or open space where you think you can land, supposedly into the wind. Of course it has to be within gliding distance of where your supposed emergency occurred. The main idea is to learn the gliding capabilities of the airplane so you don't over or undershoot the field you have chosen. Some time during every dual flight when you least expected it the instructor would retard the throttle, scream "Forced landing," and then you immediately set up a gliding landing pattern. He would hold the throttle closed so you couldn't cheat with power. Then the instructor judged you on your choice of fields, how well you executed, and whether or not you were able to reach your chosen objective. When the plane had descended to within 200 feet of the ground you opened the throttle and abandoned the approach. At this altitude it had already been determined whether you were successful.

This day there was no wind and as long as you stayed away from buildings almost any field in the practice area could be used for an emergency landing. I made three or four approaches from different altitudes and felt that I had made good choices. I decided to try one more before heading home so at 2,500 feet I pulled back on the throttle and spotted a flat, beautiful barley field directly under the airplane. This was great because I could start a descending spiral right over the field and this would give me practice in losing excess altitude and choosing the right time to start the landing pattern which would lead to the final approach. Everything had to be perfectly timed. Trying to stretch the glide would decrease the airspeed and create a stall, causing the airplane to crash. Too much airspeed and you would overshoot the field with the same dire consequences. At 800 feet I broke out of the spiral and established a base leg and at 400 feet turned onto a final approach. The barley field was as flat as a tabletop and not a breath of wind. At 200 feet I knew I had the field made, but for some reason I decided that I would wait until 100 feet to apply power. As I passed through 100 feet I was almost hypnotized by the green field coming up and by the time I reached for the throttle it was too late. The wheels were already turning in the crop and the drag caused the plane to touch down.

It was a beautiful landing; the barley was just starting to head out. The farmer had a bountiful crop and there I was sitting in the middle of it. The ground was quite firm so I taxied to the far end of the field and with full power was able to make a 180 degree turn and get back into my original tracks to decrease the ground drag. The airplane accelerated very slowly at first, but finally I was able to get the tail up and the speed increased immediately. I was airborne long before I reached the point of touch down.

I heaved a sigh of relief and headed home. It was a crazy, stupid thing to have done and certainly a good way to wreck an airplane. I kept scanning the skies but there weren't any airplanes in sight so I felt reasonably sure no one had seen me go down. The plane was okay and only the farmer would notice strange tracks in the field. No one would ever know except the farmer and me.

When I reached the base I was the last plane in the landing pattern and the old Stearman settled onto the runway without a bounce. I taxied to the flight line, parked the plane, and as I was crawling out of the cockpit my instructor came down the line and stopped by the tail waiting for me to fasten the seat belt around the stick, a procedure that was done to keep the controls from moving in case the wind came up. As I stepped down from the wing he said that he had talked with Captain Asmus. He was pleased that I had passed my two-stage checks and the captain had told him what areas I needed to work on to be a better pilot. We would concentrate on them at our next dual session. Then he walked around to the front of the plane, stopped, and I thought he was having trouble breathing. He motioned for me to come forward where he was looking at the plane. By now he had recovered his voice and said, "Where have you been? What happened?" I looked and saw that the landing struts had turned green. The front of the plane and the leading edge of the lower wing were covered with juice from the barley plants. The silver fabric was now olive drab. It looked funny, but it wasn't a laughing matter. "I'm waiting for your story," he fumed. I thought about saying maybe somebody should mow the grass on the auxiliary field, but I knew that wouldn't fly. I was caught red handed so there was only one thing to do and that was tell the truth. While I was explaining he kept saying, "No, no, oh my god."

I kept saying, "Yes."

"Oh no, I'm gonna be fired from my first instructing job because of some nitwit cadet." He looked tired and somewhat resigned to his fate.

I told him I would go to the squadron commander and tell him the truth and he wouldn't be responsible for anything. I would accept the consequences of my actions whether it was punishment or wash out. I was filled with remorse but couldn't undo what had happened. I would just have to live with it. At this he bristled and said, "Don't you dare tell anyone. I don't want anybody to know that I had a student dumb enough to pull such a trick. You're not going to make me the laughing stock of the instructor corps. Check in your parachute and meet me in the ready room on the double and forget about chow, Mister. You're in trouble." I was busy "yes sirring" and he was busy shaking his head and muttering "I don't believe it."

When we met in the ready room he had a bucket of warm water complete with suds and the chamois from his car. We did not draw any undo attention as we proceeded down the line to the airplane carrying the bucket. Since many cadets experienced air sickness it was standard procedure for them to wash out their planes. Although it didn't take very long to wash off the green juice, he kept repeating that it was students like me who gave instructors gray hair long before their time. He couldn't figure out what he had done in life that would cause him to be punished by being assigned such a student. I couldn't answer his question but only scrubbed harder.

Finally he said, "Well, it looks okay. You had better get going so you aren't late for classes. If you mention this to anybody you're asking for trouble. Believe me, you better not screw up again 'cause I'll be watching you like a hawk going for a chicken."

The following day I spent two hours in the air demonstrating every flying maneuver I had been taught while my ears were ringing to the innuendos of an inhuman screaming demon who now occupied the front seat of the airplane. It was hard to believe that this was the same kind gentleman who had been my instructor two days before. It was apparent to me that he had a split personality. I

had heard that traumatic experiences sometimes affected people
that way. Before landing there was a request to fly over the barley
field at 1,500 feet. When the tracks became visible the inside of my
knees took a terrific beating as the demon threw the control stick
from side to side. Frustrations finally vented, he requested we land
at auxilliary field #4 and then I could proceed with an hour of solo
time. As I taxied away the spent shell of a man was still shaking his
head, and I quietly gave thanks to the Dayton draft board that had
saved me from a similar fate.

By now most of the men in the other squadrons with previous
time had soloed. To the best of my knowledge there were four of
us. Over the next few days the men without previous time started
joining our elite ranks. Cadet Jim House, our cadet wing adjutant,
became the first from Squadron 8, followed closely by our cadet
squadron commander M. J. Dumont. I was particularly happy to
see them do well on the flight line since they excelled as cadet officers. Their military knowledge and expertise commanded respect
from all of us. A little more brass was starting to appear on uniforms so there was hope that we would soon look like a military
unit again.

Saturday, May 8, I received a call from Mrs. Frank Eastwood, the
manager of Hotel Oxnard, stating that Sunday she would have a vacant room with bath available. I managed to get a short pass and
paid thirty-six dollars for two weeks in advance. Sherry arranged to
take the Union Pacific stage, arriving the fourteenth. I left a note in
the room asking her to come to the base after 7:30 p.m. that night.

On May 12 Squadron 8 was assigned to fly out of auxiliary #3.
The instructors departed with their students and I was assigned
my solo lesson, which was one hour in length, after which I was to
land at auxiliary #3 and pick up Captain Asmus for another stage
check. The stage check took forty minutes. Then I was to practice
landings at the auxiliary field for thirty minutes after which the airplane would be assigned to someone else and I would return on the
bus.

Everything went as scheduled. The newly soloed cadet was told
to go up and do several stalls, get a good feel of the airplane, and
then come back and practice landings. When the student returned
for landing practice the white flag was flying. This was a signal for
everyone to land. The cadet made a good landing in spite of the
wind which was just beginning to come up. In short order all of
Squadron 8 aircraft were on the ground. The instructors were in a

huddle while the students were sitting in the airplanes with engines idling and full brakes applied. The wind was really picking up and the western sky was black.

Oxnard was only two or three miles from the ocean with an elevation of thirty-three feet. Our auxiliary field was slightly north and east of the home field. A squall line was rolling in from the ocean; moisture was not a problem, but the wind represented a real hazard for it meant a crosswind landing at the home base. While the Stearman was a stable airplane, it was jokingly known to have a built-in ground loop. This was attributed to the fact that it had a narrow landing gear. For the uninitiated, a ground loop is an accident which occurs on landing by inexperienced pilots. The pilot loses control of the plane after touch down and it does a very sharp 180 degree turn. The resulting sharp turn causes a wing to drag the ground as the airplane pivots in a tight circle. The pilot, because of inexperience, has allowed the airplane to get ahead of him and by the time he reacts a wing has been damaged and the pilot has suffered considerable humiliation to his pride and reputation. Wind in extreme cases could be a cause, but usually it was the inattention of pilots.

The instructors finished their consultations, boarded their aircraft, and started taxiing for takeoff. At this point Captain Asmus motioned for me to join him. He explained the white flag meant that all solo flights were cancelled; only dual aircraft were to be in the air and they were headed for Oxnard. There was one problem. We had one more plane than instructors so he was requesting that I fly the extra airplane back. I must have had a questioning look for he immediately said, "I know you are capable. Will you do it?"

"Yes, Sir."

"Okay. What I want you to do is fly over the base 500 feet above traffic altitude, check the severity of the crosswind and if you don't feel you want to make a crosswind landing, circle the field until the traffic slows down. Then forget about the runways, head into the wind and make your landing directly into the wind crossing the runway at an angle. You won't have any trouble so give me a head start and I will notify the tower to watch for you and they will hold up traffic until you get down."

By now the wind was becoming more severe and it was necessary for the captain to crawl in the front seat of my airplane and hold the brakes so the solo cadet could get out and give me his parachute. As soon as I was buckled in and had control, the captain climbed out and boarded his own plane while the cadet boarded the bus. Captain Asmus circled the field once to make sure I got off the ground okay, then he headed home.

As I came over the home field I saw that they were using only one runway, the same one I had soloed on. The reason for this was that the wind was so strong they had cadets stationed about two-thirds of the way down the runway. As each plane turned off the blacktop runway four cadets, two on each side, immediately grabbed the wings to stabilize the aircraft while the instructor slowly taxied to the tie-down area. I circled the field twice then decided I would land on the runway the same as the others. Pride would not let me land across the field into the wind. I would do it right or wreck the plane trying.

I entered the traffic pattern making sure I had good separation behind the lead aircraft. When I turned final I carried power to help counteract the crosswind. When I set up the crab (nosing the airplane sufficiently into the wind to counteract wind drift) and lowered the wing into the wind, it dawned on me how hard the wind was blowing, but I wouldn't back down. It was now or never. I wasn't about to make a full stall landing allowing the wind to get under the wing. I passed over the end of the runway still carrying slight power; at the last second I kicked out the crab and leveled the wings. The old Stearman behaved perfectly as I applied slight forward pressure on the stick and greased a wheel landing. Still maintaining slight pressure on the stick I slowly retarded the throttle to idle, allowing the tail to drop gently onto the runway and then applied full back pressure on the stick. It was so early in our training that the cadets had not yet been taught how to make a power-on landing, but it was a procedure I had learned in civilian flying. I let the airplane decelerate on its own and applied brakes only to turn off the runway and allow the cadets to grab the wings. I taxied back very slowly savoring every minute.

When we reached the tie-down area I remained in the cockpit until the ground ropes were attached to the wings. After shutting down the engine I slowly got out of the cockpit, realizing that the mental strain had left me weak. Walking down the line I heard one instructor, who was still sitting in his airplane, ask his student, "Who the hell is that hot rod?" The answer was inaudible but it brought on a real high. I was now walking at just about traffic altitude.

About that time a voice from below was heard to proclaim. "That's my student." Through the film in my eyes I could faintly see my instructor appearing from nowhere. No one will ever know the feeling I had at that moment and I certainly couldn't describe it.

Two days later for some unexplained reason Mr. Fletcher was transferred to another instructor, a Mr. Pulici, who had just arrived from Hawaii. Mira Loma was his first instructor assignment and it appeared to me that the instructors hazed one another the same as the cadet corps.

When I was notified of the change of instructors Captain Asmus remarked, "Fletch, I don't think I did you a favor by having you return the plane the other day. Every military pilot on the field knows about it and they are just waiting for an excuse to get you on a check ride. Whatever you do, don't make even a little mistake. You've now been warned. They won't wash you out, but they can sure make a flight miserable for you."

The role of the six military pilots on the base was to see that all of the instructors taught the students in the same manner. It was a matter of standardization. There may be many ways to perform a maneuver, but, in the eyes of the military, there was only one correct way and that was the army way. It was their job to ensure that not only were we taught the army way but also practiced it. It was possible, however, to graduate from Primary without ever having ridden with a military pilot since the senior civilian pilots had the responsibility for the final checks.

Another task of the military pilots was to give check rides to students who were having trouble with their flying. After a check ride they would decide whether the student had the potential to continue in the program or was to be eliminated. This relieved the civilian instructor of this responsibility. The instructor and the check pilot worked closely together comparing notes and discussing the student's progress and potential, but in the end the military had the final say.

Some of the students who were washed out might have been good pilots had they been able to have a little extra time, but this was wartime and pilots were needed immediately. Those who learned the quickest would succeed. Occasionally a student was held back one class, but these were students who had demonstrated good flying ability and had fallen behind for some reason, maybe a case of measles, a sprained ankle or some other mild health problem. The reason had to be related to something other than flying or ground school.

At Mira Loma we also had eight student officers in class 43-J: one captain, three first lieutenants, and four second lieutenants.

These officers from the infantry, cavalry, and other branches had applied for flying duty and were now undergoing the same training as the cadets. Assigned to Squadron 8 were second lieutenants George Kinnon and Dale Miller. They attended class with us and always sat in the back of the room. During class breaks they left the room first and stayed away from us. These men were good officers and had no desire to inhibit us by their presence. They were always cheerful and they sympathized with some of our problems, but we knew they had already experienced most of what we were going through. We also found out that they had other duties including officer of the day, which they rotated among their group. These student officers did not live on the base, although they took their meals there. While we weren't always aware of it, these men were pulling for us to succeed and provided help whenever they could, always behind the scenes. One of these student officers would eventually provide a worthy service for me.

As more of the cadets started soloing, more goofs were committed. Ground loops, airplanes standing on their noses because the brakes were applied too harshly, and damaged wings from either parking or taxiing too close together became a routine sight. The cadets who committed these blunders were awarded red stars on the squadron progress report sheet. It wasn't long until the squadron had collected enough red stars to make a Russian general's heart pound with pride.

For a small infraction the cadet had to wear a red arm band for whatever length of time the instructor prescribed—two days, a week, or whatever. This was to notify everyone that he was an accident ready to happen, so beware. A cadet who had a major infraction had to wear a cowbell around his neck while on the flight line. This was known as belling the goat, but this farm boy knew the difference between a goatbell and a cowbell. This bell, without a clapper, was worn until the next incident occurred, when it was passed on to another culprit. There were times when it changed hands two or three times a day. It was my good fortune not to wear either the bell or an arm band, but I felt sorry for those who were thusly humiliated. Eventually the cadets were able to see the humor of their mistakes and the stars, arm bands, and bell became badges of honor and were worn with pride, albeit false. Once they adopted the attitude of "don't fight it, join it," things became a lot easier.

There were times when the auxiliary fields resembled a three-ring circus. One of the incidents involved a student on his first solo. He made a good takeoff and flew a perfect pattern. The final approach was right on, but just before touchdown he applied full power and went around. We all had the feeling that he wasn't satisfied with the approach and we anxiously awaited his second try. Again it was the same thing. Before touchdown the power went on and the plane climbed to pattern altitude. We were beginning to suspect the cadet was experiencing a lack of confidence.

After the third go-around his instructor was becoming very nervous and concerned. The other instructors weren't helping by suggesting that he might have to be shot down. On the fourth go-around all the levity was gone. Up to now we had not had a personal injury or major accident, but it now appeared we had one in the making.

On the fifth approach everyone was frozen in place, eyes riveted on the airplane, following every move. More than one silent prayer was riding with the cadet as each one of us was willing him the courage and confidence to make a successful landing. As he came over the end of the grass strip the nose elevated in a perfect flare-out and the Stearman settled on the ground in a perfect three-point landing. The grim-faced cadets broke into a rousing cheer as the airplane rolled to a stop and a misty-eyed instructor ran to congratulate the cadet. It was obvious that the instructors cared more about the welfare of the students than they were willing to admit.

It was a nervous, smiling cadet who crawled out of the cockpit exclaiming, "I did it. I did it." It was a relieved, jubilant group of cadets who pounded him on the back while the instructor was explaining that was enough for one day. There would be a tomorrow. This was the most celebrated solo in Squadron 8, but it was not a cause for punishment.

By now flying was the furthermost thing from my mind. Sherry was coming. After a separation of four and a half months we would actually see one another again. My spirits were so buoyed that Friday afternoon I summoned the courage to call on the base commander after classes to request a long weekend pass. I had polished my brass, shined my shoes, and put on my best military manners in hopes that my request would be well received. It was very important to me.

When I entered headquarters the first sergeant asked what was the nature of my business. I told him I wished to see the commander in order to request a long weekend pass. He gave a faint smile and disappeared into the commander's office. Upon his return he stated that the major would see me now and held the door open. I

marched into the major's office and up to the desk while the first
sergeant closed the door. I stood at attention and held a salute until
the major looked up from his papers and returned it. The major ordered, "At ease, Mr. Fletcher. State your business." I proceeded to
tell him that my wife had arrived early that morning and since we
had not seen each other for four and a half months I was requesting, if possible, a long weekend pass.

He answered, "Request denied, Mr. Fletcher."

I immediately responded, "Thank you, Sir," saluted, did an
about face, and left the room. On the way out the first sergeant
stopped me and said he was sorry that I had not been successful
but the major was only following the policy in regard to the number
of people required on the base. I told him I understood and
thanked him for allowing me to see the major. To say that I was disappointed was a lie; I was crushed. Anyway, I would see her for
two hours that evening and we would have Saturday night together. Even that would be heaven, I was just hoping for more.

That evening just after 7:30 the cadet runner came to the cottage
and said I had a visitor at the gate. He handed me a pass and explained it was good only for a two-hour visit in the visiting area
just outside of the main gate. He also presented me with a copy of
the rules in regard to a female visitor. It would be wise to give the
copy to my spouse that she might know the rules before starting
divorce proceedings. I knew the rules but it dawned on me that I
had not prepared Sherry.

The rules were essentially this: We were required to remain in
the visiting area under the supervision of the guard at the gate. The
visiting area was a small barbed wire enclosure with two benches
facing each other about five feet apart as we were not to touch each
other. If we sat on the same bench there had to be eighteen inches
between us. An embrace or even a hand shake was out of the question. This arrangement reminded me of the prison visits I had seen
in the movies. The whole environment was very embarrassing.
The barbed wire enclosure, the guard watching our every move,
the wooden benches and dirt floor all gave the appearance of a pris-
oner of war camp. Rules were in place to make men of us, but certainly not fathers. The hard part was telling Sherry to stop where
she was and read the rules before we greeted each other. But in
spite of all of this our spirits were not dampened and she promised
not to divorce me until we had one night together.

While we were visiting, a couple came to the gate and requested
to visit Cadet Jim House. The lady was a real beauty; she was ac-

companied by a huge man with a full red beard. It was very unusual to see a man with a beard in those times. They arrived in separate cars: the lady in a new red convertible and the man in a new sedan. When Cadet House arrived we moved to the far end of the compound to allow them some privacy, but we did overhear enough of their conversation to realize that the young lady was Jim's sister. Her husband was Andy Devine, the movie star, and the reason for the beard was they were filming *Ali Baba and the Forty Thieves*. Here we were in the presence of a movie star and his family who were being accorded the same indignities.

When our time was up Jim's family left first, driving away in the sedan and leaving the convertible for him. Jim was a very pleasant, low-key person and this was the first time I realized he was close to members of the film industry. I chose not to tell any of the cadets what I had seen since I felt this was a private matter.

It was impossible to sleep that night. Mixed emotions kept nagging me awake. I was very happy that Sherry was there, but I was also miserable because of the way she and the other guests had to be treated. I could only hope that those who wrote and directed the policies of war exhibited more compassion and intelligence than those who were directing the cadet corps. I could not envision any situation where warmth, love, and pride of family could be construed to be a detriment to the service and me in particular. If a handshake or a quick embrace were to determine the outcome of the war we were in deep trouble. But as a cadet who wanted to fly you pocketed your pride and continued the farce of, "Yes, Sir. No excuse, Sir."

The next day, Saturday, I flew two hours and fifteen minutes. When I explained to Mr. Pulici that my wife was in town he suggested we fly the first hour dual because he needed to be sure my mind was on flying instead of something else. We spent most of the hour on aerial work, and then we proceeded to the auxiliary field to shoot landings. Traffic at the field was nonexistent as everyone was in the air practicing. Only the bus driver, dispatcher, and a few cadets were present. We practically had the field to ourselves.

We entered the pattern on the downwind leg. Visible to us about 400 feet inside the field boundary was an exceptionally green area about 100 feet in diameter. Just after passing the green spot Mr. Pulici jerked the throttle closed hollering, "Forced landing." I lowered the nose and set up a glide for the field. Through the gosport I heard Mr. Pulici say, "I hear you are pretty good at forced landings so let's see you hit that green spot." I nodded my head in agreement. I knew in a flash what I was going to do. Rather than risk going out too far and landing short of the green spot I would play it safe, come in high on the final approach then side-slip the airplane, a cross control procedure designed to lose altitude quickly, thereby avoiding any miscalculation. It was a recognized procedure taught in civilian flying just for this sort of emergency.

When I turned final Mr. Pulici gloated, "You blew it. You're way too high. You'll be lucky to hit the field, let alone the spot. Poor judgment, Mister. For this you get the bell." At that instant I lowered the left wing while applying pressure on the right top rudder to maintain directional control, elevating the nose slightly to keep from gaining excess speed. The Stearman was now in a slide-slip. The altimeter needle was unwinding at a highly accelerated pace. At 100 feet of altitude I released the pressure on the controls and resumed a normal glide, crossing over the airport boundary at seventy-five feet. Mr. Pulici, completely taken by surprise, let loose a barrage of screeches which I interpreted to mean "What do you think you are doing?" The airplane floated to the edge of the green and when the flare-out was completed the ship settled right in the center of the spot.

As I pulled over to taxi back Mr. Pulici gave me an earful. "Where did you learn that? Don't ever do that again. That is never done in the army and is not taught." I tried to explain it was a safe procedure designed for such an emergency. "Yes, in light planes it is okay, but in the heavy military aircraft you will eventually fly, NEVER. You can kill yourself. Because of the weight you can't recover fast enough. That's why we don't teach it."

"Okay, okay. I thought you wanted to see if I could do it."

"Not that way. Now don't ever do that again for me or any other instructor."

When he finished chewing me out he wearily climbed out of the airplane and said, "Since you are going to see your wife tonight I know it won't do any good to give you lessons to practice because you're going up to celebrate and have a good time. But please don't do any more side-slips or tear the wings off the plane and, above all, don't forget to return to the base on time. I will ride back with another student." I spent one hour and fifteen minutes doing every fun thing I knew and the instructor didn't have to worry about my losing the wings. The Stearman was a very sturdy airplane built more like a boxcar than a plane. It had withstood the stresses of pilots far better than me and even those who were worse.

On our way to dinner after flying I could tell that my roommate, whom I will now call Lester, was very moody and unhappy. I knew he lived in the Los Angeles area and had just become a father which should have been a reason for joy. His problem was that on our short pass he could not get to where he lived, visit his wife and daughter at the hospital, and still get back before his pass expired. This meant he wouldn't be able to see them until we got to be upperclassmen. I suggested that he explain his dilemma to the major and perhaps he might be more sympathetic to his plight than mine. He snapped back that he had already tried that and had been turned down. Lester was a good cadet but very moody, with light red hair and a temper with a hair trigger. While we were roomies we didn't become good friends. My other roommate was just plain withdrawn so the three of us never became close friends; each did his share of the communal chores and that was it.

When we returned from dinner we had thirty-five minutes before personal inspection. If we passed inspection we were then given our passes. I felt sorry for Lester and wanted to help him. An idea dawned on me. Every Saturday at inspection one cadet was selected out of each squadron in class 43-J and given a long pass, a gimmick to inspire us to look our best. The one chosen was known as the best-dressed cadet in the squadron. I told Lester that I would shine his shoes and brass, he could wear my new tie and maybe he would win, but we had to hurry as there wasn't much time. He said, "Do you really think so?"

"Why not? Somebody has to win." He got into the spirit of the competition and with five minutes left we had him shining and looking good. I was impressed. I had five minutes to get dressed and get into formation.

I lined up behind Lester. We had to stare straight ahead and not move a muscle during inspection, but in this position I could see Lester and the inspecting officer. I was surprised to see that this day the major was inspecting our squadron. After we opened ranks the major started down the front rank, trailed by the first sergeant who carried a clipboard with the squadron roster of names. The cadets wore name tags at all times so the inspecting officer could call your name and report violations to the first sergeant.

At the end of the first rank no demerits were given, but two cadets were ordered to remain in place when the squadron was dismissed. At the end of the second rank inspection one cadet was given a demerit for some infraction and another was ordered to stand fast. Then came the third rank: two were given demerits and when the major reached Lester he gave him a good look over and then ordered him to stay in place. I was elated. Lester was in the top four; he had a chance and I felt good about helping him. Now if his good luck could just hold he would have the long pass.

Coming down the fourth and final rank the major was speeding up. When he came to me I was frozen in place, my eyes glued straight ahead. The major gave me the once over, then seemed to be concentrating on something, maybe I had missed a button in my hurry. As he stood looking I knew I was going to be gigged so I couldn't believe my ears when I heard, "Stand fast, Mr. Fletcher."

The inspection over, the squadron closed ranks and was dismissed. The five of us remaining were ordered into a single line and the inspection commenced again. This time three cadets were dismissed; Lester and I stood side by side. I knew he was going to win. There we were, the two cadets who had both requested long passes now the finalists. Coincidence? Maybe, who knows. Anyway, Lester was a cinch. The major looked us over very carefully then commented to the first sergeant that it was certainly a tough decision and he didn't know how he was going to resolve it. He would try one more test. "Misters, let me see your dog tags." Since they were always worn on a chain around our necks, I immediately unbuttoned the next to the top button on my shirt and flipped out the tags. I couldn't see Lester since my eyes were still focused to the front. I assumed he was displaying his, but then I heard him utter, "Damn, I left them hanging on the bedpost."

We were dismissed as the first sergeant penned my name on the pass. As we walked into the cottage Lester looked at me with contempt, muttering, "You didn't even shine your shoes." But his remarks fell on deaf ears as I was heading for the Hotel Oxnard.

I ran over to tell a good friend, Don Bell, that I was ready to go as we were going to walk to the hotel together. Don was from southern Idaho, a little older than myself, having worked his way up to become a trainman in civilian life. He was a level-headed cadet and would have made a good roommate. His girlfriend was a school teacher from southern Idaho and had arrived in Oxnard on Friday to spend the weekend. Don had managed to reserve two rooms at the hotel, one for his girlfriend for Friday and Saturday nights and one for himself for Saturday night.

When we reached the hotel we found that his girlfriend had been assigned a room on the first floor and Don on the third floor. The four of us had supper together and then Sherry and I returned to her room to spend some time, which in today's vernacular would be called "quality time." She had room 62, a corner room on the ground floor. Don's girlfriend had room 60 and the headboards of our beds were back to back on the adjoining wall.

Upon returning to the room the suspense of the sleepless night, the stress of flying, and the surprise ending of the inspection were beginning to take their toll. A tired, relaxed, peaceful mood set in and I suddenly realized that in order to reach our goals all of us in the cadet corps had been running on nerve alone. We had long exceeded our own potential and stamina. Sherry and I were now reunited; I would start with renewed vigor, but only after my long pass had expired. For now I was happy and contented. My life was whole again and the entire cadet experience was pushed into the background.

It was hot in the room so I raised a window and put a stick in place so it wouldn't fall. We were visiting like there would be no tomorrow; so many things to catch up on. We could hear Don and his girlfriend laughing next door. In spite of the war we still lived in a wonderful world.

Our light went out early before Taps. As I prepared for bed I realized the room did not have a closet so I very painstakingly folded my clothes and laid them on a straight-back chair, with my shirt and blouse hung over the chair back and my service cap on top of the pile on the chair seat. My pajamas consisted of a T-shirt and O.D. boxer shorts. In my hurry to get to town I had even forgotten my shaving kit. Sherry remarked that she would probably be scared if she woke up and saw a man's clothes hanging in the room after all these months. I assured her that any clothes she saw in the room tonight would be mine. Not to worry.

Exhausted, I fell asleep. I thought I might be dreaming, but I finally realized Sherry was poking me in the ribs and whispering that someone was in the room with us. Half asleep I muttered that it was my clothes on the chair. Go back to sleep. Again she whispered, "Do something. There is someone in the room." Before I could answer something like a felt glove passed across my face. For a second I felt sharp terror. She was right, I had to do something.

It was pitch black in the room. I needed to turn the light on but the only one in the room was a ceiling light and the switch was by the entry door at the far end of the room. I jumped out of bed and bounded toward the door. Someone tripped me and as I fell I hit the footboard on the bed, jamming the headboard against the wall with a bang. I wasn't sure whether I was hurt or not but this was no place for a coward. As I jumped up I immediately flipped the light switch. Blinded by the light it took a second or two to realize I had fallen over the chair where I had placed my clothes. There did not appear to be anyone else in the room, but obviously something was wrong. At that moment a large bat dropped from the ceiling and made a pursuit pass over my head. I dropped to the floor and grabbed my shirt with the idea I would throw it over him on the next pass.

When Sherry saw the bat she screamed and immediately pulled the covers over her long blonde hair. Completely covered, she issued the muffled command, "Put on your cap. Bats can get tangled in your hair." By now I was so used to obeying commands that without even thinking I clutched the leather bill of my service cap and jammed it on my head. The bat would have had a problem since my G.I. haircut was so short even a marine would have been embarrassed. I jerked open the door leading to the hallway hoping to shoo the bat out, but for some reason he or she kept dive-bombing me. I was running around in my boxer shorts, T-shirt, and service cap, flagging the bat through on every pass.

Sherry, although completely huddled under the covers, was experiencing stark terror. Bats were never her favorite mammals. She was screaming, "Get that thing out of here." I was trying to reassure her that everything was okay even though I knew it wasn't since I wasn't having any luck chasing the bat by waving my shirt and doing a war dance. She took one more peek and screamed, "I can't stand that thing any longer. Please get it out of here." I renewed my efforts of running around the room waving the shirt and ducking out of the way as the bat was now upset too. One more "I can't stand it" echoed from the bed as I crashed against the wall running out of breath.

Just as I was getting ready for another pass there was a slight knock on the wall and a reticent voice whispered, "Fletch, is everything okay?"

I hollered back, "No."

Again a very reluctant, half-hearted voice said, "Is there any way I can help?" Before I could answer, the bat made another pass. I jumped over the fallen chair, grabbed my shoe, and threw it. Sherry responded with another "Get that thing out of here" in a trembling voice while I shouted at Bell that I needed help.

Within seconds Don appeared in the doorway in full uniform. He took one look in the room just as I was performing another "pase de pecho" with my shirt. As the bat went by he hollered "Olé" and doubled up with laughter. In between fits of guffawing he managed to gasp, "Thank God it wasn't what I thought." I didn't know what he thought but I suggested he could be a little more helpful. There was something about a camera and then, still laughing like a hyena, he gasped, "Why don't you put on your pants and I will go see if I can find a broom." I took his advice and pulled on my pants and shoes, still swinging the shirt. I suggested to Sherry that she go next door until the room was clear but she wasn't about to come out from under the covers.

Bell quickly returned with a straw house broom. The high ceiling gave the bat the advantage over us but we eventually chased it into the hall. When we went to return the broom the desk clerk, who was a young lady, announced that we were not going to leave the bat in the hall which led to the reception area. She wasn't about to have it in her domain so we opened the two large French doors that sealed off the dining area, while she hid under the front desk. After another long chase the bat flew into the dining room and we hurriedly closed the doors. The desk clerk, now mollified, thanked us profusely.

It was 11:30 and Bell, still laughing, headed up the stairway to his room. I surely wasn't going to thank him for his efforts after essentially providing the evening's entertainment. As I passed his girlfriend's door I did apologize to her for ruining her evening. She gave me a strange look and icily said they would still have some time in the morning since Don didn't have to report until noon, but I left with the impression she wasn't overjoyed with Don's choice of friends.

When I finally got back to our room Sherry was sitting up in bed pondering what Bell had said. When the meaning of his remarks eventually dawned on us we were able to have a good laugh at our perceived predicament. After finding a large hole in the screen I closed the window, rationalizing that not too much mental acumen was expected from a cadet.

We spent most of Sunday visiting, planning, and speculating what Sherry could do since she was on her own for the first time in a strange military environment. She was sure that Hotel Oxnard would not play a role in her future plans; the hotel had lost its romantic intrigue and the town fared no better.

Ventura sounded more attractive, but that was a decision she would have to make. My decisions were always made for me with a simple "Yes, Sir," but hers would not be made that easily. The responsibility for finding a place to live and a job rested on her shoulders as there wasn't any way I could help. Since we were mar-

ried adults we would not be humiliated again by the army's bull-
pen visiting policy. We would see one another only on weekends.
However, if an emergency arose or if something transpired that I
should know about, she could come any evening.

Left with her dilemma, we embraced in the room out of sight of
the all-seeing military eye. Then I hurriedly headed for the base, arriving in my room just as Taps was sounding. At the breakfast formation I was greeted with some strange all-knowing looks and
grins from close friends. Bell managed to stay clear of me, but I
would have given anything to have heard the concocted, titillative,
licentious stories he must have related to the others upon his return.

My two roommates were scheduled for a check ride that morning and both were in a foul mood. By midweek they were gone and
I was the sole occupant of the cottage. Word quickly spread that the
best way to wash out was to have Fletcher as a roommate. It was
rumored that he drove his roommates batty.

The strict rules under which the cadet corps operated can best
be conveyed by excerpts from a letter Sherry wrote to her parents:

> Gene was in some big parade Wednesday on the public school lawn
> but he didn't find out what it was for unless it was for publicity or better
> community relations. All he knew was he got hot—too hot in the sun.
>
> One of his roommates flunked out and had to leave Wednesday. The
> other one is on the verge but he doesn't know either way yet.
>
> Gene is going to get night flying while he is here so he is thrilled
> about that. All the instructors are practicing now so you hear them at all
> hours. He has a new instructor, his third one since he has been here. He
> hated to lose his old one as they were good friends and had so much fun
> together. He had about the same number of hours Gene has as he was a
> student instructor.
>
> I've been meaning to tell you that the cadets only sleep in their beds
> one night a week and that's Thursday night. You see it takes a compass,
> protractor, ruler and two fellows about an hour to make one bed. They
> don't have that much time each morning so they sleep on top of them.
> Fridays they have to change the sheets so that's why they sleep in their
> beds Thursday nights. Isn't that something?
>
> The scenery is beautiful here and the weather warm but not hot be-
> cause of the breeze from the ocean. I've seen so many new sights. Bar-
> rage balloons are flying everywhere along the coast, everyone is raising
> victory gardens and just outside of town there are huge truck gardens of
> cabbage and lettuce.
>
> Thursday a cadet wife came from Georgia, also a girl from Nebraska
> who is marrying a cadet today. There are wives here from nearly every
> state in the union—Washington sounds as if it's just in the backyard.

On Friday I was summoned to Captain Asmus's office on the flight line. He told me that he had coordinated with the commandant of cadets and that I was being assigned two roommates. Both had demonstrated good potential as pilots but were victims of minor accidents—a ground loop and a minor wing brush. He felt the cadets were experiencing a lack of confidence in their abilities, but they were men he did not want to lose. If I could inspire them and raise their morale, perhaps the army would gain two good pilots.

I knew the two men he was talking about. Both had a good sense of humor and I was pleased to have them as roommates. I could only hope the feeling would be reciprocated. This was how John D. Bride, Jr., became one of my roommates. Captain Asmus did not need to worry about J.D.'s morale. He was the second cadet in Squadron 8 to do a medium bank 180 degree turn on the runway: a ground loop. This was not a spectacular feat in itself, in fact it was rather commonplace, but what made it noteworthy was the fact that J.D. was able to accomplish this with an instructor on board. John thought the instructor was flying and the instructor was positive J.D. was in control. One thing was certain, the airplane was out of control.

Anyway, J.D. was taking it all in stride and I wasn't about to tell him how to fly an airplane since he outweighed me by about forty pounds. He always wore a pleasant smile and was a master of one-liners. When the need arose he could become very serious and you knew he was thinking all of the time. We did as much hangar flying as time allowed and I don't know if it was a help to him, but I certainly enjoyed and profited from our sessions.

J.D. had earned the nickname of the "Light Duty Kid," which simply meant he had learned how to manipulate the system. Whenever any project or physical fitness tests were scheduled he always showed up with a slip from the medics restricting his participation to light duty. Not everyone could do this. It took brains and a certain amount of wiliness to do this correctly and not cross the fine line of being a goldbricker (those who did absolutely nothing).

By now many of our instructors had acquired nicknames, all of them printable but never used in their presence. I'm sure the instructors had pet names for the cadets also, although we had no desire to learn what they were.

Our roomie had drawn an instructor we called Laughing Boy. This man wore a perpetual frown combined with a slight sneer. He had a sharp, shrill voice and was continually needling his students. It was said that he had whipped many a cadet into shape for a check ride: it was easier to pass it than to face Laughing Boy if you failed. Our roomie was complaining about him constantly. One day I remarked that he shouldn't complain, he should feel sorry for the man's wife since she had to live with him and put up with him longer than he ever would. His response was that his wife lived with him because she wanted to, otherwise she could get a divorce and leave, whereas he was stuck with him until he graduated or washed out. Unfortunately the latter came first.

Our next roommate was the victim of a nose-over, which was apparently the result of applying the brakes too harshly. His story was that the brakes locked, causing the longitudinal axis to rotate over the lateral axis while the plane was still in a three-point position. He was able to walk away so it must have been a good landing. It was his good fortune to be awarded the cowbell for several days.

In the meantime Sherry was busy scouring the rental ads in the local newspaper. By Thursday she had run out of leads and decided to try in Ventura, a small town located on the ocean about eight miles away. Ventura was a navy town and a bedroom community for Port Hueneme (pronounced *y Knee me*). There was transportation service between Oxnard, Ventura, and Port Hueneme with buses leaving Oxnard about every half hour.

She spent most of the day Thursday looking in Ventura. It was a disappointing day but she decided to try again on Friday. While on her way from the bus stop to a place where she could buy a newspaper she thought she heard someone call her name, something she knew was impossible since she was 1,500 miles from home and friends. Again a lady said, "Evelyn Sherrod, is that you?" and to her surprise she was staring at a good friend who had taught school with her older sister, Mildred, in the small town of Fairfield, Washington. Lorraine Littleton. It was a pleasant shock and surprise for both of them. Lorraine was now married to Howard McNew, who also was a teacher in civilian life but was serving as a pharmacist mate assigned to a ship stationed at Port Hueneme. Lorraine took Sherry under her protective wing and brought her to the Hoover Hotel where Lorraine and Howard had a room. Since Lorraine was acquainted with the lady manager, she felt something could be worked out. The manager said she had a room that was available immediately. The cost was seven dollars a week, but on the nights when I stayed over there would be an extra one dollar charge to cover the cost of extra towels, water, and the like. Sherry paid for the room and caught the bus back to Oxnard to pick up her belongings. Just seeing a friend and knowing that she would have the company of someone she knew during the week gave her a sense of security along with a boost in morale that was sorely needed. She called the base and left the message that she had moved and if Cadet Fletcher received a pass on Saturday to catch the bus for Ventura.

During midweek 43-I class finished flying training. They were now just marking time until orders were received which would transfer them to Basic training. It was rumored they would leave during the last week in May. The weather had been very cooperative and we were now ahead of schedule in flying time; most of us had about forty hours. In my case I had logged forty-one hours total time including twenty-one hours of solo time.

Saturday, after flying, I received a short pass and was able to catch the bus for Ventura. Cadet Bell had no desire to accompany me this time. Arriving at the Hoover Hotel, I met the McNews for the first time. I was very impressed with this handsome couple. Both exuded warmth and kindness and were the type of people you would want for lifetime friends. Lorraine was a beautiful, no-nonsense lady. I knew she would be the perfect companion and big sister for Sherry. It was a great feeling of relief to know she was in such good company in the heart of a sailor town.

We didn't have a lot of time together since I had to return at noon Sunday, but at least Saturday night was not interrupted by another bat chase. When we parted Sunday morning Sherry was very happy with her situation and excited over the prospect of job hunting.

I-class departed on schedule and 43-J became the top dogs. Their legacy to us came in story form but without title or author:

IT SAYETH HERE...

Now, verily, I say there liveth among the many of the mighty land a tribe of barbarians whose ways are passing strange. Themselves they calleth Air Cadets and woe be unto those who joineth their ranks. When they goeth to sup, their meal they speaketh of as mess. Though they consumeth the meal, the mess they leaveth behind.

Their raiment doth bewilder the eye. Of color and of texture each garment looketh alike one unto the other. But, verily, the tall among them sticketh out like four brooms in a flour sack, while the short among them becometh lost in billowing folds. Upon their heads they wear dull brown hats which doth have ear flaps and small tin horns thereon; while crost the top two bulging eyes protrudeth, which the supply room doth term goggles.

Early each morn, sure as the sun riseth unto the heavens, behold, a group of these creatures marcheth forth from their stronghold; each one singeth with lust his war chant. Rock ye not in terror, brethren, for the tale hath just begun. For these barbarians, all clad in their strange raiment, mount unto strange winged crates and soar about the heavens like birds, each one seeking to drive the other from the sky. Now, hark ye, a strange thing. While some mount crates behind the stalwart figure who graceth the front seat, there are others who go unto the sky alone, there to fly crazily about, describing great and awkward eights throughout the heavens. It is these, brethren, that righteous men fear; for in their haste and zest, they calleth unto the Being for the wrath to beat about their heads, and many times doth their engines conk out and leave they and the world in fear and trembling. Then, as the strange tale goeth, they descend from the heavens and enter again unto their stronghold, lustily trying once more their war chant.

Truly, brethren, if one doth peep about in the late afternoon, one doth see them all unto a line, dressed now in gray, sack-like apparel, describing great arcs in the air and while some bendeth on hands and knees and kicketh about their legs, others about them stand and goldbrick. Verily, these are strange men, and wise men would shun them for truly, they seem to use their heads only to keep their two ears from slapping.

Friday, finishing a solo practice session, I flew over auxiliary field #3 five hundred feet above traffic altitude to determine the direction of traffic. Our direction indicator on the auxiliary field was not too sophisticated. It consisted of two 1-by-12 boards about ten feet long, painted white. The two unattached boards were placed to form a T with the top of the T pointing to the direction in which to land. As I looked down the T was pointing to the west and I noticed two cadets walking toward the area where the T was located. I set up a landing pattern in accordance with the T and proceeded to concentrate on the landing procedure while day-dreaming about my upcoming Saturday pass.

About halfway down the final approach another airplane appeared on final from the opposite direction. A quick look down showed the T now pointing east and the two cadets sauntering back toward the bus, their mission accomplished. I immediately applied full throttle, climbing and turning away to the right, which was the correct emergency procedure, at the same time quietly hurling invectives at the cadets for changing traffic with an airplane in the pattern.

I wasn't particularly worried because the complete airfield lay between the two landing aircraft. There wasn't any danger of a collision as I had yielded right-of-way in the proper manner before reaching the airport boundary. With the new pattern set up I landed and taxied to the parking area to exchange with another student. After crawling out of the cockpit I started to remove my parachute when the cadet from the plane which had landed ahead of me came running over and said to leave my parachute on as Captain Wells, the senior military check pilot, was requesting that I report to him immediately at the airplane. The cadet was agitated and nervous so it was safe to assume that I was in trouble since this was the plane I had given way to on final approach.

Captain Asmus's warning now came surging back: "Don't make even the appearance of a mistake because they're waiting for you." I had now goofed and would have to pay the price. While there wasn't any danger involved, the least I could have done was re-checked the T while on the base leg since I had seen the cadets moving in that direction and knew their purpose.

I hurried to the airplane and saluted the grim-faced captain on board while standing in the breeze of the idling prop. He waved back a salute and motioned me into the rear cockpit. As soon as I was buckled up and had placed the gosport tubes on the metal connectors on my helmet the captain let loose with, "Mister, I want you to take off and perform the following maneuvers in the exact sequence that I will now give you." With pencil in hand I started making scratches on my knee pad indicating the maneuvers: sideways u for an Immelmann turn, o for a loop, slash for a stall, squiggle for a snap roll, squiggle with a minus for a slow roll, z for a falling leaf, and 8 minus for a lazy eight. After several minutes I ran out of symbols and could only hope that he couldn't remember the order either. Finally he ran out of maneuvers and breath and motioned for me to taxi.

This could be my last ride, but if it was it would be my best because he had a very determined cadet in the rear seat who would not wash out without a protest. Upon reaching altitude I rolled the airplane from right to left to make sure there wasn't anyone below us on either side. Then after checking above I lowered the nose, applied full power to gather airspeed, and pulled up into an Immelmann turn. Again checking to make sure we were clear of other airplanes I performed a tight loop, retarding the throttle on the downward side as we pulled out in level flight. The captain had the controls in a firm grip and the rudder locked in neutral with pressure from his feet. I wasn't sure whether I was supposed to break his control or what.

Before I could respond he shouted into the gosport, "I've got it."

I relaxed my grip on the controls and throttle, but kept them in place to follow through with his motions. For about twenty minutes he put the Stearman through the paces, then made a straight-in approach to the auxiliary field and landed without entering the pattern. It dawned on me that this was the same thing he had done when I was forced to leave the pattern. Had he flown a pattern I would have seen him across from me on the downwind leg.

Upon landing he taxied back to the staging area with a speed far in excess of what the cadets were allowed to use. When the airplane came to a full stop I was prepared for an earful, but instead he motioned for me to get out. I crawled out of the cockpit, stepped back three paces and saluted him. He gave me a stern look, returned the salute and taxied off. It was a strange flight. The only words spoken in the air were, "I've got it." Those were the only and last words I heard and no one ever mentioned anything about it: the military, Mr. Pulici, or Captain Asmus. It was just as if it had never happened and I certainly didn't bring up the subject to anyone.

Saturday evening found me back in Ventura. Sherry was in a happy mood for she had found a job as a clerk in the local store of a large chain. She and Lorraine were enjoying each other's company and they found many things to do to fill their spare time. When I left Sunday morning to return to the base, Sherry decided she would sunbathe on the sandy beach which was just about two blocks from the hotel.

Back at the base everything was routine flying and classes, both punctuated by the usual harangue of the instructor. The cadet corps had now been weeded down. We were working on more precise flying skills which included spot landings, landing after passing over a rope hurdle, and various other tactics which required more expertise. It was a challenge the cadets enjoyed, each attempting to outdo the others. The flight instructors were starting to relax a bit and enjoy watching the fruits of their labor perform.

The week passed very quickly but not nearly as fast as the weekend pass. Sherry had been promoted to cashier and was now working in the office. She had been assistant cashier in the branch store at Walla Walla and consequently knew the procedures and duties.

On her trip to the beach the preceding Sunday, she, not being used to the effect of California sun on her fair skin, received a very severe sunburn. The hotel manager, seeing her return to the lobby, advised her to get olive oil and vinegar, mix them half and half, and keep her body saturated until nature could provide healing. I don't know how successful the treatment was but she thought it worked wonders. However, the blisters and red peeling skin certainly altered the appearance of the young lady I had bid good-bye. She jokingly insisted that she was promoted into the office to keep her out of sight of the viewing public.

As we continued our flying the advantage between previous-time men and the newly soloed men continued to shrink. The cadets who were flying for the first time were now demonstrating a proficiency to be envied because of the rapid pace in which they mastered the art of flying. As their abilities increased so did their level of confidence. We knew we were watching men who would some day make aviation history. And while we all laughed and joked about the cadet/teacher relationship, we knew a bond had been forged between the student and his mentor. The cadets would later relate with pride and admiration the stories of learning to fly and the impact these Primary instructors had on their lives. If nothing else, the immense load that these instructors carried flying six days a week with as many as five or six students, risking their lives to impart knowledge and expertise, commanded admiration.

The last two weeks of flying passed in a very routine manner as we passed stage checks and flew dual and solo cross-country flights. The name is somewhat misleading since we did not actually fly across the country but flew to a neighboring town and returned without landing, testing navigational skills. For me the dual flight lasted one hour and ten minutes as we flew from Oxnard to Newhall and returned. My solo flight was to Moorpark and return, a total of forty-five minutes in the air and never out of sight of either destination. I felt it was a very trivial flight and not a test. However, the half-dozen cadets who got lost and spent more time in the air did not agree with my analysis. To me the real test was back in Civilian Pilot Training. There, to qualify for a private pilot license, the solo cross-country was a triangular flight with each leg over an hour in length with a landing at the end of each leg to have your log book signed by the airport manager. Refueling was also required, so this all resulted in more than four hours flying time plus the time spent on the ground at the end of the two vectors. That was a test.

On June 11 I received my final check ride. I was requested to take off, spend thirty minutes getting used to the flying characteristics of the airplane, and then land and pick up Captain Asmus for the final test. Even though I had flown many times with my former instructor I was slightly nervous. I wanted to perform at my best to show him that I had made considerable improvement. A check ride with anyone always creates some anxieties as you question your abilities to perform any test under stress.

The test was going along smoothly, although I had the feeling that I could have done better on some of the maneuvers. Finally it came time to do a slow roll to the right. As I lowered the nose to pick up flying speed I picked out a point on the horizon on which I could center the nose of the aircraft and hold it there while the craft rotated through 360 degrees in the horizontal position. As the plane moved to the inverted position I felt myself falling out of the aircraft. It was a feeling of sheer terror. In the same instant the falling sensation stopped; the friction catch on the buckle had allowed the safety belt to slip about two inches. My body was hanging on the belt with the seat parachute not touching the seat in the airplane, but with my feet still on the rudder pedals. With deliberate precision I made a quick shift from full right rudder to full left rudder hoping to speed up the roll so centrifugal force would overcome gravity and push me back into the seat. To the end of my life I will always remember the leg movements that were made by a frantic pilot. I got the desired results and as the roll was finished I realized that the nose had stayed glued to my check point on the horizon. It was a sober, ashen-faced cadet who finished a ride that lasted forty-five minutes. I dreaded the critique to come; I didn't want to hear about the slow roll fiasco. This was a mental block as it could be the one thing that would cause real trouble.

On the ground Captain Asmus pulled out his checklist and we started going through the flight step by step as he explained my performance on each maneuver: Snap roll, not bad, but the nose went a little too wide around the point. Learn to tighten it up. On the next: Entry speed a little too slow. Loop could have been a little tighter, and so on. Nothing too bad, just a little more refinement. Finally the dreaded slow roll. He stopped and thought a minute. By his hesitation I knew he was choosing his words and my heart started to sink. Here it comes. In slow, measured tones he said, "Fletch, I've flown with a lot of experienced pilots as well as hundreds of cadets and I must tell you that no one has ever demonstrated a slow roll such as yours." Oh, no, it was worse than I thought. "The entry was perfect. The timing on the rudder pedals and the recovery was exact. The nose never wavered. I would have to say it was the best slow roll I have ever ridden through."

I was dumbfounded but I managed to mumble, "Captain

Asmus, when I started that slow roll my seat belt slipped and I thought I was a goner. All I was trying to do was stay in the airplane. It was a survival roll as far as I was concerned. If it turned out good I can assure you it was accidental, not intentional." He smiled and said, "Well, let's hope you continue to fly accidentally. You have just completed all the check requirements to go on to Basic. You will have one more flight. That will be Monday night when you will experience your first night landing. I have decided that I want to be the one to demonstrate that. Have a good weekend. I know you have a long pass and I will see you Monday."

Even though it was Friday afternoon I could hardly wait for Saturday to get to Ventura to tell Sherry the good news. We celebrated with the McNews and they were just as happy as I was that I had passed the second hurdle in the cadet program, even though we knew this meant we would be parting company after one more weekend.

Monday evening was a real event on the flight line. The runway was not lighted, consequently the cadets and the instructors worked together to place kerosene burning pot flares about a hundred feet apart down both sides of the left-hand runway. The Stearman did not have landing or cockpit lights. The instructors carried flashlights on board but this was only to check oil pressure, altitude, and airspeed. This was known as blind flying in its most elementary sense.

After every flare was in place we waited for complete darkness. Then the flares were lighted and the whine of the inertia starter on the engines filled the air, along with a few wracking coughs as the starters were engaged and the engines sputtered to life. The atmosphere resembled that of a pep rally. Everybody was excited, including the instructors, since these demonstration rides were only given once, at the end of every class. They really looked forward to this event. I was never sure whether it was the thrill of night flying or the fact that it was the last time they had to ride with us that was the cause for joy.

When I crawled in with Captain Asmus he said, "Prepare yourself for the thrill of a lifetime." We made two night landings, never leaving the pattern. At the conclusion I now had fourteen minutes of dual night flying in my log book. The entry didn't amount to much on paper, but the thrill of being in the night air, the wind whistling by the open cockpit, the scarves around our necks snapping in the slipstream, the lights of the town sparkling in the clear night, the lighted flares marking the runway all combined to produce a feeling you don't forget. And for us it was even more momentous since we knew this was our last ride in a Stearman. What a way to end Primary training and say good-bye to the men who had brought us through sixty-five hours of arduous and dangerous training.

As I crawled out and shook hands with Captain Asmus there was a feeling of warmth and a bond. All I could say was, "Thank you for everything, Sir." That was all that needed to be said as the look in his eyes showed he understood.

The next day we started finishing up our ground school and physical fitness tests, but I received a surprise in the afternoon when I was pulled from a formation and ordered to report to the flight line in flying gear. What had gone wrong? Had the military pilot raised some doubts? Uncertainty. That was what cadet training was all about. I went on the double to Captain Asmus's office as I was sure I had completed everything, but in the military you run on doubts and rumors so this should have been routine.

When I reached his office he looked up, smiled, and said, "Mr. Fletcher, I have just been going over your log book and find that you are eleven minutes short of sixty-five hours. Mr. Pulici is on the line with an aircraft. Run out, jump in, and fly around the pattern, make one or two landings, log eleven minutes, and report back to the cadet compound."

As soon as I crawled in Mr. Pulici jumped out, insisting that I was trying to leave without finishing the course. I hollered back, "No, sir. How about letting me fly the crate to Basic?"

With a big grin he replied, "Fly your eleven minutes and get out of here. Give my condolences to your next instructor because he will surely need them."

When I was done, the log book showed sixty-five hours total: thirty-six hours solo time, twenty-nine hours of dual instruction including fourteen minutes of night flying.

With our Primary flying time completed everyone was looking forward to Basic Training. At Santa Ana, secrecy had surrounded our next destination. But here, since we were on a civilian field, we were immediately told where we were going. All four squadrons were heading for Lancaster, California.

We got our passes early Saturday morning so upon reaching Ventura I was able to tell Sherry where we were going. We knew that Lancaster was a very small town and places to stay would be in short supply or nonexistent. As we mulled over the situation we hit upon a plan that might work. If we could get to Lancaster before we were transferred we might beat the rush and find something, so we rented a car.

Once there we started asking people if they knew of any place where lodging was available. We really didn't receive any encouragement since most of the available places were already rented to the spouses of H and I classes. Finally we started knocking on doors in the residential area, introducing ourselves and asking the residents if they rented rooms or knew of anyone who did who might have a vacancy. It was the same story. When the wives of H class left we might be able to find something, but it would be on a first-come basis.

We decided to try one more home before returning to Oxnard. The door was answered by a motherly middle-aged woman. We told the lady who we were and explained our predicament. She invited us into her home for a cool drink while she thought about how to help us. After a short visit she explained that her daughter was a WAAC serving on a distant military base, consequently her room was not occupied. She was sure her husband wouldn't object to renting the room to Sherry, even though it had not been rented before, providing Sherry felt the room was large enough and was interested. We explained that any room would be large enough since we did not have any other prospects. Sherry closed the deal immediately, with Mrs. Story apologizing for the four dollar a week rent for a room without a cooler, especially with the heat of summer coming on.

It was a happy drive back to Oxnard. The mission had been a success. When I returned to Mira Loma on Sunday I knew that Sherry would be leaving on Monday for Lancaster.

In a letter from Sis received two days before, she had mentioned they were thrilled that Cap had finished Primary and they were heading to Coffeyville, Kansas, a BT-13 school for Basic Training.

That night as Taps was sounded it was the sweetest sound anyone could expect to hear. Our bugler was Cadet Boldi, a master of the trumpet. He was the first in Squadron 8 to commit a ground loop, followed two days later by J. D. Bride. Boldi could have committed any sin he wished and not been washed out. He was irreplaceable. His prominence as a bugler was well known at Santa Ana and his reputation preceded him to Oxnard. One evening during the first week at Oxnard immediately after Taps, he played two popular songs of the day. Everyone in the cadet corps thought it was great. He rendered music with such dignity, grace, and clarity of tone that we were mesmerized. We wondered what would happen as this was a total departure from tradition. If it meant tours every cadet would have walked with him. Our worries were put at ease two days later when he said that the officers were also impressed and as long as we were on a civilian field this could be a nightly occurrence.

With Taps over and lights out, the sweet sound of the trumpet permeated every nook and cranny on the base. The familiar sounds cast a spell over a life filled with responsibility and we listened in awe, each with his own memories and dreams of the future. It became a ritual that we all anticipated: a security blanket, or at least a momentary escape from reality.

Our departure date was set for June 22. Bus transportation had been arranged for the corps of cadets. We had arrived in army 6 × 6s but we were to leave in style. There were three exceptions: Cadet Jim House and two others were allowed to drive their personal autos. Just before boarding the bus I was presented a leather billfold. This same memento might have been awarded to all members, but I'm not sure. Mine contained a citation stating:

> E. R. Fletcher is hereby granted this school's Gold Star Merit Award and his name has been inscribed in the Academy's Hall of Fame in recognition of having completed the course of flying training with distinction and without accident of any kind.
>
> Signed C. C. Moseley, President
> Mira Loma Flight Academy

As we boarded the bus I noticed that Gene Jones, my classmate from Dayton who had been assigned to Squadron 7, was still with us. We had spent nine weeks at Primary and still had not had a chance to visit.

We had come to Mira Loma over 200 strong; we left with a head count of 176, plus our eight student officers. Our ranks had been thinned by more than twenty-five cadets.

4

Basic Flying School

Lancaster, California

We arrived at Polaris Flight Academy, War Eagle Field, in the afternoon of June 22. We were somewhere in or near the Mojave Desert, too far to walk to civilization. The buses parked by the main gate and the drivers started unloading our bags. There was no welcoming committee; it must have been siesta time. The heat was stifling, putting a damper on any activity that required physical exertion.

While the bags were being unloaded several of us walked over to a large flatbed trailer parked not far from the front gate. The trailer appeared to be loaded with scrap aluminum and junk. It didn't take us long to realize that we were looking at the mangled components of one or possibly two Basic trainers. Upon closer inspection we saw small flecks of bone and shreds of material that might have once been a flying suit. I turned away with a sick feeling having seen enough to remind me that not all flying was fun and games. Sometime, somewhere, someone was paying the ultimate price to provide our nation with pilots and air crewmen. I will never know why this spectacle was allowed to greet us. Maybe it was meant to be a reminder that we were training in a hazardous occupation, but more likely it was just an oversight. We had already found out that two former members of Squadron 58 had perished in a head-on collision and a third in a spin. But those were letter statistics. This was grim reality, a sight that could not be pushed to the farthest recesses of the mind. For that reason I suspect I unconsciously became a more cautious, conservative cadet.

Filing into the central compound through the main gate, we realized that Polaris Flight Academy was almost a complete replica of

War Eagle Field, Polaris Flight Academy

Mira Loma, only on a grander scale. The same style: cottages in circles enclosing a courtyard with a flag pole in the center. There was green grass and all the buildings were bathed in a new coat of paint. There was only one drawback immediately apparent and that was the burning sun. Later we would find others.

We had been told that all Basic flying schools were completely militarized. But here we were on a civilian field also owned by Major C. C. Moseley: another Country Club of the Air. We suspected this was the only civilian Basic school in the country.

We were eventually told that the base had been built to train English cadets for the Royal Air Force. The European conflict had made it difficult to train cadets in England, and the RAF had sought a safer haven to pursue this endeavor. British cadets had been arriving since 1941. Their last class of pilots had departed Number 2 British Flying Training School, Lancaster, California, about February 1943. All British trappings had been removed, but many letters of commendation from the British government were framed and hanging in the headquarters building. Apparently a new name and a fresh paint job was all that was necessary to convert to an Army Air Force Basic Flying School.

As we filed into the courtyard we were met by a contingent of military officers. We were assigned cottages and told to report in formation at 0900 the next morning wearing fatigue uniforms. At this time we would be briefed on our schedule and the rules of the post. We were then dismissed to settle in.

D. C. Bell

The cottages were slightly different from those at Mira Loma in that four cadets were assigned to a unit. A unit consisted of two rooms separated by a common latrine and a hallway. Don Bell and I were assigned as roommates. He said that this was his choice. Since he had to look after me at Primary we might as well be roomies and make the job easier for him. He had already received a Dear John letter from his girlfriend, for which he thought I was responsible. Once he made up his mind whether this was good or bad he would be able to make life miserable for me or thank me on a twenty-four-hour basis. But I had the feeling he already counted it as a blessing.

At supper that evening we learned that both classes shared the common dining hall but each was assigned a designated area. The regular military officers and student officers had a separate dining facility in another building which housed the small post exchange, a facility which was deemed necessary due to the remoteness of War Eagle Field.

After Taps we were again treated to the melodious sounds of George Boldi's trumpet. So what had changed? We were still on a campus-style civilian field; our flying and ground instructors were all civilians; we still had a military cadre only slightly larger than

Primary; Sherry was already in Lancaster. What more could a cadet ask? When I was explaining all of this to Don Bell he exclaimed, "Fletch, if you think you've died and gone to heaven take a look at the thermometer over there. We're probably nearer to shoveling coal than growing wings, possibly closer than either one of us would care to admit."

"Knock it off and let's see what tomorrow brings."

At 0900 we assembled in the inner court and received our usual welcome including all the threats and no-nos. We would retain our cadet officers who had served us so well at Mira Loma, but apparently there were several rule differences here. One: There were many female employees on the base and there would be no fraternizing. Two: We would not fly on Saturdays. Three: We were not placed under quarantine as we had been led to believe. It was obvious the hot sun had sterilized everything including the cadets. We received the usual pep talk and an announcement that we would meet our ground school instructors Friday and our flying instructors on Monday. The ensuing time would be spent on orientation. We were then introduced to our first orientation instructor, a second lieutenant who was in charge of the physical training unit.

We were greeted by a ninety-day ground-pounding wonder who had just reported to the base a few days before. It was his first assignment from Officer Candidate School. He was formerly a high school coach and he would not be satisfied until all of us were as physically hardy as himself. To show us how he was going to accomplish this we were to fill our canteens and he would personally lead us on a ten-mile forced march along the desert roads.

We marched off the base in formation singing the Air Force Song with the temperature well over 100 degrees, but once out of sight of the base we were allowed to break formation and continue at our own pace. One mile down the blacktopped highway we turned off onto a sandy desert road.

The desert sun was cruel. Trailing us by about fifty yards was an ambulance. The instructor smirkingly stated that if anyone could not keep up he could show his true colors and ride in the ambulance. However, he was challenging the wrong group of people. We had been in training for six months compared to his ninety days.

We were in top physical condition, but none of us was used to the searing heat. We made regular rest stops and visited while resting. Eventually we gave up the visiting and merely tried to convince those who were suffering from heat and blisters on their feet to get in and ride a ways, advising them that they were more valuable as pilots than desert rats. But pride kept most of them on their feet. Eventually two cadets fainted from sunstroke and were placed in the ambulance.

It was sheer torture. Some of the cadets were picking up sunburn and showing signs of heat exhaustion. Those of us with darker skin were spared the sunburns but we still suffered from the heat. The lieutenant was slowing down and he started limping, a sure sign of blisters. When the instructor showed signs of stress the cadets pushed harder and became more determined. We were finally able to convince several cadets to ride a short distance to recuperate. We did not want to see anyone's health or flying career ruined because of some misguided nut who happened to be wearing gold bars.

At the next stop it was evident that the lieutenant was in trouble with blistered feet. We implored him to ride in the ambulance; it was ridiculous to continue in his condition. We made it clear that no one would think any less of him. No one doubted his stamina or resolve, but it was foolish to continue with swollen feet and blisters. He let us know that he would not get in the ambulance. His pride was just as great as ours; he started out leading and he would continue to lead until we reached the field.

We had been following roads which formed sort of a rectangular pattern around the field. There was no question that everyone had had enough by the time we reached the blacktop. One last rest, and then we would go the final mile. We used the last of our water from the supply on the ambulance. The driver was willing to drive to the base and bring back more, but we all felt we could make it.

During the rest the lieutenant removed his shoes. His feet were so swollen and blistered that he could not put them back on so he tied the strings together and draped them around his neck and started down the hot blacktop highway in his stocking feet. We felt sorry for him but it was his decision to push ahead. At this point we just wanted it to end. We didn't believe in martyrs or miracles; we just wanted to fly.

When we entered the base it was a sad lot that silently passed through the gate, a direct contradiction to the marching, singing group that left. As we headed for the showers we were advised that the medics were standing by to treat blisters, sunburn, and any other problems we might have. We did not see the lieutenant for at least a week and to my knowledge no one asked about him. The four of us in our unit could hardly wait to get the two coolers turned on and the shower running. It was a day we could not easily forget.

All of the cottages were cooled by swamp coolers, a primitive form of air conditioning. The unit was mounted in the wall so that air could be pulled in from the outside by an electric fan mounted in the back. Water was allowed to drip down through excelsior-type filters and the air was cooled as it was forced through the saturated filters. As water built up in a sump in the bottom pan it was pumped back up to trickle down again. These units were quite effective in the desert climate and most of the cadets left them on all night in order to sleep more comfortably.

We soon found we had a problem with the cooler in our room. The room had been freshly calcimined in a strange green color but, unfortunately, the painter had decided to calcimine the inside of the cooler and had also spilled some in the sump. Just as soon as the water was turned on and the unit started, the smell became unbearable. We decided it was easier to sweat than to put up with the stench. We tried several times to clean it but without success, so we decided to leave it off and hopefully gain some relief from the cooler in the other room.

We received a short pass on Sunday and were assured that our regular permanent passes would be available before the next weekend. I caught the bus into Lancaster and headed for the Story residence to check on Sherry. She had arrived Monday on the Pacific Greyhound Lines bus and was the only passenger to get off at Lancaster. Upon stepping to the ground she turned around to wait for the driver to open the side hatch so she could claim her suitcase, but instead he closed the door and drove off. She had only the clothes on her back, the lingerie on her bottom, and her purse. She notified the station agent who advised her not to worry, they would track down her luggage and it would arrive in three or four days. Mrs. Story provided her with a dressing gown so she could wash her clothes every evening. The hot, dry air of a Lancaster night provided a perfect dryer so she was able to have clean clothes every day; however, the choice was limited.

Mrs. Story told Sherry that many young ladies were employed at Polaris Flight Academy, and perhaps she could put her name on the list. Consequently, Tuesday morning she caught the local bus for War Eagle Field and proceeded to the employment office. The man she needed to talk to was on the telephone. When he finished his conversation, she told him she would like to place her name on the list to be notified if they had a vacancy. His response was, "Can you start to work right now?" She assured him that she could. He explained that the phone call was from the manager of

With Sherry

the officers' dining hall. They were short a waitress and needed one immediately. The paperwork could be taken care of later. She received two meals a day and worked through the dinner and supper hours.

She had seen us arrive and at this point she knew our schedule better than we did. The job was a blessing for her since her work area was air cooled and she was there during the hottest part of the day. It sounded great to me even though I knew I would never see her on the base.

I was able to meet Mr. Story, but it would be another week before we really became acquainted. My few hours were up; it was time to return. Sherry's suitcase had been found and returned on Friday, so she now could change clothes.

Monday we reported to the flight line for instructor assignments. Bell and I wound up with different instructors. Four of us were assigned to Eugene Bowen, a fine looking man endowed with a pleasant, outgoing personality with the right blend of sternness and humor to command respect and at the same time make you feel at ease. I could sense that my usual luck on the instructor draw was holding; our personalities meshed on the first handshake. Now if I could just fly and make progress, Basic would be fun. Mr. Bowen said we would spend all morning on the line but we would not fly. There was an instructor's meeting he had to attend which probably would last two hours. In the meantime we were to go out on the flight line and inspect the basic trainers, crawl into the cockpit, familiarize ourselves with the location of controls, and then report back. We would go over everything we had seen and he would explain the function, location, and operation of everything in the cockpit.

"Pay attention to what you see and what I tell you. Before you solo you will be placed in the cockpit and blindfolded, then as I call off each control, gauge, or lever you must instantaneously touch or grasp the object. You will not be allowed to grope. In an emergency you have to react on instinct, you won't have time to look for something. Now it will be best if you work in pairs. Eventually you will perform buddy rides so let's start right off that way. Mr. Fletcher and Mr. Hoffman will work together. Mr. Littlefield and Mr. Marchant will function as a unit starting as of now. Mr. Fletcher, do not report to the flight line again in your work shoes."

I stupidly suggested that I thought the uppers on the work shoes would give ankle support in case of a bail out. He smiled and said, "My students are trained to fly, not to bail out. Wear the thinnest soled shoes you have so you can actually feel the amount of pressure you are placing on the rudder controls. Report back in two hours. Dismissed."

It was a pleasure to be assigned to learn and fly with Cadet Robert Hoffman. He was known and liked by all in the cadet corps. He was a good-looking cadet with a deep bass voice, a pleasant grin, a heavy suntan, and a sense of humor which worked overtime. Every morning as he greeted his fellow cadets it was always the same. In my case it was, "Mornin' Fletch." Then dropping his deep voice one octave lower he always growled, "How you doin', old dawg?" It was a greeting that was pleasant to hear and always brought a laugh from the recipient, but it also led to his being nicknamed "Old Dawg" since the response was always, "Fine, Old Dawg, how are you doing?"

It didn't take Old Dawg long to find us an unoccupied BT-13A, a low wing monoplane manufactured by the Vultee Company and known as the Vultee Valiant. However, previous cadet classes had already nicknamed it the Vultee Vibrator. It was equipped with a 450-horsepower nine-cylinder radial Pratt Whitney engine. It had a maximum gross weight of 4,490 pounds, a wingspan of 42 feet 2

(Left) With Gene Bowen in front of the BT-13A Vultee Valiant, nicknamed the "Vultee Vibrator." Note our dress shoes. (Right) In the "Vultee Vibrator"

inches, length 28 feet 10 inches, height of 12 feet 5 inches, and a top speed of 156 miles per hour, along with a service ceiling of 16,500 feet plus a range of 516 miles.

As he climbed up the wing he called, "Fletch, I'll take the front cockpit, you get in the rear and we'll compare notes." The glass canopies were open to keep the heat from building up inside, but it was still hot. We climbed aboard, each exclaiming to the other all of the new things we would learn about. We knew we were in an airplane with a complete electrical system including a self-starter plus cockpit, wing, tail, and landing lights. With electricity we had two-way radios and an intercom system to communicate, complete with headsets. We had a plane with a two-position propeller as well as navigational and flight instruments necessary for blind flying. There were toggle switches everywhere, trim tab controls, and, above all, wing flaps to be lowered to slow the aircraft down and provide additional lift to make landing easier. There were so many goodies we did not find them all and some we did find we did not know their purpose.

Here were two cadets who were having a ball, just like two kids turned loose in a candy store. This was an AIRPLANE, not a box kite with an engine, an airplane completely wrapped in aluminum and glass, or so we thought then. It was going to be a challenge to fly. We could hardly wait to get started. Old Dawg commented, "Now, Fletch, you know what it is like to be in hawg heaven. Say, did you notice this airplane is equipped with a gosport system? I'll bet it's a back-up system, in case of an electrical failure."

"Well, Old Dawg, I don't see any tubes back here and I don't know how you would hook them to the headset anyway."

"If you don't have electricity the headset wouldn't do any good so you'd take them off and stick the hoses in your ears."

"Whatever, but I haven't found the hoses yet."

"Well, while you're looking I'll speak into the funnel and you see if you can hear me. Fletch, old dawg, I'm speaking into the funnel. Can you hear me?"

"Yes, but since the engine isn't running I can hear you without the hoses."

"Then I'll speak a little lower to see if you can hear it come out the end of the hose. Maybe that will help you find them."

After a few minutes it dawned on us that our time was about up so we had better report. We joined Littlefield and Marchant on the way back and found they were just as enthusiastic as we were. We sat down with Mr. Bowen and he started explaining many of the things we saw in the cockpit, telling us the procedures we would use and some of the flying characteristics of the airplane. He talked to us for over an hour, then said that we would receive a short orientation ride the next day, probably only a takeoff and landing. From then on we would fly full periods.

Did anyone have questions or remarks? Littlefield said he would like to know something about the gruesome sight of mangled metal that we had seen when we arrived. Mr. Bowen said all he knew was that the accident involved one airplane. It had crashed head-on into the dry lake bed, killing two cadets on a buddy ride. He did not know whether there was a mechanical problem or pilot error involved and no one would ever know. He stressed that the BT-13 was a good, safe airplane but it was not a toy. Treat it with respect, fly it properly, and you won't have any trouble. The plane was not known to have any chronic mechanical problems, so forget it and concentrate on the positive.

Were there other questions? Old Dawg replied, "I don't have a question but I think it's neat that the designers put a gosport system in as a back-up in case of failure of the electrical intercom."

Mr. Bowen looked quite puzzled and said, "Mr. Hoffman, I'm not aware of a gosport system in the BT."

"Well, there is one. It is a black synthetic funnel hooked onto a tube that leads down into the fuselage. The funnel is shaped a little different than in the Stearman, but otherwise it looks the same."

"Where was it located?"

"On the right-hand side of the fuselage just about in line with the front of the seat. The hose could have been a little longer but I could lean over and talk in the funnel."

Mr. Bowen started to smile. "You talked to Mr. Fletcher?"

"Yes, Sir."

"Did he hear you and talk back?"

"Yes, Sir, he said he could hear me, but he couldn't find the hoses in the rear cockpit."

"Well, Mr. Hoffman, if Mr. Fletcher had been more observant he would also have found the hose and funnel slightly to the right and below his seat. This tells me you men have to be more alert and be able to spot these things."

By now Mr. Bowen had a huge grin and was obviously trying to suppress an urge to laugh. "Mr. Hoffman, I don't know how to tell you this, but the BT does not have a gosport system. It has a longer range than the Stearman and, consequently, some provision must be made to afford pilot comfort on a long-range flight. Now if you had traced the hose through the fuselage you would have noticed it was vented to the outside. Speaking in the funnel only vented your voice outside and that really isn't its purpose. That little gadget is known as a pilot's relief tube and its purpose is to relieve the pilot's discomfiture. Do you understand what I'm talking about?" Old Dawg, with a look of horror on his face, started gagging and requesting that he be excused to look for a water fountain. The instructor could not contain his laughter any longer and dismissed the four of us with, "This is just the beginning. Wait till they start to fly."

The following day when we reported to the flight line, Old Dawg told the instructor he was quite embarrassed over the gosport incident. Mr. Bowen praised his inquisitiveness and ingenuity, saying these were qualities of a good student. He said he was sorry he had laughed in Hoffman's presence but the incident was so funny he couldn't help himself. Besides, very few students provided an instructor with an opportunity to laugh. He said, "I was laughing with you, not at you. This incident should be one which we can both look back on in fun and not embarrassment." We knew we had a diplomat and a gentleman for an instructor and that he would bring out the best in us, an ability which was sometimes lacking in others.

Mr. Bowen then placed the four of us in a circle on either side of him and proceeded to explain the functions of all the "new to us" equipment on the airplane. After a lengthy session we went out to the flight line and each of us received a ten-minute ride which consisted of a takeoff and landing with the cadet following through on the controls. It was a real thrill and we could hardly wait to experience more, especially when we found out the cadet now rode in front with the instructor in the rear cockpit.

We soon settled into a routine reminiscent of Primary: one-half day on the flight line with the rest of the day spent in ground school, physical training, and the usual drill. A few night classes were also thrown in once or twice a week. The classes became more advanced and the magnitude of the new material piled on every day boggled the mind, so again the cadets set up study groups in the evening led by those who excelled in a particular subject.

On June 29 all of the cadets received their permanent passes. The passes authorized us "to be absent from this post (within a radius of 150 miles) at all times when not on duty." Of course the catch was all cadets were considered to be on duty twenty-four hours a day seven days a week, so this required another pass to be issued stating you were not on duty. This was the procedure that allowed us to receive Saturday nights off. There were no procedures set up to allow the cadets to receive visitors on the base, which was okay since we didn't have time to visit anyway.

My first overnight pass came on Saturday, July 3. Mr. and Mrs. Story were salt-of-the-earth people and insisted that we have our meals with them. We were a family and they enjoyed having young people in their home again. Sharing meals was for them more than a courtesy, it represented a sacrifice on their part because this was a time of rationing.

Since I was a part of the military I did not have a food ration book, but Sherry contributed her food coupons to the family since she was taking her meals on the base and had no need for them. Meat especially was in short supply with only twenty-eight ounces per week allowed each person. All butter went to the military while the civilians made do with butter substitutes.

Things weren't too rosy on the home front. People were contending with ration books for food, shoes, gas, and tires. Ladies' skirts were shortened and the cuffs removed from men's trousers to save fabric. Silk and nylon stockings were replaced by leg make-up, which was just as well since there wouldn't have been anything to hold up the stockings. Garters, girdles, and anything containing rubber had already been turned in to help in the war effort and substitutes were not available.

A permit to buy replacement tires was obtained through the local rationing board and was not easy to come by. Gas coupons allowed essential travel only, with the speed limit set at 35 miles per hour to save wear and tear on cars and tires. All kitchen fat and meat drippings were saved to make soap, and tinfoil was collected and balled. The local Boy Scouts and Camp Fire Girls took on the project of collecting and turning them over to the government receiving stations.

Price controls were in effect on all consumer items including rents. Wages were frozen and this allowed the economy to function without inflation. Consequently, windfall profits and profiteering were virtually eliminated. Some bartering occurred, but this was minuscule given the size of the big picture.

Mr. Story was the local butcher and also a Technocrat, a believer in a theory in which government and our social system should be controlled by scientific technicians. Every Saturday night we discussed technocracy while Mrs. Story and Sherry did the dishes. Once the dishes were over I would lose interest in the conversation, since I was more interested in other subjects and activities. Mrs. Story could always sense when my patience was wearing thin and would intervene with, "Come on, Dad, you can continue this conversation some other time. We must allow these young people some privacy." Thank you, Mrs. Story.

Sherry's room was quite small, containing only a closet, bureau, and a single bed. It was a corner room with cross-ventilation which only meant the hot night air was allowed to enter from two directions. I will not address the size of the bed except to say that it created a feeling of togetherness.

The local churches were practically filled every Sunday morning with the influx of the cadet corps of both classes. My roommates and some close friends usually joined Sherry and me for Sunday services and we would spend part of the day visiting together. The small town afforded few opportunities for dates for the single men, so most who wanted to talk to someone other than another cadet had to settle for a short visit with the wives. Sometimes it would be for suggestions of gifts to send home to family or girlfriends. Since the stores weren't open on Sundays, many times it was a request to make a purchase in town or mail a package. Other times it was just a desire to hear a female voice.

The first full week in July was spent learning all we could about the BT-13. Not all the aircraft were the same. Some had better instrumentation and excellent radios. These planes were to be used for instrument and cross-country flying. Others with poorer instrumentation were to be used for aerobatics, and still others had a plywood empennage and were not to be used for aerobatics. Aircraft were assigned on the basis of the mission, but it was up to us to make sure that the right airplane type was used for the proper purpose.

After six hours of dual instruction, I was allowed to solo on July 12, and during that week most of the other cadets soloed. After that it was a wonder we had any airplanes left for instrument flying. The field looked more like a rodeo grounds than an airfield because the landings were like riding a bucking bronco with the cadets cheering "Ride 'em cowboy" as the trainers bounced and bucked. Two or three landings were made with a single approach. No one was hurt but the aircraft took a beating. At night the cadets shared their stories of close calls and an occasional incident showing surprising expertise.

We had one incident that really caught our attention. The heat was terrible. In fact, we used gloves to keep from burning our hands when we touched the metal on the airframes. The heat also attracted rattlesnakes and we were told to watch out for them. Most of us took this as a joke but on this day an instructor and cadet were seen to jump from the plane on the flight line screaming "SNAKE." A rattler had curled up for his siesta on the fuselage and it seems they had disturbed him when they attempted to climb aboard. We all took this pretty seriously except for one cadet who had had Laughing Boy as an instructor at Oxnard. He couldn't see what the fuss was all about, insisting it would have been a pleasure to ride with the rattler after putting up with Laughing Boy.

Again we were flying as in Primary using auxiliary fields and buses. The auxiliary fields were on Muroc Dry Lake. It was possible to land anywhere on the lake but certain areas were designated and marked only with a strip of oil sprayed on the ground to indicate a runway. In addition to the buses a jeep with radio receiver and transmitter was driven to the auxiliary field to serve as a portable tower. We were now initiating all takeoffs and landings using radio communications.

Going out to the auxiliary fields on the bus was quite an experience. You could see what looked like a lake in the distance but you never came to the water. At one particular place the silhouette of a battleship always appeared, but it was never visible from the air. The bus driver once said the battleship was a wooden mock-up used by the Navy for gunnery practice, but because of the other wild tales he had told us his credibility factor with the cadets was zero. The reports of mirages became a full-time conversation topic. We cussed, discussed, and speculated but we never arrived at a conclusion on how these visions were formed.

Mr. Bowen was on my tail constantly trying to get me to practice more aerobatics and spins. I kept asking him to spend more time demonstrating some of the things he wanted me to work on, but it seemed we were always in the wrong type of airplane when I made the request. He kept insisting that his making the maneuver wouldn't help me. Only by practice could I really learn how to do it. "You know the procedure so practice on your solo time."

Finally it got to the point where he would ask me every time I returned from a solo flight what aerobatics I had done and how many times. I always told him the truth even though I wasn't doing as many as he thought I should. He kept inquiring about spins and I would honestly tell him that I wasn't practicing them. He had demonstrated one sloppy spin and I didn't feel comfortable with what I had seen. The spin is probably the easiest of all maneuvers to do in an airplane but, for some reason, maybe it was what we saw when we came on the base, I had a built-in resistance. Finally I told him, "If I ever get up to 10,000 feet with nothing to do I'll try it, but right now I'm working on other things."

His response was, "If you're going to fly, either master all the arts of flying or forget it." I knew he was right but there was something about his reluctance and lack of demonstration that held me back.

The time finally arrived when I felt it absolutely necessary to practice spins. Mr. Bowen probably took my 10,000 feet of altitude stipulation as an attempt at humor, but in this regard I was definitely serious. Since the elevation at Lancaster was about 2,300 feet I set the altimeter at zero on the field. This procedure allowed me to read my actual height above the ground directly from the altimeter. I then flew out over Muroc Dry Lake to a deserted practice area as I did not want an audience or, for that matter, any airborne traffic.

On the way to the practice area I maintained a constant climb but at 8,200 feet the plane was not climbing as fast as I desired. In ignorance I decided to manually crank down about fifteen degrees of flaps and hopefully get more lift to speed up the climb. This act did not speed up the climb but I slowly reached 10,000 feet.

I do not wish to bore the nonflyers with a long, drawn-out flying lesson, but I will tell you the control of an airplane is maintained by a smooth flow of air over the wings and tail surfaces. As the control surfaces such as the rudder, elevators, or ailerons are moved, they extend into the smooth airstream and cause a reaction. An example: If the control stick is pulled back the elevators are extended upward into the airstream; the tail is forced down and the nose rises. The same principle applies to every control surface. In this manner the pilot exercises control over the airplane and, theoretically, it flies where he wants to go instead of just wallowing around in the sky. As I said earlier, the spin is probably the easiest maneuver to enter and the easiest to recover from, especially in the trainers which I had flown.

Upon reaching 10,000 feet I picked out a reference point on the horizon while sliding the front canopy open. I'm not sure why except that in case of a bail-out the hatch would be open. I repeated to myself "Here goes nothing" and retarded the throttle while slowly applying back pressure on the stick. When the stick finally reached its limit of travel the aircraft had lost its airspeed and was completely stalled. At this point the aircraft is out of control and can only nose over and fall off on a wing. In this case I had determined to spin to the right so I applied full right rudder causing the plane to fall off on the right wing.

The airplane fell over into a vertical dive and was now in a spin to the right. As the plane spun around my eyes focused on the reference point and I knew I had completed one complete revolution. This is how orientation is maintained and the number of revolutions determined. I had decided to do a two-turn spin. This meant that spinning would be stopped by the exact time the nose reached the reference point for the second time. To stop the spinning, full left, or opposite rudder, is applied before reaching the pull-out point, in this case about ninety degrees before the reference point is reached.

Once the spin has stopped the back pressure on the stick is released. The stick is returned forward to the midpoint of its travel; the controls are now neutralized and the control surfaces are streamlined, putting the aircraft in a dive. The smooth, steady flow of air is again crossing the control surfaces. All that remains is to slowly ease back on the stick and the nose returns to level flight as power is added to maintain normal airspeed.

Three-fourths of the way around the second revolution I applied full left rudder and felt the spin slowing down. I realized that I was overshooting the check point but I wasn't concerned about accuracy. I just wanted a recovery this time, I could work on precision later. The spin slowed down but did not stop, in fact, it suddenly became tighter and faster. No problem. I neutralized the rudder pedals and started the recovery again. As before, the spin slowed but would not stop. The nose dropped lower and again took to a tighter spin with increased speed. By now I wasn't concerned with recovering on the point; I would recover any place I could around the circle. After four unsuccessful recoveries it became apparent that I had a problem. The airspeed was far greater than I wanted it to be and was approaching the red line. There wasn't time to panic, the ground was rushing up, but for some reason I could not stop the spin. I made a decision: Two more attempts at recovery, if nothing happened I would bail out. Those two attempts were made very hurriedly, but again with no success.

Since the canopy was open it was only a matter of getting out of the airplane. Before unfastening the safety belt I looked over the side to establish how I was going out when I noticed that the flaps were still in the down position. I had failed to retract them before starting the spin. In that instant I knew the flaps were disturbing the airflow, making recovery impossible. As I immediately cranked up the flaps with my right hand and stood on the left rudder the spin stopped. The airspeed indicator was past the red line and the altimeter was passing through 1,500 feet, the plane still in a vertical dive.

It took every ounce of willpower to keep from jerking the stick back. A quick movement would have created either a high-speed stall with no response from the airplane or if the plane did respond it could have lost a wing or tail section and disintegrated. I bit my tongue and slowly eased back on the stick. The nose started to raise ever so slowly and finally returned to level flight with the altimeter reading 700 feet. As the airspeed finally settled down, the power was eventually restored. My supposed two-turn spin had consumed 9,300 feet of altitude.

My flight suit was wringing wet with sweat, but still in better shape than my nerves. As I flew around trying to regain my composure and flying confidence I kept thinking of the poor judgment I

In front of a BT-13A

had exhibited. The dangerous predicament was precipitated simply by my own stupidity. I thought of the trailer at the gate and
wondered if the two cadets had pulled something similar. After flying around for approximately fifteen minutes I knew what I had to
do: either fly back to the base and quit flying or go back upstairs
and practice spins in the proper manner.

I climbed back up and flew the aircraft through three more two-
turn spins. This time all three hit the reference point right on the
nose. Flying back to the base I knew I had conquered a self-
imposed adversity. If I didn't kill myself some day I would be a pilot and a good one at that.

Sitting on the ramp after landing I started filling out the Form
One, in which the pilot notes anything that is inoperative or anything unusual that he has observed about the aircraft. The ground
crew then has to check and repair any abnormalities before the airplane can be flown again, unless the next pilot signs that he has
read the notation and accepts the aircraft in its "as is" condition.
While filling out the form I walked around the airplane to examine
the exterior and realized I was flying an airplane with a plywood
tail, one which was not authorized for aerobatics. Again it was decision-making time: Do I ignore what has happened since no one

would know or do I tell what happened and face the wrath of the instructor and squadron commander and probably a military check ride? Knowing that other people would fly this airplane, my conscience dictated only one course. Among other things the entry in the Form One read: "Aircraft was flown at a speed in excess of the red line and was spun several times. Check for undue stress. Signed, Cadet Fletcher." It sounded better than Stupid Cadet Dodo.

At critique Mr. Bowen inquired about my flying activities to place in the record. I was able to report that I had practiced spins, which seemed to make him happy. I went on to say, "but in an aircraft with a plywood tail."

"So? Do you think you're the only cadet that has ever done that?"

"Well, I don't know but I also exceeded the red line. However, I have written that up in the Form One."

"Every airplane on this field has had the red line exceeded but we don't make a practice of it. So what else is new?"

"I guess that's about it, Sir, but I can assure you at the next stage check I will be able to recover a spin on the point." By now I had learned that there was no need to overburden an instructor with graphic details. They were already aging prematurely from the stress of their occupation.

A perfect example occurred a few days later. I had finished my lesson and landed at one of the auxiliary fields. Old Dawg took over and would land back at War Eagle Field while I returned on the bus. Most of the auxiliary fields had a shelter resembling an igloo to provide a place for the cadets to study out of the desert sun. On this field a crew was building an igloo. I walked over to see how these shelters were built. They had constructed a frame of narrow mesh chicken wire, and then they proceeded to blow, from a large tank truck, a mixture of water, sand, pea gravel, and cement into the frame. The mixture set up very quickly in the daytime heat. It was a fascinating procedure but the heat compelled me to seek the shade by the side of the bus.

While walking back I noticed a parachute blossom quite high in the sky. I ran to the jeep where radio traffic was being controlled by a sergeant and a lieutenant. I explained that I had seen a parachute open in the sky in the direction of the morning sun. Since it was not visible at the moment in the brilliant sunlight they thought I was reporting a mirage or hallucination. They were sure if someone

The "igloo," where pilots waited their turn to fly

had trouble there would have been a radio transmission or a distress signal.

Finally the sergeant also saw the chute, and started calling on the radio to alert the planes to watch for it. A very meek voice came on the radio and asked if they were inquiring about a man in a parachute. The controller answered that he was. The meek voice replied, "That's my instructor."

"Please repeat your transmission."

"That's my instructor."

"What happened?"

"I don't know. He just asked me if I had control of the airplane and when I said yes, he opened the back canopy and bailed out."

The cadet was ordered to return to War Eagle Field. "Should I finish my lesson first?" the voice inquired.

The lieutenant shouted into the mike, "Return immediately."

"Yes, Sir."

The lieutenant made one more transmission notifying everyone that the auxiliary field was closed since radio communications were suspended. The jeep took off in the direction of the parachute, leaving a trail of dust on the lake bed.

The bus driver requested the cadets board the bus for home since the auxiliary was closed. By the time we reached the base the incident had been reported. Mr. Bowen told us that because of occupational fatigue the instructor had decided to quit teaching and since he had always wanted to make a parachute jump he had achieved both goals that morning.

I would like to say that all my problems were confined to the flight line but that would not be entirely true. The physical fitness instructor who had taken us on the forced march was now back making life miserable for us in the 120-degree temperature. Pushups, chinups, situps, side straddle hops, running, anything to produce a sweat seemed to give him great satisfaction.

There was a huge swimming pool in front of the unit where Bell and I lived. The pool was officially off limits and was used only when the instructor scheduled a class. Recreational swimming was not allowed even on time off or during weekends. This didn't particularly bother me since I couldn't swim anyway. But one day he announced that one phase of our final fitness test would be to swim two lengths of the swimming pool. Anyone incapable would be failed. I had never been around a pool or lake and had never learned how to swim, in fact, I couldn't even float. In the several classes we had in the pool I had been able to dog paddle about twenty feet and that was it. Finally two close friends who were Eagle Scouts and expert swimmers decided they would teach me how to swim, but the time in the pool was limited so we were not making much headway. I would battle the water with my arms until I was worn out, then the two cadets would swim alongside and grasp hands under my chest using a modified side stroke. That way they would keep me afloat until we were at the end or at least out of deep water. They decided I had to have more time in the pool if I was going to succeed. Consequently, they decided that since I had helped them with ground school during our evening study sessions they would now reciprocate by helping me.

Since the pool was right in front of my cottage they met at my unit just after dark. We would put on our bathing suits and quietly slip into the pool. Several other cadets served as lookouts. If anyone besides a cadet left headquarters and started around the large housing circle a flashlight would be turned on, a signal to get out or hide. We had had several sessions and were making some progress, but I had the feeling they were placing themselves at risk simply to help me. Their attitude was, "What are friends for? This is not cheating; we're just breaking the rules by being in the pool."

Friday night after our session I had just returned to the unit and was standing still dripping in the shower removing my bathing trunks when there was a knock at the door. Bell responded and the cadet runner informed him that Cadet Fletcher was to report to the officer of the day at headquarters on the double.

Bell delivered the message that I had already heard. I knew then that someone had seen me in the pool and it was time to report and face the music. I could only hope the other two cadets had not been seen. Several of the cadets rallied around shining my shoes and polishing the brass on my uniform while I finished my shower. As soon as I dried off, my uniform was hastily laid out spic-and-span. I hurriedly dressed among words of encouragement from the cadets, but I was beyond cheering up. I had obviously been caught; now it was suffer the consequence. A better solution might have been to drown while taking the test. I thanked the guys for their help with my clothes and their moral support and started off on the double for headquarters.

I was very relieved not to see the other two cadets on the way. Maybe they hadn't been seen or maybe I would be asked to identify them. Who knows what a fertile imagination is capable of? Wash out, walk tours; the answer was just several steps away. I marched into the commander's office, came to attention, saluted, and stated, "Cadet Fletcher reporting as directed, Sir."

The O.D. was one of the student officers. He returned the salute, hesitated for a few seconds, long enough for some more unpleasant thoughts to come and go, then stated, "Mr. Fletcher, how would you like a pass?"

I couldn't answer. I wasn't even sure I had heard the question correctly. My mouth was dry but our military discipline kept me from shaking. Again he asked, "How would you like a pass?"

This time I responded, "I would like that very much, Sir." He immediately handed me the white slip that activated our permanent pass. I stepped forward, took the slip, backed up two paces, "Thank you, Sir," and saluted.

He returned the salute with, "Be back on the base before Taps Sunday evening." I did an about-face and hurried from the office. I ran all the way back to the unit to get my shaving kit as the bus would be leaving for Lancaster in fifteen minutes.

As I entered the cottage I realized that the place was crammed with cadets all waiting to see what punishment had been meted out. All I could do was exclaim, "I got a two-night pass."

"What for?"

"I dunno, but I'm getting out of here before somebody changes his mind. See you Sunday night." I grabbed my shaving kit and as I started out the door I told the two cadets who were helping me to forget the nighttime lessons. I would rather drown than go through that again. I caught the bus still wondering what had happened, but I certainly wasn't going to look the gift horse in the mouth.

It was almost 10:00 when I greeted Sherry at the Story residence. I told her I had just received a two-night pass but I had no idea why. She explained that at dinner that day one of the lieutenants wanted seconds on dessert. She told him she couldn't do that but he insisted, saying he would do a favor for her in exchange. She asked him what kind of favor and he asked her what she would like. She said that what she'd like would be for her husband to have extra time off the base. He said that he was O.D. for the weekend and he could make it possible. Against the rules she served the extra dessert but with no anticipation that I would really get the pass as the officers were always kidding those who worked in the dining room. So for a paltry piece of apricot pie I was given an extra night off.

Saturday night I was just about ready to convert to Technocracy when Mrs. Story intervened. Sunday morning Bell and several cadets came by and we went to church together. On the way I told him the story Sherry had told me. "I am glad," he replied, "because after Friday night half the cadet corps thinks you're crazy."

"How about the other half?"

"They know you are."

I-class finished on schedule and were to ship out the next day. By the time we joined them at dinner in the restaurant they were having a good time laughing and joking within their own group. There was one staple that we were always served at dinner and it was always prepared in the same manner. "Case hardened potatoes" was the name used by the cadets, although the cook probably used a more appetizing terminology. The potatoes were small, ranging in size from a large marble to a golf ball. They were peeled, boiled, and then placed in a greased pan and fried as they rolled around in the hot grease. The outside of the potato became very hard, hence the name "case hardened." The potatoes tasted good and were served piping hot, but the problem was trying to cut through the hardened shell to make them bite size and allow the inside to cool. Most attempts to fork or cut them caused them to jump off the plate, roll around the table, or even onto the floor.

The door to the restaurant was always open during mealtime but a screen door functioned to keep the flies out. As one of the J-class cadets opened the screen door to come in, an upperclassman seated just beyond our table picked up one of his potatoes from the floor and with the exclamation, "I've chased these potatoes for the last time," proceeded to toss it out the open screen door. Unfortunately a captain chose that moment to enter the dining hall. The potato hit him on the forehead. The only damage was to the captain's pride.

It was an act which was done in jest and the cadet had not deliberately thrown at the officer, but it was an indiscretion that could not be overlooked. Some form of punishment was not only expected but required. However, none of us anticipated or were even prepared for the harsh sentence that was meted out. The cadet was removed from the shipping roster. He was told that if he desired to remain in the cadet corps he could join J-class but since his flying was completed he would be required to walk an eight-hour tour every day in Class A uniform, which meant wool blouse, trousers, and visored cap. He would carry a rifle and constantly march between the headquarters building and the flag pole. Upon reaching the flag pole he would present arms, shoulder arms, do an about-face, march back to headquarters, and repeat the procedure. He was allowed to rest five minutes out of each hour in the headquarters latrine.

The cadet was confined to the post and denied any visiting privileges for the rest of the time J-class would be on the base. His wife and two small daughters lived in Lancaster. Further, he was not allowed to converse with any of the cadets and was assigned to an isolated unit. If he could not accept these conditions or failed to perform properly he would be washed out immediately.

He refused to quit and accepted the challenge. It was obvious that the military had underestimated his desire to be a pilot. Every cadet on the base knew that we were witnessing cruel and inhuman punishment as the temperature on the base was now reaching 120 degrees every day. The unfortunate cadet had the support of all of us but we could not vocally express this support; we could only give a veiled thumbs up sign at a chance meeting. The military took the attitude that he could quit anytime he wanted to and, therefore, they felt no responsibility.

At the end of two weeks the cadet could hardly walk because of blistered feet. He was called before the commanding officer and asked what he desired more than anything else. The cadet replied that he would like to see his wife and daughters. The commander expected him to respond that he wanted to fly. Consequently, he was ordered to complete the punishment or quit. The cadet went back to marching. It was obvious that as long as he could move he would not give up. We groused to every civilian instructor on the base about the type of punishment and the contest of wills that was going on, but their reply was that they did not have any influence with the military.

We also had to exhibit a very low profile since any display on our part would also affect our own flying careers. Even so, it did have an impact, which surfaced when we eventually reached a position of command. It could be seen in the humanitarian manner in which we tried to exercise this authority.

The incident was eventually resolved after nearly three weeks. The cadet had withstood the ravages of the desert sun with his head held high. His feet were giving out but he still hobbled his rounds. At this point the medics intervened, stating that his health was being endangered and the humiliating public display had to stop. They insisted that his family be allowed to visit him in the infirmary and that the incident had to be resolved: Either eliminate him from cadet training or honor his commitment to duty and his attempt to comply.

While this human drama was being played out, J-class was busy learning formation, instrument, and night flying. Formation flying was a real challenge but was enjoyed by all of the cadets. The BT-13 was perfect for this. It was a heavy airplane but very stable in flight as it responded immediately to power changes and control movements which made it ideal for flying in formation. Old Dawg and I liked nothing better than to fly formation on Mr. Bowen's wings, each trying to see who could consistently fly the closest without being warned by radio to back off. We finally reached a level of expertise where we could change wings with one crossing over the top while the other crossed underneath, all without causing the instructor undue alarm.

At this point Mr. Bowen decided we were ready for formation takeoffs and landings, a procedure in which the students watched only the wing of the lead aircraft and by imitating its every movement would become airborne, circle the field, and come in for the landing. As the flaps came down on the wing of the lead ship we immediately cranked ours down, perhaps five degrees lower. The leader then brought us over the runway and again, with our eyes glued only to the wing, we would execute a perfect landing without

BT-13As in formation

ever realizing where we were in relation to the ground. It was fantastic and gave a feeling of elation I have never forgotten.

On instrument rides a hood was placed over the pilot's head, blocking off the windows, and he learned to fly by using only the instruments for orientation. Since the pilot was flying blind, a cadet rode in the rear cockpit to serve as an observer, keeping the aircraft away from other airborne traffic. These were known as buddy rides. Only the pilot logged the flying time; consequently, we spent more time in the air than the log books showed. We gained valuable flying experience by observing and evaluating the actions of the pilot under the hood.

Old Dawg and I flew most of the buddy rides together, each being more critical than an instructor would ever be. We spent hours in the Link trainer (a static flight simulator) practicing all phases of instrument flying and navigation, trying to keep ahead of the operator who could simulate all forms of conditions, hazardous or otherwise, that we might encounter on any flight. Needless to say, many times we heard the operator's voice saying, "Sorry, you just crashed. Let's start over again." As long as these mishaps were confined to the ground trainer everything was okay, but eventually there came a time when I had to face an emergency in the air.

Most of the airplanes had taken off. Mr. Bowen and Old Dawg had taken off on a stage check and I was assigned an aircraft for a one-hour solo flight and was to land at an auxiliary field where the aircraft was to be used in other stage checks. I taxied to the end of the runway and proceeded with the engine ground check. The magnetos checked okay, well within the 100 rpm loss that was allowed. All gauges were in the green and the engine responded well to a full power check.

Confident that everything was okay I called the tower and received permission to take off. The takeoff went perfectly; I was airborne with one-third of the runway left. At 300 feet, still climbing and just passing over the airport boundary, the engine coughed and sputtered. I lowered the nose and remembered a cardinal rule: With engine failure on takeoff you keep the airplane under control and land straight ahead. There was one problem: The area around the field was filled with Joshua trees. An emergency landing under these conditions meant you would probably not walk away.

As the engine sputtered I suspected the engine fuel pump had failed. I took my left hand off the throttle, leaving it in the wide open position, grabbed the control stick and using my right hand activated the wobble stick, a hand operated back-up fuel pump. Rocking it back and forth did not produce the desired result as the engine continued to cough and sputter. The altimeter fell to 150 feet and the little Joshua trees looked like huge telephone poles with outstretched arms. I switched techniques. This time I used my left hand to pump the throttle back and forth, hoping that some fuel remained in the accelerating well that could be discharged to the engine.

The engine responded and I was able to regain a little altitude before the engine started acting up again. Something must have worked but I wasn't sure which, the wobble pump or pumping the throttle. As the engine sputtered the second time I held the rudder pedals in neutral by applying an equal amount of pressure on each. Then with the control stick clasped between my knees I started pumping both the throttle and the wobble stick. The engine responded with intermittent power but it was impossible to gain altitude. By leaning my knees slightly to the right I could execute a slight bank and by more pressure on the right rudder I was able to make a skidding turn to the right.

I desperately wanted to call the tower but I only had two hands, two feet, and two knees and they were already all occupied. The engine continued to sporadically respond and then quit. By now I had one hope and that was to circle the base to the right, staying outside the boundaries, and with good luck maybe I could reach the same runway that I had used for takeoff. There was one frantic ca-

The tower at War Eagle Field

In the BT-13, calling the tower for permission to take off

det in the cockpit flying with his knees, pumping with both arms, and shouting obscenities at a balky engine.

Each time the engine responded I gained a few feet of altitude only to lose an equal amount on the cut-out. The altitude fluctuated from 200 to 250 feet, while the Joshua trees kept providing the impetus to pump and wobble faster. I heaved a sigh of relief as I turned onto the base leg. In two or three hundreds yards I would be past the trees.

As I skidded onto the final approach I was almost blinded by the green light from the Aldis lamp in the tower. The color made no difference to me; I was committed to land whether I reached the runway or not. I placed the throttle half open and grabbed the stick with my left hand while still pumping like crazy. The engine settled down and began running smoothly. Passing over the boundary I quit pumping, switched hands on the stick, and closed the throttle. The engine idled perfectly and the landing, under the circumstances, by my standards was a success. I slowly taxied back to the flight line with the engine running as smoothly as a sewing machine.

I was completely baffled. I didn't know what was wrong. How could an engine run so smoothly on the ground and refuse to run in the air? One thing was certain, I did not have time to think or worry about my safety while in the air, but now taxiing on the ground the gravity of the situation was starting to register. I considered myself very lucky to be able to land with the airplane intact and my body in one piece. Little did I know as I shut off the engine and crawled out of the cockpit that there was even more trouble to come.

I looked up to see an instructor advancing toward me. I waited by the airplane wondering if he had seen my flight or if maybe I would be assigned a different airplane. Instead he sneeringly demanded to know why I had not taken the aircraft to the auxiliary field as I had been told. I explained that I had taken off, had engine trouble, and returned. The instructor cynically replied, "Look, if you're scared to fly your lesson, at least take the airplane out to the auxiliary field where someone can use it. We are very short of planes and we need them all in the air." I protested that the airplane was mechanically unsound and I had no desire to fly it again until someone from maintenance had checked it. His next reply burned me to the core. "You cadets are all alike. Forty hours of pilot time and you are all expert pilots and mechanics. Now get that airplane in the air and deliver it."

I tried to explain that my not flying the airplane had nothing to do with hours of flying time but involved mechanical problems. If he was giving me a direct order to fly it I would have to refuse because I considered the airplane unsafe. In a very arrogant, scornful, and condescending manner he asked, "If I fly it once around the pattern will you deliver it?"

"Yes, Sir, but I don't think it is wise. The plane performs perfectly during the ground check but it will not run in the air."

"Give me your parachute, get out of the way, and let a pilot on board."

As he donned the parachute I tried to explain the procedure of opening and closing the throttle and using the wobble pump to stay airborne. "Mister, when I want your advice I'll ask for it."

"Yes, Sir, I'll be waiting when you return."

He taxied off and I watched as he went through the ground check. The airplane appeared to function in a normal manner as he proceeded into position for takeoff. I was suddenly hit with the dilemma of what to do if the airplane performed satisfactorily. I hadn't imagined what had happened, it was real, but now if it performed okay I would look like the idiot he had portrayed me to be. No one likes to be humiliated, but at the same time there is only one life to live and I didn't want to end mine because of some overconfident, insulting instructor. But it was possible that this time it might fly okay. Then what?

Straight as an arrow in flight the aircraft went down the runway and lifted toward the sky out across the field boundary. It was a beautiful sight. Then in an instant the engine sputtered and coughed, and the plane started a nose down descent. I was sure that a crash was imminent, then the engine caught again and I hoped the instructor's ride would be as successful as mine. I watched intently as the airplane went out of sight behind the buildings which obstructed my view. I could hear the engine sporadically cut in and out and finally realized the instructor was using the same pattern to return to the airfield that I had. I don't believe he was ever able to get over 200 feet above the ground but he eventually made it down.

I waited for him to taxi over but it appeared that he was avoiding me. He would not look in my direction but kept on taxiing down the line. I was mad. I knew we would have one more encounter if I had to chase that airplane all around the field. Finally it dawned on me that he was taxiing to the maintenance hangar so I headed for it on the double. By the time I got there the instructor was out of the airplane talking to a mechanic.

When he finished I walked over not caring whether I flew again and remarked, "Do you still want me to fly that crate over to the auxiliary field?"

With wide eyes and a grim face he looked me over from head to foot then said, "She was one sick son of a gun."

Spinning on my heel I replied, "I guess you'll return the para-

With Gene Bowen under the wing of the BT-13A "Vultee Vibrator"

chute since you used it last." Without waiting for an answer I took off on the double for the Link trainer building, hoping to find a trainer not in use. At least I could practice instrument flying from the safety of the ground while waiting for the airplanes to return from the auxiliary field.

The following day Mr. Bowen and I sat down to discuss the incident. He had heard that engine trouble had prevented me from reaching the auxiliary field. I related what had happened from my point of view and said that while I didn't know the name of the instructor I had tangled with, he was certainly the most arrogant, stupid individual I had ever met in the flying community. Mr. Bowen said that he was aware of part of the story and the man in question, who was from a different squadron, was not the most popular person on the base. He thought a moment then said, "Fletch, there is one thing you cadets have to realize and that is you're probably being trained to shoot down, in some instances, better people than you are being trained to protect."

It was several days before I could get back to the maintenance hangar to find out what was wrong with the airplane. The fellow who worked on it was gone for several days, but he had told someone that the problem was in the carburetor. Something was loose. At full throttle with the engine drawing maximum power it would

run for about three minutes or until the fuel supply in the carburet-
or was exhausted. Then whatever was loose, it could have been the
butterfly valve, caused the engine to starve for fuel. He said that
working the wobble pump did not help since the engine fuel pump
was okay. Moving the throttle to off and then advancing it was the
procedure that kept it trying to run. In fact, the engine would have
run perfectly for any length of time if no more than two-thirds
throttle had been applied once it was in the air. Since the full power
ground check lasted only a few seconds, the problem wasn't detected. At full power on takeoff the two and a half to three minutes was
just enough to get airborne before the engine was starved for fuel.
"But," he hastened to add, "these are not problems a pilot can di-
agnose or correct ahead of time. It is only something you can react
to. Luckily you both reacted in the right manner; however, the second flight was probably superfluous."

     With perfect weather we were flying every day, but the schedule
was very tight since we were experiencing a constant shortage of
airplanes. It seems that the wash-out rate was not as high as had
been anticipated so we were overloading the system.

     Our graduation day had been set for Saturday, August 28. This
meant that a lot of us would have to fly on Friday in order to finish
on time. Our ground school courses were completed and the final
tests were administered with everyone receiving a passing grade.
The potato cadet from I-class was brought to the flight line and allowed several hours of refresher flying. This gave us all a good feeling when we learned he would be allowed to graduate with us.
Thursday all that remained was the completion of our physical fitness test, including swimming two lengths of the pool. Then Friday night we would have to complete the last phase of flying which
was a night solo cross-country flight.

     I dreaded the swimming test. In my own mind I wasn't even
sure they could wash me out if I failed, though that threat was
made by the physical fitness instructor. But I had learned one thing
by now: Anything can happen in cadet training and most threats
were carried out as a matter of principle.

     We were divided into groups. One group at a time was allowed
in the pool while the others completed different phases of the test.
Finally our turn came for the swimming test. It was not a speed
event, only a requirement to swim two lengths without a break. As
the cadets dove into the water my two cadet swimming instructors
dove off one on each side of me. They had cautioned me ahead of

time not to panic or try to swim too fast, just take it easy and keep up a slow easygoing rhythm. They would swim beside me to instill confidence and if I should flounder there was a promise of rescue.

About halfway through the first length we met most of the others on the return lap. When I turned around at the end of the first lap three-fourths of the group had already finished and were clinging to the edge of the swimming pool. Several others circled back and joined us. I wasn't sure I could finish the last half length. I was getting very tired and not making too much headway but I could hear the reassuring voices of the two cadets repeating, "Come on, you can do it." They had more hope than I did. Finally I closed my eyes so I couldn't see how far it was to the end.

Eventually I felt my hand hit the end of the pool. Opening my eyes I grabbed the edge and wasn't even sure I could pull myself out. Then I realized that all of the group was still in the water. Immediately hands grabbed my legs and waist as I was shoved up and out of the pool. Gasping for breath I saw the instructor making a checkmark on the roster as the other cadets crawled out. I might have been the last to finish but I was the first one out of the pool. No one in the group said a word as we went on to other tests.

The following night at briefing we learned that our solo night cross-country would entail flying from Lancaster to Mojave to Daggett to Palmdale and back to Lancaster. Mr. Bowen stated that Littlefield would take off first, followed by Marchant five minutes later at an altitude 500 feet lower than Littlefield. Hoffman would take off five minutes later climbing to the same altitude that was assigned Littlefield. I would take off last, five minutes after Old Dawg, and fly 500 feet below him. In this manner everyone had a five-minute, 500-feet separation.

Several other routes had been established and other groups were also taking off at the same time. We were using two parallel runways with both right- and left-hand traffic and were to return and land on the same runway from which we had started. From the time I took off it would be at least another twenty minutes before anyone else would take off using our route. The purpose of this procedure was two-fold: First was safety; second, it would be impossible to just follow the lights of another airplane instead of navigating on your own.

We were assigned to the right-hand runway, the same one on which I had made the emergency landing. Everything went as scheduled. It was a typical desert night—not a cloud in the sky and the stars were sparkling bright. As I approached Mojave from the south the engine was running smoothly. It was a peaceful flight as the radio traffic from War Eagle Field had slowly faded out. I made the turn over Mojave heading east by southeast, and in due time the lights of Barstow appeared just slightly left of my course. Everything was proceeding according to plan, on course and on time, with the lights of Daggett slightly south and east of Barstow.

In the vicinity of Barstow the radio crackled to life with the message, "Fletcher, this is Hoffman. Do you read?"

"Roger, Hoffman, receive you loud and clear. Transmit your message."

"This is to inform you that I inadvertently spiraled down below your altitude and am now climbing back up through your airspace and request that you watch for me."

"Roger. Will keep watching for you. Do you have mechanical problems?"

"Negative. Just wanted to warn you that I'm passing through your altitude."

"Roger. Thank you."

Within a few minutes I made the turn over Daggett and headed west toward Palmdale. The compass headings were right on, an indication there wasn't any wind. Passing over Palmdale I turned north and could see the airport beacon at War Eagle Field only a few miles away. When I reached the airfield there was lots of air traffic as other units were also returning. Finding a break in the traffic I entered the pattern for the right-hand runway. While making the right-hand turn onto the final approach I flipped on the landing lights and was suddenly struck by the beauty of the lighted runway ahead of me. There was a feeling of nostalgia as I realized that I was landing at War Eagle for the last time. I retarded the throttle and the aircraft floated over the airport boundary and down the center of the runway while I executed the perfect flare-out. The aircraft stalled and in the instant that followed, before the plane hit the ground, I realized I had leveled off too high. It was the hardest landing I had ever made. The airplane just dropped about ten feet to the runway in the three-point position.

Turning off the runway I taxied to the line and hurried to the ready room. Littlefield, Marchant, and Mr. Bowen were in critique when I joined them. Mr. Bowen inquired how the flight had gone. I explained that everything had gone fine. Every checkpoint was reached right on time and the ETA (estimated time of arrival) at the field was off about five minutes, but some of that time was spent entering the pattern. The only problem was the landing. I thought I was making a good one but leveled off too high and was just lucky the airplane held together. Mr. Bowen laughed and asked if I knew what happened. I said I suspected since there was so much traffic and absolutely no breeze there must have been a dust cloud hanging just above the runway. "You're right," he interjected, "and your landing lights reflected off of the dust layer. You made a perfect landing on the haze and so has everyone else. Luckily so far the only damage has been to the pilots' pride. While we are waiting for Hoffman I want you guys to tell me what you thought of the course and the instruction you received. This is your chance to tell me what you think. I want you to be as honest with me as I have been with you throughout the course. So let's have it, good or bad."

At first we were a little timid, but he assured us that he really wanted to know, and since we were through flying we should level with him. Surely we could find something to criticize. He was sure he wasn't a perfect instructor and while we were good our flying wasn't perfect either. "We'll start with Marchant, then Littlefield, then you, Fletch, and Hoffman when he shows up."

Each one expressed his opinion. We were all very happy to have had him as an instructor. We felt he was more than just an instructor, he was a person we had come to like. He was someone who understood our problems and was never found lacking when we needed advice. He was certainly a gentleman at all times and we hoped that we would be able to emulate his example. I did suggest that in the beginning there was a time when I felt I could have used a little instruction on spins and aerobatics. He smiled and said that yes, he felt we were shorted in this regard. There were times when he felt a little inadequate in this situation, but remember, he was learning too. Then came the surprise remark, "Besides, Fletch, I thought the hot pilot from Mira Loma could figure out a few things on his own."

"Wait a minute. What have these guys told you?"

"Nothing. I was on the field at Mira Loma and watched you bring the Stearman home one windy day not too long after J-class arrived." He explained that he was an instructor in another squadron at Mira Loma while we were there. He had applied to become a Basic instructor and when our class finished he was transferred to Polaris. He had arrived three days before us. When we received our orientation rides he had only five hours and thirty minutes flying time in the BT-13. We were his first Basic students. "Does that answer any of your questions?" It certainly did and it only increased our admiration of the man and his flying ability.

By now I had been on the ground for over forty minutes and Old Dawg had not arrived. If he had been on schedule he should have been down before me. Mr. Bowen was showing some signs of concern that maybe he got lost. After another five minutes I felt compelled to tell him about the radio contact that I had with Old Dawg near Barstow. I didn't know whether it was relevant or not, but I knew he was okay then even though I did not see his lights and felt he must still have been ahead of me. Only an occasional plane was landing now and most of the instructors and cadets had already left the line. I was sure something had happened but I didn't know what. Mr. Bowen assured us that it was too soon to start worrying as the BT carried plenty of fuel and he would probably show up in a little while.

Sure enough within a few minutes, to the relief of everyone, Old Dawg walked in with a big smile on his face. Mr. Bowen exclaimed, "Well, we're all down. Let's go home. It's getting late and tomorrow is your big day." He shook our hands, wished us well, and hoped his next class would be as much fun as his first.

On our way back to the cottages, when no one else could hear, I asked Old Dawg what had happened. What took him so long? Did he get lost? "No," he said, "I was on the ground and saw your sloppy landing and watched you park two airplanes away from me."

"What were you doing? I was really worried about you, especially after your radio transmission and then not showing up at the ready room."

"Well, it's like this. Since this was our last flight I decided to use that relief tube to see if it worked. I had just passed Daggett with all systems go when I realized the tube was plugged. In the excitement I fell off into a spiral. That's when I called you. You can guess the rest. When I got to Polaris I stood outside by the airplane for about an hour waiting for things to dry. Do you think I was going to walk into that ready room with a wet flying suit? No way."

The graduation ceremonies were set for 10:00 a.m. Saturday. We had received a new commanding officer and he, along with Major Moseley, put forth considerable time and energy planning a major publicity event. Several representatives from three states, all members of the House Subcommittee on Appropriations, were present along with the Army Air Force Commandant of Cadets as well as the head of Basic Training for the West Coast Training Command. In a spirit of cooperation and a show of solidarity high ranking members of the Navy, Army, and Coast Guard participated in the review of the cadet corps.

The citizens of Lancaster were also invited to attend the open house and ceremonies. The Muroc Army Band was bused in to provide martial music. A feeling of euphoria returned as the colors were posted and the cadets passed in review. We were then allowed to watch as a test pilot from Lockheed Aviation roared a few feet above the runway in a high speed fly-by in a P-38 Lightning pursuit plane. On his second pass over the runway at 500 feet with one prop feathered he proceeded to do a slow roll, then pulled up into a victory roll while restarting the dead engine. At that moment I knew I wanted to be a P-38 pilot. Any airplane that could perform like that certainly could make a pilot out of the likes of me.

The cadet corps performed with precision complete with new white gloves, the gift of Mr. and Mrs. Herman Gold of Lancaster who donated 700 pair. It was a proud, confident, happy group who marched into the huge hangar for ceremonies commensurate with the elite guest list. Lieutenant Rudy Vallee, resplendent in the white uniform of the Coast Guard, acted as master of ceremonies and sang several songs, including *Mad Dogs and Englishmen,* to the delight of everyone present. At the conclusion of the festivities the wives were allowed to join their husbands and received a complete tour of the base. We were given the orders transferring us to Advanced flying school, the last school in the cadet program. If we could survive this last hurdle we would win our wings and become commissioned officers in the Army Air Force.

That evening as George Boldi sounded Taps, we eagerly awaited the two selections he would choose to play at the conclusion. We were treated to the euphonious sounds of *Stardust* and *Till We Meet Again.* When the last note sounded I was swept up in a feeling of nostalgia as I realized this was the last day we would enjoy his company and hear the trumpet sounds that had become so much a part of our lives. Before I fell asleep the events of the day filtered through my mind.

Twenty-two of us were selected to go to the twin-engine Advanced Training School at Douglas, Arizona, which in my fantasy was the first step to the P-38. This made up for the fact that all of my close friends were being sent in small groups to other fields throughout the Southwest. Lieutenant Scott, one of the student officers, would drive Sherry and two other wives to Douglas with

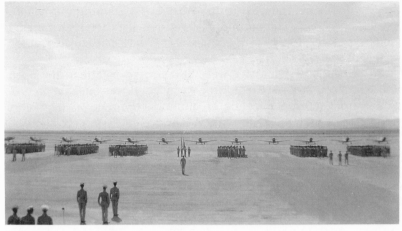

Ordering the massed formation to pass in review

Graduation day parade

only the stipulation that they share the expense of the gasoline.

My log book showed 36 hours and 20 minutes of dual instruction and 43 hours and 40 minutes of solo time, added to the 65 hours of Primary. I now had 145 hours of military flight time, not counting time flying as an observer on buddy rides.

I was not sure what the future would hold, but I could tell Mr. Pulici that the BT-13 could perform both forward and side-slips just as easily as the Stearman.

5

Advanced Flying School

Douglas, Arizona

After a bus ride to Los Angeles and a long train trip we finally arrived at Douglas Army Airfield on August 31, 1943. Douglas, located in the extreme southeast corner of Arizona, was right on the Mexican border with an elevation of over 4,000 feet. It was a thriving modern city with a population of 14,000, the third largest city in Arizona. The climate was warm and sunny with very low humidity. The annual rainfall, around fourteen inches, created a more scenic locale than Muroc Dry Lake. The temperature was quite pleasant compared to the Mojave Desert.

As our group entered the base we were immediately subjected to cultural shock. Most of the buildings were wrapped in black tarpaper held in place with a few wood strips for batten. We were truly on a military base: back to barracks style living. Everything that moved on the base wore the insignia of the Army Air Force. The beauty of the bases, the privacy and frills of Mira Loma and Polaris, faded into the past and were only a dream which had suddenly turned into a nightmare.

As others reported in we were suddenly a squadron of approximately 250 J-class cadets. The cadet corps consisted of an equal number from I-class. There was also a contingent of Nationalist Chinese cadets on the field. It was a sprawling unsightly base whose only redeeming feature was the flight line and the endless rows of AT-17 Cessna "Bobcats," twin-engine fabric-covered airplanes powered by two radial seven-cylinder Jacobs air-cooled engines generating 245 horsepower each. The aircraft had a wingspan of 41 feet 11 inches, length 32 feet 9 inches, height 9 feet 11 inches,

AT-17 Bobcat, advanced training plane, Douglas, Arizona

gross weight 5,700 pounds, top speed 176 mph with a range of 750 miles and a service ceiling of 22,000 feet.

There were dual controls with side-by-side configuration for a pilot and copilot. All of the flight instruments were located in front of the pilot on the left-hand side of the instrument panel. The engine instruments were on the right side of the panel in front of the copilot. There was a bench seat in the rear of the cabin which could comfortably accommodate two passengers or a crowded three in an emergency. Being as observant as possible I was unable to locate either a gosport system or relief tube.

We could hardly wait to start flying this rather strange looking aircraft. We had hoped to find an airplane of metal construction and much more streamlined, but it had controls, wings, and engines. What more could a pilot ask for?

Our first trip to the mess hall confirmed the fact we had indeed been pampered while attending two civilian flying fields. We knew that some of the finest cooks and chefs in the country were serving in the army, it was just unfortunate they were assigned to the motor pool.

As we received our barracks assignments we realized it was being done in the true army tradition: alphabetical order. It meant that all close associates would now have surnames starting with E, F, or G. The list of twenty-two cadets coming in from Lancaster did not contain any E's, only one F and one G, then jumped to M. Cadet Gajda and I found it relatively easy to make new friends since all of us shared a common bond. Somewhere at sometime we had all been chewed out and maligned by some individual who felt it his duty to return us to our proper mental status in the cadet community.

Monday we reported to the flight line and were given our instructor assignments. With my good luck still holding I was assigned to Second Lieutenant Kenneth Dye. Lieutenant Dye was a gentle, good-natured, humorous individual who felt that it was easier to talk a person into doing a good job in the beginning rather than having to resort to verbal abuse to correct a mistake already made. He was small in stature with light blond hair, blue eyes, and an infectious grin. His physical size was obscured by an overabundant knowledge of flying, expertise, and good common sense. It was my first experience of being able to stand flat-footed and look directly into the eyes of an instructor, an attribute which could only enhance a feeling of competence.

He explained that it was not his responsibility to teach us how to fly. We were here because we had already demonstrated this capability and were now considered to be pilots who needed only to hone our skills and learn more advanced techniques. He would show us how to take off and land a twin-engine aircraft and acquaint us with all the emergency procedures pertaining to the aircraft. Once we mastered these techniques we would begin flying as teams of pilots and copilots. New techniques would be demonstrated, our progress would be monitored, and help would be given on an "as needed" basis. He would talk, explain, and demonstrate, but the execution of the maneuvers was left to the student. The first two weeks of the course he would be an active flyer in the right seat, but from then on his position would be one of an observer, adviser, and monitor. We were cautioned to do our best and stay out of trouble because we had the meanest squadron commander on the field along with several other disagreeable persons.

On our first flight three cadets were put on board, one in the left-hand pilot seat and the other two cadets in the bench seat at the rear of the cabin. I had the privilege of being the first in the pilot's seat, and with the others watching, we received a lengthy cockpit check and explanation of the controls. We were shown a toggle switch located under a red plastic cover along with the admonition to never touch it while on the ground since this was the landing gear retraction switch.

While taxiing out for takeoff I mentioned to Lieutenant Dye that this would be only the second time since I had joined the military that I had been accorded the privilege of flying with an army pilot. He feigned shock and dismay that I had been denied the opportunity of such a pleasant experience and said he would certainly try to make up for this deficiency in my training program. I wasn't sure whether this offer was good or bad but I suspected with his sense of humor and dedication that things would turn out okay.

We received our first open post on Saturday, September 11. Sherry had already written me that Lieutenant Scott had dropped them off at the Gadsen Hotel August 30. The three young ladies, Mrs. Saling, Mrs. Meeks, and Sherry, spent the night at the Gadsen where they rented a room for three at six dollars. This was a luxury hotel built in 1906. The lobby was impressive with a leaded stained-glass mural and a curved marble staircase leading to the second floor. The next day they were all able to rent rooms in private homes at a more modest rate.

Sherry found a room with an outside entrance in a very lovely stone house. The room was much larger and nicer than the one at Lancaster; it even contained a double bed. The lady who owned the home was very nice and quite friendly, but this could not match the close family relationship which had developed with the Storys. On several weekends when the lady was gone, Sherry was granted kitchen privileges in exchange for looking after the house and a pet cat.

She had no trouble finding a job and was working six days a week in the mail order department of a major chain store. Because of the proximity to the border a large percentage of the customers were of Mexican origin and most did not speak English. Sherry's two years of high school Latin and two years of French at Whitman College did not help much, but since it was a catalog department they could point to pictures and guess at sizes.

She had also become close friends with the family who lived across the street. They had several teenage daughters and had welcomed her into their home. Since Sherry was a music major they spent many evenings together playing the piano, singing, and visiting. Here she was introduced to her first Mexican food. I was greatly relieved to find that she had such nice friends including

Sherry in front of the house where she was rooming

several cadet wives. It was a pleasant way for her to fill the time between our short overnight weekend passes.

As time went on I became more impressed with Lieutenant Dye.
The AT-17 was an easy airplane to fly and land and everyone
caught on very quickly. When I asked when we would start doing
something other than just flying level Lieutenant Dye laughed and
said in a joking manner that was all we were going to do. This
wasn't a P-38, it was a wood-and-fabric "bamboo bomber." Our
greatest thrill would probably be a stall; forget the aerobatics. Here
the emphasis would be on instrument flying, formation day and
night, and navigation in all its forms. The fighter pilots had already
been weeded out and we had been selected for a different role in
the flying military, but at this point no one knew what that was.

I wasn't very happy with this analysis. In fact, I was downright
disappointed. However, I would play the game. The important
thing was to win the silver wings and then, as an officer, again
make a bid for the P-38.

Our schedule now was very similar to the other schools. We still
had our half day on the flight line, ground school, physical training, and drill. The ground school courses were more advanced and
new courses were introduced, many of which pertained to leadership, customs and courtesies of the military, the responsibility of

Cadets marching to class

command, and the need for censorship and military security. Everywhere we looked there were signs: "Loose lips sink ships," "Button your lips," "Don't spread rumors," "Remember the enemy is listening," "The life you save may be your own." But the one that brought a hearty laugh to the cadet corps was an anonymous verse tacked to the bulletin board entitled *A Military Secret:*

> Absolute knowledge have I none,
> But my aunt's washerwoman's son
> Heard a policeman on his beat
> Say to a laborer on the street,
> That he had a letter just last week
> Written in the finest Greek,
> From a Chinese coolie in Timbuctoo,
> Who said the negroes in Cuba knew
> Of another man in a Texas town
> Who got it straight from a circus clown
> That a man in Klondyke heard the news
> From a gang of South American Jews
> About somebody in Borneo,
> Who heard of a man who claimed to know
> Of a swell society female rake
> Whose mother-in-law will undertake

To prove that her husband's sister's niece
Has stated in a printed piece
That she has a son who has a friend
Who knows when the war is going to end.

As we settled into our flying routine the tempo picked up because we were spending more time in the air. The flights were
longer and we still used auxiliary fields but they were much farther
from the home field. Buses were no longer practical and weren't
needed since we could carry the instructors and two or three cadets
with us. This eliminated the study time we used to have at the auxiliary field as we now spent all our time in the airplane.

Every Monday morning we followed a little ritual as we saluted
and reported to Lieutenant Dye. His response was always the
same, "Please, gentlemen, don't salute so loud. Woe is me. Poor
little Kenny has had a rough weekend and now you expect me to
touch my aching head to acknowledge your presence. Misters,
please show a little respect for your superior who has to spend all
weekend with a jug and some female company in order to forget
your errors of last week and work up nerve enough to fly with you
again this week." We assumed that it was all a charade, but only he
knew the truth. He was a good looking single lieutenant in his early twenties. This verbal exchange was always done on the ground
for once in the air everything was business and no foolishness. I'm
sure this relaxed approach resulted in a better flying performance
by the cadets.

There was only one exception of light-heartedness in the air and
that I suspect was to keep our minds from dwelling on what could
have been a rather frightening experience. During our second week
of flying Lieutenant Dye was giving two of us a stage check. The
other cadet had received the first check and had done well. I was
now in the left seat with the instructor in the right seat and the other cadet belted in on the bench seat. My check had just been completed and all of my mistakes pointed out. I was told to head back
to Douglas and land as our time was up.

Navigating back to the field was no problem. Douglas was the
site of a large copper smelter which contained four tall smoke
stacks of which at least one was always spewing forth tons of yel-
low smoke. The active stacks were visible for miles during the daylight hours. We didn't need a compass heading; we just flew toward the stacks.

Approaching the field I called for landing instructions and upon

Students of Lt. J. H. Connell and Lt. K. R. Dye. (Standing, left to right) *Feuerstein, Fisher, Fall, Ferry, Folsom;* (kneeling) *Foley, Fletcher*

entering the pattern we started the landing checklist. Lieutenant Dye flipped the gear switch to the down position and nothing happened. He immediately called the tower and explained we were leaving the pattern since we were experiencing landing gear problems. While he was making the radio call I moved the landing gear switch to up then back to down, but still no response. The instructor then turned to the other cadet and told him to crank the gear down manually.

He located the crank and placed it in the emergency slot to start the long process of manually cranking the gear down. In a few minutes he reported he could not turn the crank, which was now connected to the long screw which lowered the gear. Lieutenant Dye told him to turn it clockwise since he was probably trying to crank it up instead of down, but the cadet said, "Sir, I am trying to turn it clockwise, but it won't budge."

"Can't you guys do anything right? Mr. Fletcher can't flip the switch correctly and now you can't crank the gear down."

I interjected, "But, Sir, you flipped the switch down."

"I did?"

"Yes, Sir."

"Well, jeez, that's the trouble. I have to do everything: flip the switch, crank the gear down, next I suppose I'll have to do the flying too. Now, Fletcher, climb up another 500 feet and keep circling the field while I show your buddy how to put the gear down and please don't run into anyone while my back is turned."

"Yes, Sir."

After a few more minutes of grunting and griping I finally gathered that the screw had loosened up and the gear was very slowly going down. After another five minutes they announced the screw wouldn't turn any more so the gear must be down. I reported that the red light was on indicating that the gear was not down and locked. "Take off your sunglasses and look again."

"It's still red, Sir."

"Well, maybe we hit a hard spot on the screw. We will try some more."

Another couple of minutes of grunting and it was decided that the gear had to be down because the screw wouldn't move. Whether it was locked or not was another question. Lieutenant Dye slipped back into the right seat exclaiming, "Oh, my aching back. I flip the switch, I crank the gear down. Fletcher, the least you could do is turn out the red light."

"I can unscrew the cover and remove the globe if the red light is too bright."

"Forget it. Call the tower and let's go in. We've done all we can up here."

I notified the tower that we were reentering the pattern, that we had cranked the gear down manually, but still had a red light indicating that the gear was not down and locked, but suspected the light was not functioning properly. The tower recognized we had an emergency and responded by sending out the fire trucks and an ambulance. Lieutenant Dye watched the activity on the ground

then turned and said, "Fletch, you had better make the best landing you've ever made because if you mess up my Saturday night
they won't need that meat wagon."

"Are you sure you want me to land it, Sir?"

"Yes, I want you to make the landing. You're the one who needs
the experience and I feel more comfortable following you through
on the controls since that is my job. Besides, if anything happens I
can lay the blame on you."

With his constant bantering there wasn't any time to think
about the consequences, but I did notice my buddy was white
knuckled even though he wore a slight grin. As we settled onto the
runway we all held our breath for a few moments until we were
sure the gear was not going to collapse. Then we all exhaled at the
same moment.

As we turned off the runway we had quite a caravan following
us: two fire engines, the ambulance, and the fire chief's control vehicle. Lieutenant Dye, grinning from ear to ear as he watched the
parade, broke the ice exclaiming, "Men, it looks like we disappointed the vultures this time."

As we taxied on down to the line the emergency vehicles left us.
Before we reached our parking area we passed an AT-17 sitting on
the ramp with the gear up and the wooden props splintered. After
we crawled out of the airplane we proceeded to give the crew chief a
bad time about the gear switch. Then Lieutenant Dye gave the
Form One to the other cadet saying, "Fletcher made the landing
and since you got to crank the gear down you get to fill out the
form. To vent your feelings make it good and I will sign it in the
spirit of a cooperative endeavor."

We then asked the crew chief about the AT-17 sitting on the
ramp sans wheels. He grinned and said one of the Chinese cadets
had somehow managed to flip the gear switch to the up position
and apparently that switch had worked better than ours. Maybe
they wouldn't even repair our switch, but just assign the airplane
to the international group.

The following weekend the four alphabetic couples, Ellsworth,
Fisher, Fletcher, and Foley, decided to spend Sunday in Douglas'
sister city, Agua Prieta, Mexico. It was just a short walk to the im-
migration and customs building where by showing identification
we were allowed to cross the border.

Agua Prieta was a small, sleepy border town. The shops contained many of the things that were in short supply in the U.S. The
four ladies had fun trying on shoes which were plentiful, but they

knew they couldn't buy them since we had been told by the customs officials that anything that was rationed in the U.S., if pur-
chased in Mexico, would still require giving up a ration coupon
when we came back across the border. Somehow the regulation did
not make much sense. Things were rationed because they were in
short supply. It appeared that something bought in Mexico would
extend U.S. supplies. But after ten months in the cadet corps we
were well aware of the fact that rules do not have to make sense,
they were only made to be obeyed.

The following Monday we were scheduled for a solo night flight.
Lieutenant Dye was going through his usual Monday ritual and in
his perceived condition he was glad he did not have to fly with us
since our rough landings would only jar his head and prolong the
ache. Feeling rather brave I suggested that if he were married he
would not have these problems since the state of matrimony outlawed most of his indiscretions. "Mr. Fletcher, please do not resort
to blasphemy. I've washed out cadets for just thinking about this
word which you have found it necessary to utter. If you wish to
keep flying never mention *that word* again. Why would you deny all
of these young southern belles the pleasure of my company? Have
you no compassion? You must seek forgiveness."

"Yes, Sir. I'll speak to the chaplain, Sir."

"Okay, but when you do don't mention my name.

"Now let's get on with the flight that has been planned. It's not a
true cross-country flight but a rat race cross-country to give you experience in night landings and takeoffs from strange fields. You
will take off from here in trail at thirty-second intervals, then proceed to the auxiliary field at Rodeo, land and join the line for takeoff, head for the auxiliary field at Cochise, then to Fort Huachuca
and back to Douglas. You will fly two cadets to a plane, pilot and
copilot, but at Cochise you will change seats and split the time in
each position. Now plot your courses and keep in mind that you're
flying between mountain peaks that range in height from 8,500 feet
to almost 10,000.

"There will be an instructor parked in an AT-17 at each field who
will act as the tower for radio communications. All of these fields
are well lighted with flare pots but there is always the possibility
that some will blow out so use caution. You will transmit on one
frequency and receive on another. This way you will not be able to
block out the tower ship with your transmission. It also means that
you will not have airplane-to-airplane communication. All communications will be conducted through the control ship."

It was a beautiful moonlit night when we took off from Douglas. I flew as pilot for the first leg, making the landings at Rodeo and Cochise. We were in the middle of the pack and by the time we reached the auxiliary fields they were enveloped in a haze of dust. These were grass fields without runway markings. In the daytime we just landed near the center of the field after passing over the boundary, but at night the flare pots outlined a runway in the landing area. The dust did not create the problem which I had encountered at Lancaster; we had learned how to land without completely stalling the aircraft and could feel our way through the haze until the wheels actually touched down.

As soon as we cleared the landing runway we changed places in the cockpit and taxied back toward the takeoff point. Since I was now in the copilot's seat it was my duty to initiate the radio calls and free the pilot of this chore. With this routine he could devote his full attention to the hazards of night taxiing and the location of other aircraft. Since there weren't any defined taxi strips everyone left on his landing lights. Upon turning toward the runway I called the control ship and requested permission for takeoff. The answer came back to hold our position as there was an aircraft on final. We could now see the other aircraft coming down the final approach. Just before he reached us at about 100 feet of altitude the other cadet remarked that the landing craft didn't look right. At this instant I realized what was wrong and immediately called the control ship reporting the airplane landing did not have its gear down.

Instantly the control ship requested the ship landing to pull up immediately, go around, and check the landing gear. The pilot responded by pulling up and exiting the traffic pattern. By this time there were two more ships in the pattern and we had to hold for about five minutes before receiving takeoff clearance.

In the meantime my partner wondered why the airplane left the pattern. I speculated that he was hoping they hadn't copied his call number. Since we couldn't hear his call number we didn't know what it was either. He could delay and come in later and no one would know his identity. If this was the purpose it obviously worked since the incident was not mentioned at critique after we completed the rat race.

The next day I was telling a good friend about the airplane that had tried to land with the gear up and if we hadn't noticed it some dumb cluck would have smeared a trainer across the Cochise countryside. His reply was, "Fletch, I resent you talking like that."

"What do you mean?"

The obstacle course

"Your calling me a dumb cluck just because I overlooked the small matter of flipping the gear switch to down."

"I'm sorry. I didn't realize it was you."

"That's okay because no one else does either, but thanks anyway."

Our training continued on schedule. The physical fitness instructor was a little more humane than the one at Lancaster and allowed time for recreational swimming at the cadet pool. He did not feel it necessary to make swimming a part of the final test; he was more interested in the obstacle course that he had designed. The impediments were rough and varied but the cadets seemed to enjoy the rugged course. It was a good place to vent frustrations. For ten months we had been climbing mental walls trying to remain in the corps. Now it felt good to be climbing and jumping physical ones, especially in the more temperate climate.

The ground school instructors were shoving us through the courses at top speed. It was still reading, lectures, and testing.

There was no time for classroom discussion, only an occasional question. The only way we could possibly keep up was to assume that retention equalled survival and this provided the incentive to absorb all that was given.

I was still having problems in radio code. We were using the international Morse system. I could maintain a minimum passing grade but felt I should be doing better. It was so easy for some of the cadets that they couldn't imagine anyone having difficulties. One day the opportunity arose to explain my problem to the instructor. He thought that I had reached a plateau and the lack of rhythm was preventing me from improving. He suggested we try an experiment. "What do you hear when I say dah dah dit dah?"

"Well, I hear two dashes, a dot and another dash which is the letter Q."

"All right, you repeat it back to me."

"Okay, dah dah dit dah."

"I heard payday today, Q. Repeat it over and over, pick up the rhythm, dah dah dit dah, payday today, Q. Pretty soon you will only hear the jingle that you know means Q." At this point he proceeded to give me a whole group of jingles that corresponded to the letters in the alphabet. It did make code more fun and there was a little improvement, but not the breakthrough for which I had hoped.

In the meantime, all the cadet wives were attending, once a week, classes on the base sponsored by the Officers Wives Club. Most of the classes were supervised and led by the commanding officer's wife. The wives were instructed in the art of military protocol as it pertained to an officer's wife. They were expected to provide a wholesome, warm, family home atmosphere whether they lived in humble or luxurious quarters. The wives were instructed to establish a simple but gracious, hospitable style of living. They must be prepared for any emergency and were expected to devote some of their free time to worthy causes sponsored by the base. There were certain functions which a wife was obligated to attend, only one of which was to be present when her husband presented his card to call on the commander, at his home, at each new base.

The classes also included these suggestions: Their husbands, who would soon be commissioned as officers, were not to carry packages, children, or babies in public. A wife should always walk on the left side of her husband, leaving his right arm free to salute, draw weapons, or whatever. Hand-holding in public was outlawed as well as taking hold of an officer's arm. In addition to making a good home it was their duty to be good hostesses and support their husbands at all times. They must always keep in mind the rank of their husband and defer to those whose spouses were of a higher rank. Above all, they must do nothing to embarrass their husbands. A wife's conduct reflected upon the husband's character and had great influence on his progression in the chain of command.

As Sherry related these new positive suggestions to me it seemed best to remain noncommittal. I could only smile and nod inwardly. After all, I still wished to maintain a marriage and there might come a time when I would be a civilian again.

On the flight line the only thrills generated were in recovering from unusual positions, a procedure in which the student closed his eyes and bent over until his head was parallel with his lap. At this point the instructor would make several turns and pull-ups to disorient the student, then he would place the airplane in an unusual position and tell the student to recover and return to level flight by using only the flight instruments for orientation. One of the favorites was to go into a dive, pick up excessive speed, and then put the airplane into a climbing turn and holler "RECOVER." When the student saw the excessive airspeed he would think he was in a dive and pull back on the stick, or yoke as it was now called in the AT-17, which only exaggerated the climb into a stall and the plane would fall off in the direction of the lowered wing.

Eventually we learned to read all the flight instruments in one glance: the artificial horizon, airspeed indicator, turn and bank instrument, and rate of climb or descent indicator. This would give us the attitude of the airplane and we could apply the correct recovery procedures immediately.

Lieutenant Dye was right, the stall and the unusual positions were the only self-imposed thrills that we could experience. Any others came as a result of something unexpected: mechanical malfunction, a near aerial miss, just plain poor piloting technique or judgment on the part of the student.

Unlike Basic where buddy rides were almost always with the same cadet, here we found ourselves flying with a different cadet almost every time. In my case the situation was exaggerated because one of Lieutenant Dye's students was eliminated, and that left three of us with me becoming the odd man. The advantage of this was that I was exposed to the flying abilities and temperaments of a great many more students. Standardization in flying and procedures was still required and adhered to, but personalities varied from student to student and this was a true lesson in human attitudes and individualism in a regimented society. It also kept everyone on his toes, alert, thinking, and ready to react since we were not lulled into complacency because of familiarity.

After days of the humdrum of routine flying our interest was greatly enhanced by an announcement that we would be taking a long cross-country trip to Santa Ana where we would all undergo tests in a static high-altitude chamber. We would leave on Monday morning, spend Tuesday and Wednesday at Santa Ana, and then fly back to Douglas Thursday night. The outgoing flight was a day-time cross-country while the return flight would be at night.

Eventually all of J-class would make the trip, but we were in the first group. Our twenty airplanes were divided into two groups, and a flight commander in a separate airplane was assigned to each flight of ten.

The two flight commanders were pilots who were involved with administration rather than flight instructors, and we weren't famil-iar with them. We were buddied up two cadets to an airplane and I was not acquainted with the cadet who was paired up with me. I had never seen him before and was sure he was not in our squad-ron. On the outbound trip I was assigned as copilot and navigator.

The airfield at Blythe, California, was designated as our refuel-ing stop. There was a Green westbound airway that ran from Cochise to Tucson to Phoenix to Blythe to Riverside, just northeast of Santa Ana. I didn't like the idea of flying the airway since it took us through areas of very heavy air traffic so I plotted a course from Douglas direct to Tucson. This was one traffic area I could not avoid and still have a highly visible checkpoint. From there we would fly to Casa Grande, then to Tonopah where we would pick up the airway and head due west to Blythe for refueling. From Blythe we would fly to Indio and then direct to Santa Ana.

There were two mountains on the route. Old Baldy at 9,500 feet, was approximately thirty miles south of Tucson on our first leg. Then after Indio, there was San Jacinto, a peak of 11,000 feet north of the course on the final leg. Since it was a daylight flight the peaks would not be a hazard but actually would make good landmarks.

The flight commander went over the plan thoroughly, and then he asked what I would do if I missed Casa Grande. I answered that we would tune in the Phoenix radio and home in, then pick up the airway to Blythe. We chose an altitude of 8,500 feet since all visual westbound traffic flew at even thousands plus 500 feet.

The course was approved and we took off on a fun flight. After

Cross-country briefing

passing Tucson we picked up the outline of a dry river bed and followed it to Casa Grande which appeared right on time. Continuing on we crossed the Gila River near Buckeye which was twenty miles south and east of Tonopah. From there it was just 100 miles due west to Blythe.

Landing at Blythe we realized we were the talk and envy of the cadets. Here we were advanced cadets flying in from some unknown place in twin-engine aircraft heading on west for some purpose which was beyond their imagination. We did our best to ignore them and perpetuate the myth that we were probably gods from the heavens merely pausing for a brief moment in the span of perpetual life.

After refueling we had lunch and took off for Santa Ana, 200 miles distant. After passing south of Hemet we let down to 6,500 feet and kept a sharp lookout for other traffic, which we knew would be heavy in the Santa Ana area. I was just starting to question our course as we reached our ETA and the airfield was not in sight. I wondered if we could be slightly north of course. Then I saw the tall mooring masts and the large quonset-shaped hangars that housed the lighter-than-air craft that were stationed in the area. In a matter of minutes we were in the traffic pattern at Santa Ana. The cadet made another good landing while I was busy congratulating myself on a good job of navigation. I just hoped my counterpart would do as well on the way back, but that was two days away.

Within the space of the next hour all of our ten aircraft had landed. The flight commander had already made arrangements for our billeting and messing. It seemed strange to wander around our Preflight base not in formation or wondering whether someone was going to chew us out. It had been a long trip out so we turned in early.

Before entering the chamber the following morning we were given a lecture explaining the effects of anoxia or hypoxia and how this condition would alter our personalities, but nothing could prepare us for the actual test that we were going to experience. The chamber was a huge metal tube with extra thick walls and hatches. We entered through a very small hatch at one end into a small chamber which would accommodate three or four people. This was the outer chamber. Then we crawled through another hatch into a larger cylinder. The sides were lined with long benches separated by a narrow aisle. These benches seated ten people on a side and there was barely headroom to stand up in the aisle. Since I was one of the first to enter I was literally shoved to the end of the tube-like chamber.

When all twenty of us were seated, three enlisted instructors entered the chamber and explained how to use the oxygen masks which were located at each station. Once everyone demonstrated that he could use the mask the instructors ordered the inner hatch closed. As it clanged shut I experienced a feeling of claustrophobia and only the presence of the others kept me glued to the seat. The attendant in the outer chamber turned the huge wheel which locked the hatch in place. From the looks of the eyes surrounding me I realized that I was not the only one who was having trouble adjusting to the enclosed area.

As soon as the inner chamber was sealed the attendant exited and closed the hatch which led into the outer chamber. Again we knew the huge wheel was being turned although we could not see it since the hatches were solid. We donned our masks again and hooked up our headsets to the intercom system so we could receive instructions from the three attendants. There was an altimeter which started to measure the lessening pressure as soon as the pumps were started. We were told that we would be elevated to a pressure of 25,000 feet.

In the meantime we would be given tests to prove to us that we could not function without oxygen. Several candles were lit so we could see the effect of a lack of oxygen on the flame. At 10,000 feet two cadets began exhibiting signs of claustrophobia. An outside attendant was ordered to enter the outer chamber and when the pressure in the two chambers had equalized, the inner door was opened and the two cadets were removed to the outer chamber. With the sealing of the inner door we continued our ascent into lessening pressure while the attendant and the two cadets in the outer chamber started their descent to ground pressure.

The flames on the candles shrunk to a slight glow. They were eventually extinguished. In the meantime each cadet, one at a time, removed his oxygen mask under the supervision of an instructor, and was asked to write his name and state how he felt. Most of the transmissions made little sense and the signatures were illegible. In my case there was a false feeling of well-being, but the signature didn't prove much since mine was illegible even when I was on the ground.

We all realized that we could not on our own recognize the danger of anoxia since in most cases it was preceded by a carefree feeling and a sense that all was okay. We felt we were functioning normally when, in fact, we weren't functioning at all. When everyone had completed the individual test we were warned to be ready for an explosive change in pressure. The hatch in the inner door contained a round window which was sealed with a thick layer of a red cardboard-type material. A large mechanical knife was attached to a spring on a lever just inches away from the cardboard barrier. The pressure was increased in the outer chamber to where it greatly exceeded ours. At a signal from the instructor the mechanical restraint was removed allowing the spring to plunge the knife into the cardboard barrier. The result was an immediate explosion from the outer chamber as the pressure neutralized in both chambers.

Recovering from the shock, we realized the cardboard was now confetti settling to the floor of the chamber. The on-rushing pressure created a vapor which looked like smoke and it was a few seconds, which seemed like minutes, before we could see. This ended the demonstration. Our pressure was slowly increased to ground level and then the hatches were opened and we were allowed to stumble out. It wasn't something that you wanted to do every day. In fact, I had the feeling that one time was once too many; I should have joined the two cadets who had to be removed. They were not washed out since this was not a test, only a demonstration. Their problem was not related to high-altitude pressure but only to being enclosed in a cramped space, a phobia which affects many people.

We now had renewed respect for the sailors who manned our submarines.

The rest of the day was spent attending lectures relating to the dangers of high-altitude flying and a demonstration of various types of equipment used in this endeavor. The lectures were given by flight surgeons and we took them seriously since we were all aware that the atmosphere represented an even greater danger to us than that posed by an enemy.

The next day we had free run of the base until our late afternoon briefing at the flight line. Since our return flight was at night, our course was laid out for us. We would fly from Santa Ana to Riverside and pick up the Green east airway, proceed on over Blythe, and eventually break away just before Phoenix with ten planes landing and refueling at Luke Field. The other ten would proceed to Williams Field. After refueling we would continue on the airway south and east to Tucson and Cochise, then leave the airway and proceed on to Douglas.

I was in the group landing at Williams. I knew some cadets at Williams, but our arrival time was around midnight, so it would be impossible to visit anyone.

As we buckled ourselves into the seats I mentioned to the other cadet that I hoped he had as much fun navigating back as I did on the outbound trip. We knew his course would be longer since we were following the airway and he would not be able to take the shortcuts that I had used on the way out. We also knew the night course would keep us away from all the high peaks en route, including San Jacinto and Old Baldy, and was the safer of the two routes.

We fired up the engines and took off just after dark. We knew we were flying a gas guzzler as we compared the fuel used on the way out with some of the other pilots, but we didn't feel this would be a problem. We were assigned an altitude of 9,500 feet on the return flight. This corresponded with eastbound traffic rules on the airway of odd thousands plus 500 feet under visual flight rules. Once on the airway at Riverside we flew on the right side of the civil airway which was deemed to be ten miles wide with a light line running down the center.

We were over halfway to Blythe before we picked up the light line. Wartime regulations prohibited the beacons from being lighted within 150 miles of the coast. The lights were spaced about fifteen miles apart depending on terrain, with each one flashing a code number when viewed from above. The numbers ran from one though nine to zero, each one coded to the nearest ten-mile increment. The first beacon we could identify flashed a number eight which we knew was number eighteen on the airway since the course lights flashed only the last digit of the beacon number.

The airway started at Los Angeles so we knew we were 180 miles from there. All of the beacons were numbered from west to east on the line. Thus the signal would be the same for 80, 180, or 280 miles. Beacons having the same signal would be approximately 100 miles apart. This was a good system as long as you knew which 100-mile segment you were in. Its main drawback was that it was only usable in periods of good weather since it relied on visual contact.

This was a perfect night, not a cloud in the sky with a forecast to remain that way all over the Southwest. We continued to check off the beacons. The other cadet remarked this was so simple it was just like shooting ducks in a rain barrel, and he was right. Only a fool could get lost on a night as beautiful as this. Eventually the lights of Phoenix came into view and there was no reason to identify the beacons any longer.

We chattered about the chamber experience and were glad it was over. The city lights still well ahead in the distance became a sight of beauty, a view which always brought a thrill to a pilot. We decided we would fly toward them until we could see the beacon at Sky Harbor airport, the civilian airport at Phoenix.

All civilian airports were marked by a rotating white and green beacon. The beacon, which was shaped like a barrel, had a white lens in one end and a green lens in the other. As it rotated through 360 degrees you saw two flashes of light, one green and one white, 180 degrees apart. The military fields were marked with the same kind of beacon but had a white lens in each end and showed two split white beams. Thus it was possible from a long distance to differentiate between civilian and military airports at night.

As we continued on I asked the other cadet how many miles we were from Phoenix. He replied, "I dunno. We can see it so what difference does it make? We'll just fly till we get close, then head for Williams."

"I think you should be keeping a log."

"What for? You kept one on the way out and nobody asked to see it. It's a lot of work for nothing."

"Well, we got there."

"Yeah, and we're going to get to Williams too."

All of a sudden there was a horrendous noise drowning out not only our conversation but the noise from our two engines also. Our airplane was pushed downward by a cushion of air, then started rocking and rolling while I fought to keep it flying straight and level. In the same instant I saw four flaming exhausts which had just passed at an angle overhead and were now streaking away at a tremendous speed. I realized that we were floundering in the prop wash of this huge airplane.

We did not panic but were shocked beyond belief by the sudden appearance of the monolithic craft and its deafening noise. We actually became weak as we realized what could have happened had we been even inches higher. The beautiful night sky, a dwelling place of angels, had suddenly become a black sinister home to the demons and spirits associated with fear and horror. We only wanted to break loose from this inhospitable environment.

How we escaped a midair collision I will never know. This airplane had come at a forty-five degree angle from behind us on the left side of the ship, passing over us so close the distance could not be measured. It was obvious they never saw us as we were overtaken on the airway at the same altitude. The other cadet suggested that maybe we should get off the airway while we were still alive; one near miss was enough. The traffic could only increase as we continued on course. I readily agreed and altered our course to a more southerly direction.

In a few minutes, with the lights of Phoenix still ahead, my partner spotted a military beacon south and east of our course. He immediately exclaimed, "There. That's Williams Field right over there." I responded that I was sure that we were not far enough east yet since I could now see the green and white beacon of Sky Harbor airport still ahead. But his reply was, "That beacon is farther east than you think. Besides there aren't any other airfields in the vicinity except Luke, Sky Harbor, and Williams. That has to be it." With that he threw the maps in the back seat. I altered the course to fly to the airfield but it didn't look right. I still had apprehensions, but since he was the navigator I didn't make any big fuss.

The lights of Phoenix disappeared before we reached the military field. It was farther away than I thought. Eventually we came over the field and I started circling while the copilot called Williams Field for landing instructions. After three attempts and no answer I was sure that either the radio didn't work or we were not where we were supposed to be, or possibly both. On his fourth try the radio crackled to life with the response, "Ship calling Williams tower, this is Gila Bend tower. We hear you loud and clear and believe you are in our pattern. Do you wish landing instructions?"

The copilot asked me if I wanted landing instructions and I asked if he knew where Gila Bend was. He said, "No."

"Well, I don't either. The maps are in the back seat so we had better land and find out where we are."

In just a few minutes we were on the runway. I turned off at the first taxi-strip and headed in the direction of the control tower. As we braked to a stop near the tower a staff car pulled up and an officer with an O.D. (officer of the day) arm band on jumped out, crawled up on the wing and opened the door to the cabin. His first words were, "Welcome to Gila Bend Army Airfield."

We both gasped, "Where's that?"

Remembering the events of the night we weren't surprised when he said, "Right at the crossroads of hell where the devil bid the owl good-bye."

"Thanks. We suspected as much but we still don't know where that is."

He flipped his flashlight on and picked up our map as I turned on the cabin lights. He took one look at us and said, "Well, look what we've got here: two RONs." This was a reference to a military order which stated that any time a cadet landed at night at a strange field which was not on his itinerary he had to "remain over night" and finish his flight during daylight hours.

We acknowledged that we understood the rules. We explained that we were on our way back to Douglas from Santa Ana and were supposed to land at Williams to refuel. He showed us where Gila Bend was located and said that we had turned off course too early. We were thirty-five miles south of course. It was seventy miles northeast to Williams.

We could now see that he was a first lieutenant. "Look fellows," he said, "I don't want to cause you any trouble. If you want to take off and head for Williams I'll pretend I never saw you and won't make a report."

This was an offer we should have accepted, but after checking the fuel supply, which was low, I wasn't sure I wanted to take the chance. I thanked him but said we had already made one mistake. We could probably make Williams okay but we wouldn't have any reserve and this could be another mistake. Two in one night might be too much.

"You're probably making the right decision, but if I have to re-fuel you then I have to report you as a matter of record to cover the transaction."

"That's okay. I don't feel we have much choice. Common sense tells me to refuel, spend the night, and proceed in the morning."

"Sounds like a reasonable decision and I don't think anyone can find fault with it."

The other cadet replied, "Sir, you don't know our flight commander."

Giving us a funny look he requested us to shut down the engines and head for the mess hall. I grabbed my pilot's briefcase, crawled out, and joined the other two in the command car. On the way to the mess hall the lieutenant was doing his best to put us at ease. He seemed to enjoy having someone to visit with even though it was only two lowly, lost cadets.

By the time we reached the mess hall he had raised our confidence level 100 percent and we were actually starting to see some humor in our predicament. Once in the mess hall the O.D. shouted to the cook to bring coffee and rustle up some chow for the two hungry fliers. The cook brought the coffee and wanted to know if some Spam, toast, and eggs would be all right. At this point we weren't too hungry, but anything he wanted to fix would be fine. We weren't used to being asked ahead of time whether something would be okay.

As soon as the coffee was poured I asked the lieutenant if he could notify the O.D. at our base at Douglas where we were, assure him everything was all right including the aircraft, and that we would fly out in the morning. He said that he could do that but he had a better idea. He explained that since our flight commander was at Williams maybe it would be better to call there since he would be waiting for us. If he could locate him he undoubtedly would give permission for us to take off and join the group at Williams. Sounded good to us; anything was worth a try. The lieutenant left to make the telephone call while the cook brought out four plates filled with Spam and eggs along with a plateful of toast. The cook joined us at the table expressing an interest in our flight.

Upon the lieutenant's return the four of us pitched in and made quick work of the chow. He explained that he had reached Williams and they were trying to locate the flight commander. In a few minutes a sergeant poked his head in the door and said that the lieutenant had a telephone call. He excused himself saying that he would probably have us airborne in a few minutes. We couldn't get over the relaxed atmosphere, courtesy, and treatment we were receiving. As cadets we just weren't used to being treated like people.

Soon the lieutenant returned and apologetically explained that the flight commander had refused to give permission for us to take off. Instead we were to wait where we were and he would fly down and deal with us personally. It seemed that he had aircraft scattered all over the Southwest. Right now he knew where three airplanes were including ours.

The cook brought out more coffee and we all decided to wait at the mess hall for the flight commander. The lieutenant said he couldn't understand why the captain was so upset. After all, we could be at Williams in a little over half an hour, which would make more sense than having us sit around while we were waiting for him to fly down.

"Lieutenant, we don't know the captain very well as he is not one of our instructors. He is a Flight Operations Officer in administration."

"Well, whatever he is he sounds as if he has a cocklebur under his blanket."

While we were visiting I opened my flight case, spread out the map, and started plotting a course from Gila Bend direct to Douglas. I wanted to make sure that going direct wouldn't force us to fly into Old Baldy in the Tucson area. It turned out to be twenty-five miles south of the course so it didn't appear to be a problem.

I asked the lieutenant if he had been to Douglas. "No," he said. "All of our flying here is out on the gunnery range or towing some darn target sleeve around. Occasionally we get a break and fly to Los Angeles or up to Phoenix, but I guess we're stuck here for the rest of the war. Maybe you fellows will have better luck and get to see some action."

We kept on visiting and drinking coffee for about an hour when a sergeant came in and told the lieutenant there was an airplane in the traffic pattern. The lieutenant told him to take a vehicle down to the flight line, pick up the pilot, and bring him to the mess hall. In just a few minutes the captain made his presence known by banging through the door and asking where the two knuckleheads were. The lieutenant jumped up to meet him and I heard him say, "Hey, take it easy. We have a lot of planes land here thinking it is Williams."

The captain looked at him with contempt and said, "Lieutenant, nobody in his right mind would mistake Gila Bend for Williams.

Nobody lands here. This is probably the first transient aircraft that you've seen in six months so don't give me that malarkey."

As he strode over to the table I rose to attention amid a query of, "What do you think you're doing, MISTER Fletcher?"

"I've just finished plotting the course to Douglas, Sir."

"Put your maps away. You don't need a course. Get your tail end in that AT-17 and I'll show you the way home."

"Yes, Sir."

He completely ignored the other cadet and was still sputtering as he went back out and crawled in the jeep with the sergeant. The lieutenant looked at us and said, "The timing just didn't seem right to offer him a cup of coffee. You can count yourselves lucky that you don't have to fly back in the same airplane with him."

With that he proceeded to take us back to the line in the staff car. The refueling crew had just finished with our airplane. As we got out of the staff car one of the crew asked the lieutenant if they were supposed to refuel the AT-17 that had just landed. "No," he dryly responded. "The captain has all the gas he needs."

We thanked the lieutenant for all that he had done for us, saluted, and started to climb aboard. The lieutenant waved and hollered, "Feel free to drop in again anytime." We couldn't think of a pleasant reply because we weren't even sure if we would still be flying after the events of the night were reviewed.

While we were starting up the engines we heard the captain call the tower requesting permission for two AT-17s to taxi to the takeoff position. Permission was granted with the notation that there wasn't any other ground or air activity in the local area. As the captain taxied by he called on the radio for us to follow him. On takeoff he would circle the field and "Mister Fletcher, I want you on my right wing before the circle is completed. If you get more than ten feet away from my wing on the way back to Douglas your flying career is over."

We didn't bother to acknowledge, we just started taxiing behind him. Once we were airborne we swung around to join up in formation and the earphones pulsated with, "Mister Fletcher, what is your position or are you lost again." I radioed back that I was approaching him from behind on the inside of the circle, would pass underneath and pull up on his wing in a couple of minutes. He radioed back, "Mister Fletcher, I hope you are better at formation flying than navigating."

The other cadet remarked, "I think he's just trying to humiliate you." I was doing a slow burn because the other cadet didn't exist in the captain's mind and I was catching all the blame. But I did point out to the other cadet that the captain wasn't trying, he had already succeeded. The more I thought about it the madder I got and kept easing in a little closer. In fact, I had learned that one of the best ways to work off frustration was to fly tight formation. The closer you get to the other ship the more concentration is required. Consequently, you block everything else out of your mind except the navigation light on the wing of the lead aircraft.

The other cadet finally started to fidget and squirm in his seat remarking, "What are you trying to do, Fletch, stick the left wing in his window?" I thought to myself, neither you nor the captain have been much help on this leg so you both can squirm. I'll keep pushing in till someone cries "Uncle."

The closer I got the better I felt and the easier it became to maintain position. In fact, I was just starting to enjoy the cadet's uneasiness when the captain called and said, "Mister Fletcher, do you think you could move out a little bit? The red wing light is blinding my copilot."

The cadet grabbed the mike and with relief in his voice answered, "Yes, Sir." I eased off a little and the other cadet yelled, "You heard his transmission, didn't you?"

"Yeah, but remember he said ten feet and he didn't say which ten feet so I'll use the inside ten."

Eventually the lights of Douglas came into view. As we passed over the airfield the captain came on the radio and in a very sarcastic voice intoned, "Mister Fletcher, do you see those lights beneath us?"

"Yes, Sir."

"Well, that's Douglas Army Airfield. Do you think you can possibly land there without getting lost?"

I jerked the throttles to idle and fell away calling the tower for landing instructions. The other cadet said, "Thank the Lord. I thought you were going to kill us."

"Shut up and quit whining. I have taken the heat on this flight and the first guy that calls me Mister in civilian life is going to have a fight on his hands. In your case it might happen sooner."

Before we could touch down the captain was back on the air proclaiming to anyone within receiving distance of Douglas Army Airfield that the two cadets will report to the squadron commander's office at 10:00 a.m. today. It was now well past 2:00 a.m., but I knew I probably wouldn't sleep too much in the next few hours. I also knew that if by some miracle I finished the course and received a commission I would never ridicule, discipline, or humiliate another person in my command in public or within earshot of someone else. This individual certainly was not my ideal of a commissioned officer, but he had the bars and rank which I could respect, if not the person.

By 8:00 a.m. I was at the flight line where I asked Lieutenant Dye if he could spare some time for a private conversation. He obliged and I told him the whole story including the near miss on the light line, only it was impossible to describe, it had to be experienced before you could relate to the events that followed. I explained that it appeared that I was being held responsible for the whole flight. I didn't know whether I would be around much longer, and I wasn't sure where they dug up the cadet who had been assigned to fly with me.

"Let me give you some advice. First, keep your cool. At this point the Army has too much money invested in your flying career to wash you out on one incident which did not endanger an airplane or personnel. Now be prepared to receive another chewing out. Accept it as coming from a squadron commander who, just like the squadron operations officer, is envious of you because you're probably going on to combat and he is stuck in the training command."

"Maybe they should request a transfer."

"They say they have, but I think if it were granted both would certainly look at their hole cards a long time before they made a bet. Now about the cadet that went with you. He is a holdover from I-class who had some problems with navigation and this was his chance to get back on schedule and graduate with J-class. That information you can use if you want to, but remember this: As your instructor my input would be needed before anyone could wash you out for something that involves flying. Insubordination or discipline problems are a different matter—I wouldn't be consulted. So go get your chewing out and then we'll get on with your flying."

"I hope you're right. Anyway, I feel better about the meeting."

At 10:00 I reported to the squadron commander's office. The other cadet was already waiting when I arrived. The first sergeant informed us that the squadron commander would see us one at a time. I was first and he ushered me into the commander's office. After salutes were exchanged I was ordered to stand at ease. The commander stated that he understood that I had had some problems on the cross-country which probably involved some errors in judgment and a demonstrated lack of knowledge in navigation. Did I care to recount what happened?

I explained that in briefing for the trip out I was assigned the position of copilot and navigator. We had flown the course making every checkpoint on time. Our positions were switched on the return trip. We hit our checkpoints on schedule and eventually we saw the lights of Phoenix. I had no intention of telling about the near collision and the part it played in our leaving the airway. I had explained it to Lieutenant Dye and he was the only person who would hear the story. Maybe it was tantamount to admitting fear, but you had to experience it to fully appreciate what happened. Words would only fall on deaf ears and true feelings could never be transmitted.

At the mention of the lights the captain interjected, "I know exactly what happened. I can see the two of you right now in the cockpit. You saw the lights of Phoenix and thought you had it made so you tossed the maps in the back seat and flew to the nearest military beacon."

His insight unnerved me somewhat but I managed to say, "Well, that's not quite the way it happened. The other cadet chose the beacon and we flew there. It was my understanding that I was responsible for the navigation to Santa Ana and he was responsible for the trip home."

That was as far as I got before he exploded with, "Mister Fletcher, the pilot in the left seat is always responsible for anything that happens on an airplane or where it flies and is held accountable for every action. Now I gather you are trying to shift the blame on the copilot."

"No, Sir. This is the first time anyone has ever mentioned this accountability. It has never been mentioned before at briefing or any other time. This was described as a lesson in navigation in which each one of us was assigned a certain area of responsibility. I am not trying to shift the blame, I'm only telling you what happened as you requested."

"You have just violated the cardinal rule of navigation: how to get from here to there without going somewhere else. Now go ahead with your version."

At this point I knew any further discussion was impossible, I was already pegged the loser. I relied on the one thing that everyone in the military understood. I came to attention, fixed my gaze on the wall just above the commander's head and replied, "Sir, in the light of what you have just told me about accountability I have nothing further to add. I accept full responsibility for what happened and the consequence that goes with it. I have no excuse, Sir."

This brought on a seemingly endless, vehement lecture on responsibility and leadership, but the only part that really registered was "dismissed." I saluted and got out before my ears burned off. Before I reached the headquarters door I heard the first sergeant tell the other cadet he was free to go as the squadron commander had no desire to speak to him.

When I got back to the ready room Lieutenant Dye inquired how the confrontation had gone. I explained that he was looking at one well chewed-out cadet who probably wouldn't be able to sit down for a week. "Did he mention any disciplinary measures?"

"I don't think so. The mind can only retain so much abuse before it blocks everything out, but I did hear him say dismissed. Beyond that I'm not sure what happened."

"Well, it's obvious that is the end of it because the captain has a way of making sure that you not only know but understand any further consequences. The incident is closed. The choice you have now is do you want to go tell it to the chaplain or fly the Link trainer?"

"I'll take the Link. The chaplain probably has enough trouble of his own."

The Santa Ana trip was the last major event before graduation. We were soon informed that upon graduation we would receive a $250 clothing allowance. It would take time to order and alter uniforms for a class the size of ours. Since the base clothing store had a very limited selection and rather poor quality, most of us chose to use Levy's Military Shop in the town of Douglas. These people offered good service and carried a top line of military apparel for both officers and enlisted men. They also had a monopoly and were assured a good business with a new class graduating every four and a half weeks. Two weeks before graduation my uniforms arrived and were altered to a perfect fit. Now all that remained was to make sure I didn't foul up and get the axe before graduation since these uniforms were sold on the basis of no returns or refunds after alteration.

Graduation day was set for Wednesday, November 3, 1943. A cadet graduation party was scheduled for the evening of November 2 at the base officer's club. Wives and girlfriends were invited to attend a buffet dinner and an evening of dancing. The end was in sight; the brass ring was within reach. Most of us were amazed that we had survived and were now just days away from the goal which we had hoped to attain: the winning of the coveted silver pilot wings of the U.S. Army Air Force.

My last flight was set for the day of the cadet party. It was an instrument cross-country. I had practiced the flight several times in the Link trainer so was quite familiar with the procedure involved. All I had to do now was actually fly the course under the hood and all my training requirements would be met.

Reporting to the flight line I was assigned an airplane and Lieutenant Dye wanted to know if I understood the mission. I told him that upon takeoff from Douglas I would fly to Cochise, let down on the auxiliary field there, pull up and go to Rodeo, let down on the field there, again pull up and come back to Douglas utilizing all three radio ranges. Upon arrival over the Douglas range I could come out from under the hood and land. My flying would be done and I would get ready for the graduation party.

"You've got it. Get going."

I was flying with another cadet I did not know who was the observer. After takeoff I went under the hood and the observer flew around for a little while. I shielded my eyes so I couldn't see either the compass or the directional gyro. When the observer felt that he had flown long enough to confuse me in regard to location I took over, tuned in the Cochise radio range, then turned to an average bisector heading corresponding to the N quadrant, which was the signal I heard. Using the following procedure I switched off the automatic volume control, flying the chosen bisector until I could determine whether the signal grew stronger or weaker. If it was stronger I would know that I was headed in the direction of the beam and the station. But it turned out the signal was fading so I knew I was flying away from the station and proceeded to make a 180 degree turn.

Once on the beam I flew to the station and entered the cone of silence which is directly over the station. At this point I turned to the heading leading to the auxiliary field at Cochise, at the same time setting up a rate of descent which would place me in a position to land if I had worked the problem correctly. At 500 feet above the ground the observer took over, added full power, and we climbed back up to altitude. At this point I removed the hood to see how successful I had been. We were right over the field. I went back under the hood, tuned in the Rodeo range and, since my position was now known, flew east on the west leg to Rodeo. Once over the station, I took the southbound heading to the airfield. As we descended to 500 feet the observer opened the throttles screaming, "Get out from under the hood. We just lost the number two engine."

I jerked down the curtain that separated us in the cockpit as well as those covering the windows and tossed them back behind us. We were at 400 feet, just short of the field but too high to land straight ahead. The nose was high and the airspeed dangerously low. I grabbed the yoke, lowered the nose to gain airspeed, then standing on the rudder rolled in rudder trim to counteract the loss of the right engine. The number one engine was at full throttle. The wooden butter paddles which served as a propeller on the number one engine were churning the air while the number two propeller was windmilling, creating considerable drag. Both were very inefficient airfoils. I realized we could not maintain our altitude but only stretch the glide. Immediately I decided to make a 360 degree turn to the left into the good engine which, if successful, was the shortest way to set up a landing approach. I asked the other cadet if he had seen any aircraft in the vicinity. He answered that the field was deserted. He had seen only one aircraft in the air but it was well beyond the airfield.

Then he queried, "Do you want to make the landing just coming out from under the hood?"

"You better believe it. I have it on good authority that the left seat is responsible for the airplane. Don't worry, if we don't make it you won't be held accountable."

By now we were halfway around the turn and still had 300 feet of altitude left. We continued flying the wide almost flat turn which provided the best lift possible with the airspeed below cruise speed, but well above stalling speed. As we finished the turn we had 200 feet between us and the hard ground. I hollered at the other cadet to make sure his safety belt was cinched tight just in case we didn't make the field. The ground was level enough if we had to land short, but there was a six-foot fence which served as the airport boundary and kept range livestock off the landing area.

I kept holding pressure on the throttle to keep it wide open and hopefully eke just a little more power out of the engine. In a few seconds I was positive if we didn't hit a down draft we would make the field. I asked the other cadet to roll out the trim when I gave him the signal which would be just as I started to reduce power, but I wanted to get over the fence first. We were now below 100 feet and the fence posts looked like trees.

Before we reached the boundary the other cadet hollered, "Fletch, there's another plane landing from the opposite direction."

I yelled back, "I see him, but the field is wide enough for both of us. I'll hold as close as I can to the right fence. Roll out the trim now. We're over the fence." I hauled the throttle closed and we touched down, a good 300 feet inside the field. On the roll-out we were about 100 feet from the right fence. As the other airplane rolled past on our left we waved to two surprised pilots.

As we braked to a stop I decided to taxi a little closer to the fence so as not to pose a hazard to anyone else landing. This proved to be wishful thinking as the airplane would not taxi on the grass field. It would only pivot in a circle. I tried holding the outside brake, then it wouldn't move at all. The old butter paddles just blew dust while the engine made noise. It was obvious we were trapped where we were. We shut down the engine and crawled out.

The other cadet said, "Fletch, I was sorta worried there for a few minutes. I wasn't sure whether the Bobcat would make it or not."

"That was sort of foolish, you know, worrying about it."

"What do you mean?"

"Well, I was worrying enough for both of us. Our Polecat turned out to be a real stinker. What a way to finish our last flight."

By now the other airplane had taxied up to us and the instructor was crawling out. We felt good because we could see that there was only one other person in the airplane which meant there was room for us to fly home. The instructor came over, commenting, "Fellas, looks like you've got problems."

"Yes, Sir, we just lost the number two engine and would sure appreciate a ride home."

Our hopes were dashed as he answered, "No, you guys stay with the airplane and when I get back to Douglas I will send somebody back for you."

I interjected, "Hey, wait a minute. Nobody is going to steal this airplane with an engine out. It won't even taxi, let alone fly."

"MISTER, you heard what I said. Stay with your airplane."

Again it was, "Yes, Sir" verbally, but if he knew what we were thinking we would have been court-martialed on the spot.

He proceeded to take off and left us in a cloud of dust. It was almost 3:00 and we had hoped to be back at Douglas by 4:00. Happy Hour preceding the party was scheduled to begin at 6:30. Sherry had already made arrangements to ride out to the field with Mrs. Foley. They were one of the few who had a car. In fact, she was bringing a carload including Mrs. Ellsworth, Mrs. Fisher, and Mrs. Gassman.

We sat around hoping another plane would land with a more charitable pilot on board, but there didn't appear to be any air traffic at all. As far as we knew, with the exception of ourselves, only

K-class was scheduled for flying. We knew we were only forty-five miles from Douglas so it wouldn't take long for somebody to fly up and pick us up. In the meantime, we kicked the tires and spun the prop on the number two engine. It moved easily with grinding sounds; obviously it was no longer connected to the crankshaft.

Five o'clock came and passed and still no ride home. We were sitting on a deserted field feeling sorry for ourselves when the other cadet piped up with, "What if that blankety blank instructor forgot to notify anyone about us?"

A few minutes before 6:00 we could hear an airplane in the distance. We grabbed our pilot cases, slammed the door shut on our crippled plane and watched as the AT-17 settled onto the field. The airplane braked to a stop a few feet away from us. We clambered on board and buckled into the back seat. The plane was piloted by two stern looking lieutenants, strangers to both of us. There was no sign of greeting. Finally over the roar of the engines the other cadet remarked that we weren't sure after waiting three hours that anyone was coming to pick us up. He didn't get an answer so we flew back to the base in silence. I didn't care whether they spoke or not but was surprised they didn't ask about the airplane or express some interest in what had happened. This was just one of the many times in cadet training that nothing made sense.

As we crawled out of the plane at Douglas one of the lieutenants said, "Mister Fletcher, you're to report to the squadron commander at 8:00 in the morning."

"Yes, Sir."

That was the total conversation. But who cares, this is party night. I ran all the way to the barracks, which were deserted as everyone was at Happy Hour. I quickly showered, shaved, and donned my new uniform.

It was 7:30 when I walked in the door at the Officers Club. There were cadets, wives, and girlfriends everywhere. Everyone seemed to be talking in whispers. I thought I was going to a party, but the atmosphere was more fitting of a mortuary. I looked for Sherry and our friends, but they were obviously obscured in the crowd. I finally decided that there must be some officers present and that was putting a damper on the crowd. They had told us the club was reserved strictly for graduating cadets and their guests, but the usual exuberance of the cadet corps was missing. Oh well, the thing to do was locate my friends and get the party rolling.

As I started walking through the area I received some startled, questioning looks. The same kind that would greet you walking into a party with your fly unzipped. I had dressed in a hurry but I knew I was safe on that count. There was no reason to check. I spotted Sherry and the others seated at a round table in a far corner of the club. Then I saw Larry Gassman leaving the punch bowl carrying drinks to the table. I hurried over and asked if I could help. He turned around and his grim expression mirrored surprise, then a big grin. "You better believe it, Buddy. Where in the hell have you been?"

"Well, all afternoon and early evening I've been sitting in the cow pasture called Rodeo auxiliary field with an engine out waiting for someone to come and pick me up."

"Then you haven't heard?"

"Heard what?"

"We lost an AT-17 this afternoon and two cadets were killed, but nobody knows who they are because the names have not been released. When you didn't show up people were starting to jump to conclusions. Get over to the table and make your presence known. Sherry and the rest are worried sick."

In that instant all of the unusual actions of the afternoon fell into place. Further discussion brought out the fact that most people knew two airplanes were missing, one from J-class and the other from K-class. With my arrival all J-class planes were accounted for. This meant the missing aircraft carried two underclassmen. The party continued on a lighter note, but was far from the lively celebration we had all anticipated.

The following morning at 8:00 I reported to the squadron commander and his demeanor was still adversarial, consistent with our last confrontation over the Gila Bend blunder. But this time I was not the scared cadet who had previously been cowed in his presence. In three hours I would be a commissioned officer. This time my eyes locked on his in the stare down.

He started off with a barrage of questions regarding the engine instruments, namely oil pressure and other readings before engine failure. I could only give one answer. "I don't know, Sir. I was under the hood and all engine instruments are located on the right-hand side of the panel, unavailable to me. I don't know what the readings were. I can only tell you what they were after the engine malfunctioned."

"In other words you let ice build up in the carburetor until the engine, starved for fuel and air, conked out."

"Sir, I learned about carburetor ice long before I joined the cadet corps. How many cases of carburetor ice have you seen in seventy-degree temperature? We reported a mechanical malfunction and that is what we had. We also know the propeller is not connected to the crankshaft, a fact which can be verified by pulling the propeller through several revolutions."

He lowered his eyes, rattled the papers on his desk and harshly ordered, "MISTER Fletcher, you are dismissed."

There wasn't time to go back to the barracks as all graduating cadets were scheduled to pass in review at nine. I headed for the parade ground, but on the way I couldn't help but think about the egotistical captain and his carburetor ice bluster. There wasn't anything in his personality that could let him believe that a cadet could do anything right. I felt we had done a good job making the emergency landing. The airplane was intact sitting on an airfield and would fly again, but the captain could not bring himself to acknowledge that something must have been done right. It was a good lesson for me as I made another mental note: If you are going to criticize and chastise a poor performance then you have the obligation to recognize and compliment that which is out of the ordinary.

At 9:00 sharp we passed in review and then were arranged alphabetically in a single line on the parade grounds. It was explained that we would walk by several tables. At the first we would sign our resignation from the cadet corps. At the second table we would receive orders showing our appointment as officers, sign the oath of office, then at the next table receive orders which placed us on flying status with the rating of pilot. At the last table we would receive our new assignment orders.

As the front of the line moved past the tables a controversy started to develop. Word was quickly passed down the line that we were not receiving the Regular Army commission which was promised in our original enlistment papers. I asked some of the fellows what that meant and why we were being denied that which was promised. One cadet replied, "It means we are the bastard sons. They need us but no one wants to accept responsibility for us so they have created a temporary army in which we receive temporary appointments for the duration plus six months."

There was a little acrimony as the cadets realized they were being short-changed and stated their objections as they passed the tables, but no one was refusing. Then all of a sudden the line was halted. Apparently one of the administrative officers, fearing the worst, decided that the first two tables should be switched.

The table order now was: You signed the oath of office, received your appointment, and then signed your resignation from the cadet corps. This was an apparent violation since you were not allowed to hold two offices at one time, but it also meant that you couldn't sign a resignation from cadets and walk away without accepting the commission that was offered. This official certainly didn't understand the aviation cadet when he panicked and switched tables. We were there because we wanted the silver wings which allowed us to fly. We had a legitimate gripe, but we would have signed anything that granted us the privilege of flying. This was our primary goal; everything else was secondary.

The line started to move again and when I finally reached the first table I read the paper placed before me. It stated that I was appointed a temporary second lieutenant in the Army of the United States (Air Force). The line above, which read second lieutenant Air Corps in the Officers Reserve Corps, was crossed out, as well as the line below which read Flight Officer Army of the United States (Air Corps). The officer remarked, "Come on, sign the paper and keep the line moving."

My answer was, "I've learned to read everything before I sign and even that doesn't mean anything."

After every one of our group, which was now 237 in number, had progressed through the line we gathered at 11:00 in the Post Theater where we were presented our wings. After the oath of office was administered, the graduating class sang the Air Corps Song (which was only a different version of the one the cadet wives had been singing for months):

> Off we go leaving our homes back yonder
> Into the lands we never knew
> Joining those who we love and cherish
> And we're both loyal and true.
> We have known plenty of joy and sadness
> And we'll stay ready for more
> We have no dough but still we know
> We'll always follow the Army Air Corps.
>
> With such pay there's no way
> For us to lead a happy normal life
> And you'll find there's no kind
> Of work to get when you're a cadet wife
> There's never any rooms within the town
> The Army looks upon us with a frown
> Still we go, cause we know our husbands are
> The Army Air Corps.

Silver pilot wings were presented to 239 members. The increase represented the two student officers who were a part of the class. It was a moment of sincere pride when Sherry pinned the silver wings and gold bars on my blouse. She was a popular lady as several of our single friends asked that she do the same for them. During this little ritual I was amazed to see Larry Luzader, my friend during Preflight, cross the stage and receive his wings. I had not seen him since Santa Ana and did not realize he was on the field. He disappeared in the crowd and, unfortunately, we were not able to meet.

It was a real melee as everyone hurried to clear the theater and get off the base. We were authorized a ten-day delay en route and every minute that ticked by at Douglas was one less we would have at home. We bolted from the theater with the speed of a bride and a groom leaving the altar and heading for the honeymoon.

Outside the theater many of the top ranking NCOs (non-commissioned officers) were waiting. They were well aware of the old custom that a newly commissioned officer would present a dollar bill to the first man to salute him after commissioning. As Sherry and I ran out the door the sergeants were saluting as fast as the right arm could move while the left held a sheaf of bills. Not wishing to patronize the money grabbers we ducked our heads and kept on moving in the crowd, ignoring the flapping arms.

We finally disengaged from the group and within a block from the theater a young corporal rendered a salute as I responded, "Corporal, do you know what happens to a soldier when a commissioned officer is saluted for the first time?"

Startled, he froze in place with eyes as large as saucers, "No, Sir, I do not."

"Well, custom dictates that the officer is required to present him with a dollar bill." With that I handed him the bill. He looked very perplexed but took the dollar and saluted again. "Hey, no seconds. On your way, soldier." He broke into a grin and continued on his way. I wondered what his story would sound like as he would surely recount this strange encounter to his friends.

We had known about the delay en route after graduation for several weeks. Sherry had managed to purchase two train tickets to Salt Lake City, where we had made arrangements to meet Cap and Sis. From there we would continue on in their car to visit our families in southeast Washington. Cap, who had also been flying AT-17s, graduated at Altus, Oklahoma, in the Gulf Coast Flying Training Command and we received our commissions and wings the same day. We had lots to be thankful for as well as to celebrate as it was a milestone passed for the four of us.

Our Texas friends, the Foleys, accommodated by transporting us and our baggage to the train station for a late afternoon departure before they headed for Corpus Christi. The Army had issued me a new watch, a pilot's briefcase filled with navigation computers and other pilot aids along with a fleece-lined flying suit complete with boots, a backpack parachute, oxygen mask, helmet, goggles, and other related flying articles. Not knowing what to do with all this equipment, which was packed in a large bag, I finally decided to have it shipped by Railway Express to Sherry's parents' home in Tekoa.

We boarded the dirtiest coach car that I had ever seen in service in the railroad system. The coaches were filled to overflowing with a raunchy-looking group of individuals. All were wearing dingy, civilian clothes. Sprawled over the seats and in the aisles, they looked and acted like refugees from a chain gang. They were slovenly and raucous. Since there weren't any seats available we moved to the end of the coach, plunked our suitcases down, and used them for seats. The group pretty much ignored us but we weren't entirely comfortable in their presence. They weren't the kind of people who would offer a lady their seat and I wasn't about to suggest it.

After about an hour of bumping along the rails a sergeant entered the car. Seeing the two of us he hurried over and said, "Sir, why are you sitting in the aisle?"

"Well, Sergeant, the train appears to be overloaded and this seems to be the only space available."

"I'll fix that in a hurry." With that he moved to the end seat in the coach and the occupants immediately disappeared into the next car. He returned and helped us move our bags to the vacant seat. As we moved in he leaned over and in a low voice stated. "I'm sorry, Sir, that you had to sit in the aisle. We just ran these draftees out of the bayou and we're headed for boot camp in California. By the time I get them in uniform and I've had them for two weeks they'll not only be broke to lead but will have enough manners to offer a lady a seat as well as show respect for an officer."

We were a little overwhelmed with the encounter, but I was sure the tech sergeant knew what he was talking about, and if these young men even suspected what the next few weeks held in store for them they would probably jump train.

As we settled back in the seat I opened my briefcase and sorted through the papers as well as my thoughts about the past few days. It dawned on me that I had not been able to say good-bye or thank you to a very fine instructor, Lieutenant Dye. The realization that I would no longer be scurrilously referred to as MISTER started to register. By an Act of Congress and an order by the President I was now an officer and a gentleman. I made a solemn vow never to violate this trust. I would find a way to carry out my duties in a manner consistent with the characterization of both. I had seen examples of the best and the worst. I knew which I would emulate.

Going through the orders I was surprised at some of the assignments. Ninety-four members were ordered to report to the Eighteenth Replacement Wing at Salt Lake City. These men were destined to become copilots. The list included my friend Lieutenant Luzader and the student officers, plus three officers who were already stationed at Douglas. The cadet who had flown to Santa Ana with me received a Flight Officer's commission and was also on the list. In all, thirteen out of the twenty-two who came from Lancaster, including Lieutenant Gadga, were subject to this order.

Five lieutenants were sent to Del Rio, Texas, for B-26 training, twelve were ordered to the Central Instructor School at Randolph Field, Texas. Lieutenant Ellsworth, the only other person from our Portland days, was in this group.

Four went to Selman Field, Louisiana, for unspecified duties. Seven were sent to Albuquerque, New Mexico, for B-24 Transition and twenty to Mather Field, California, for B-25 Transition. Seventeen stayed on the base at Douglas to be trained as instructors or whatever. Forty-seven were sent to Hobbs, New Mexico, for B-17 Transition.

Thirty-six of us were ordered to report to Roswell, New Mexico, for B-17 Transition training. All of the assignees for transition training knew they were being trained as first pilots in their respective aircraft. Our friends Lieutenants Foley, Fisher, and Gassman were included in this list, so the wives could look forward to another nine weeks of shared company.

I had received 26 hours and 30 minutes dual time, 52 hours and 20 minutes solo pilot time, plus 48 hours of copilot time for a total of 126 hours and 50 minutes in the AT-17. I had now flown 271 hours and 50 minutes in military aircraft.

Oh yes, Mr. Pulici, you can perform both forward and side-slips in the AT-17. In fact, it responds to these maneuvers very well.

6

B-17 Transition
and Crew Assignment

The dirty coal-burning train chugged into Los Angeles station about 9:00 a.m. The train was behind schedule which was probably normal, but it meant we had missed our connection and nothing else was scheduled until the following day. I ran to a phone booth and called the bus station, hoping that we could avert the long delay and continue on by bus. The station agent said the bus to Salt Lake City was due to leave in five minutes and only one seat was available. I immediately replied that I was a military flyer traveling on government orders and was accompanied by my wife. He stammered a bit and then said they would hold the bus for fifteen minutes and there would be two seats.

We hailed a cab and in a few minutes were at the bus station. I paid for the tickets while the driver loaded our two bags. Boarding the bus we found two seats, one in the middle and the other near the back. Within an hour after leaving the station the person sitting next to Sherry offered to change seats with me so we could sit together. Maybe the bars and wings brought some compassion from the bus load of civilians.

It was a long overnight drive to Salt Lake City. We arrived in the afternoon and were to meet Cap and Sis at Sherry's brother's home. He was an Army Air Force captain with the supply department stationed at one of the bases in the area. In civilian life he was a food broker but now he was a purchasing agent buying for the military. We had never met, so I wanted to make a good first impression. As we got off the bus we realized we were a mess. I was still in tan summer uniform which had changed color with smoke and coal dust from the train, and a two-day growth of beard did not enhance

187

my military profile. I was out of uniform for the area, cold, shivering, and dirty. The snow was about six inches deep.

We decided it would be best to rent a hotel room and clean up. That would also allow me to get into the proper uniform before being picked up by the military police. We tried two hotels but there were no rooms available. At the third I was sure we were in luck because a man was filling out a guest card at the front desk. When he finished I told the clerk we would like to register for a room but his reply was that the gentleman ahead of us had rented their last vacant room. Then I asked if it was possible to rent a room they might be holding for someone just long enough for us to bathe, clean up, and change into winter uniform. The clerk was sorry but he could not help us.

The gentleman who had just rented the room heard the conversation, stepped up to the desk, laid his key on the counter, and asked the clerk to let us use his room long enough to clean up. I offered to pay for towels and whatever was necessary. The clerk smiled and said the arrangement was all right with the management and they would have the housemaid clean up after us and supply the gentleman with clean towels at no charge to either of us. It was the least they could do for a military flyer and his wife.

We used the room and upon leaving thanked both the gentleman and the clerk for their hospitality. They seemed pleased to have helped. The silver wings employed magic qualities which were now becoming apparent. Anyway, before the day was over, clean-shaven and dressed in the proper winter uniform, I was able to meet Sherry's brother and his lovely wife and daughter. Cap and Sis arrived shortly after 6:30. We were all treated to a delicious dinner. Then the four of us loaded into a Champion Studebaker and started a nonstop, rotating drivers drive to Dayton.

On the way home I read Cap's orders. He had been assigned to the Central Instructor's School at Randolph Field, San Antonio, Texas. We both had the same reporting date, 15 November 1943. His orders read that "dependents will not accompany or later join the officer at this station."

During our time with Sherry's folks in Tekoa I went to the train depot and reshipped all of my flying gear back to Roswell. We had several days of visiting friends and relatives, then all too soon it was time to travel again.

Since Sis could not return with us the three of us started our around-the-clock drive south. We entered Roswell about 4:00 p.m. November 14 in the middle of a snowstorm. We stopped at the first motel in sight and by good fortune they had one vacancy. We very hurriedly removed our bags from Cap's Studebaker and bid him good-bye and good luck. He was due at Randolph Field the following day.

While we were moving our bags in, Lieutenant Norment Foley and his wife, whose nickname was Bill, pulled in looking for a place to stay. The motel was now filled so they drove off to continue their search. About nine that evening there was a knock on the door; the Foleys were back. They had not been able to find lodging and it was too cold and late to continue looking. Luckily we had two double beds separated by a wall divider so they could spend the night with us. It was an invitation they could not refuse.

The next morning Sherry and Bill toured the town looking for a home for the Foleys while Norment and I caught the bus for Roswell Army Airfield. After signing in we went down to the flight line to inspect the airplanes which we had now been assigned to fly. We were very impressed by the four-engine "Flying Fortress." It seemed almost too large to fly.

While we looked in disbelief at this aluminum-covered flying machine we were approached by a very proud crew chief who offered to guide us through his airplane. We accepted his offer and crawled into the largest cockpit we had ever seen. The crew chief very patiently explained in great detail the many mechanical features of the plane. His hands caressed the controls and his soft voice conveyed a sense of pride and love as he explained the various controls and their functions.

It didn't take him long to overload our minds as he related the specifications of the B-17F: gross weight 55,000 pounds, a crew of ten men, wingspan of almost 104 feet and a length of approximately 75 feet, powered by four Wright-Cyclone engines each capable of producing 1,200 horsepower and a top speed of 310 miles per hour. These numbers were beyond comprehension compared to the twin-engine AT-17. The jump in horsepower from 490 to 4,800 was almost ten times and every feature seemed to correspond to this same ratio. It was truly a mechanical marvel. To say we were overwhelmed would be a gross understatement. Here was an airplane that could fly for over ten hours, but there was no pilot's relief tube.

We could hardly wait to get home to tell Bill and Sherry what we had seen. When we finally exhausted their listening span and they were allowed to converse they explained that no housing could be found, so the spare bedroom invitation was again extended. It turned out to be an arrangement which lasted nine weeks.

B-17F cockpit and instrument panel

The next day we turned in all of the flying equipment we had shipped from Douglas. In classic army tradition it was the wrong issue.

Classes got underway immediately and we found that we had very little time for socializing even though we lived off the base. Drill and physical training were dropped, but new classes were added as we continued to learn about airframes, power plants, and all the mechanical marvels installed on the "17." A working knowledge was required of every system: mechanical, electrical, and hydraulic.

We met our flying instructors and again I was assigned to one of the finest flight instructors on the field. He was a very patient man who understood human nature just as well as he understood the mechanics of the airplane. He could teach anyone to fly the airplane whether they wanted to or not. In my case that was a plus since I was not happy looking forward to being responsible for nine other men. We had been told in cadet schools that the small men would become fighter pilots due in part to the small size of the cockpit. Wanting to be responsible for only myself, I was still dreaming of a twin-engine P-38 and its crew of one.

I started griping and suggesting that maybe a transfer was possible from the first moment we met. He took it all in stride and told me I was sent there because they thought I had leadership qualities and would make a good first pilot. But I didn't want flattery. I wanted a transfer to a P-38 fighter school and I kept on griping. Finally he told me that he would reluctantly sign my request for a transfer but that I would be making a big mistake. Most people wanted a command and here I was trying to turn one down, even though I was making good progress flying an airplane which many pilots would love to fly.

Together we filled out the request for a transfer, both signed it, and sent it to the squadron commander for approval. The next day as I was going down a deserted hall in Squadron Operations, I had just passed the Instructors' Room when I heard someone call "Lieutenant Fletcher." I turned around and saw a major standing in the doorway with a paper in his hand. He was just about my height and build, certainly not any bigger.

I immediately came to attention and held the salute. In a very nasty manner he stated, "Don't bother to salute me." Then he said, "I understand you can't fly the B-17."

I answered, "What do you mean I can't fly the B-17?"

Then he waved the request for transfer under my nose. "This paper means you can't. When you asked for a transfer it told me you can't do the job and are trying to shirk your responsibilities."

By now I was red-faced and trying to explain that I would like to fly fighters and it had nothing to do with my lack of ability to pilot a bomber. He kept on needling me to the point that if I hadn't been outranked I would have taken a swing at him. After a few more exchanges I lost my temper, looked him in the eye, and said, "You learned to fly the B-17, didn't you?"

He said, "Yes."

Completely out of control, I stated that I felt I was every bit the man that he was and if he could do it I could do it. Probably even better.

At this point, with a cynical smile, he tore the transfer in half, handed it to me, and said, "Good, now we will see whether you can." Then he spun on his heel and disappeared, leaving me shocked as I looked at the two pieces of paper. At this instant my instructor appeared and asked what happened.

Very sheepishly I said, "I think I just flunked Psychology 101."

With a smile he answered, "I know. I heard. And I'll tell you one thing, we better get busy because you are going to fly a check ride with him before you leave here." A note was made for the mental file as I learned another valuable lesson which I hoped would help me through a flying career and perhaps stay with me the rest of my life. It was essentially this: No matter how mad you get, don't let it affect your judgment. In other words, if you're going to race your motor, keep your brain working and take your mouth out of gear.

While the bar and wings seemed to hold magical qualities in the civilian sector, on the airfield we were still low man on the totem pole. The rank of second lieutenant was not a solution as we had hoped, it was only the beginning of the problem. With no recourse and the blunder of the day clearly in focus, I knew I had to exert every effort to become the best that my physical and mental limitations would allow. The old challenge of competition in the air, on the ground, and in the classroom returned. If I had to be a commander, those who would eventually fly with me were certainly entitled to the best that I could muster.

Learning to fly the "17" was hard work. We practiced emergency engine-out procedures which required maximum physical stamina to fly without trim control and manhandle a huge airplane whose controls were only aided somewhat by using natural opposing forces. The instructor worked our tails off but in a positive, constructive manner. We were challenged on every flight and in a matter of days I realized that the squadron commander was a very shrewd, knowing individual who knew how to motivate.

It wasn't long until I could relate to the attachment that the crew chief had shown for his big bird. The airplane captured our imagination and affection. We soon realized its capabilities far exceeded our imaginations. Its forgiving ways with student pilots brought admiration and a sense of security which no other airplane could match.

Lieutenant Foley and I had a ball as we tried to out-fly one another on our numerous buddy rides. Each demanded more and more of the other as we rotated from left to right seat. We picked the brain of every person who flew with us, including the instruc-

B-17 trainer

tor flight engineers whose total mechanical knowledge was tested on more than one occasion.

The second lieutenant syndrome vanished as we realized that it was the silver wings which provided us the opportunity to fly this "Queen of the Skies." Flying the left seat of the airplane elevated our status in our own eyes far beyond the meager rank pinned upon our shoulders.

As our flying progressed the group commander stated that we would not receive any leave time before reporting to our next station. But if everyone would cooperate and we fulfilled our requirements ahead of time we would be allowed to leave early and perhaps have two or three days extra travel time. This incentive caused everyone in Group Two to push to the limits.

Eventually it was time to fly the final check ride with the squadron commander. By this time we had both overcome the emotions of our first confrontation. It was a clear victory for him for he had kept his command intact. It was also a victory for me in that I was now flying an airplane in which I could exhibit pride and affection. Much of this confidence came from the fact that I could lose two engines and still be able to fly. Certainly there had to be safety in numbers.

The major had also demonstrated that he was too much of a gentleman to allow a petty squabble to affect his personality and judgment. But this is not to say that I got off easy on the check ride. In fact, my check lasted an hour longer than the others.

Yes, Mr. Pulici, I even demonstrated a forward slip in the B-17 and it responded perfectly. The major's only comment was, "We don't usually use or teach that maneuver, but you're going to a combat theater where you will have to use every maneuver you know in order to survive. That is the sole purpose of your training."

We were scheduled to finish on January 19 so it was a happy group that assembled in the base theater January 16 with all requirements satisfied. We knew we were going to hear the magic words "Well done. You have finished early and have earned two extra days."

The group commander was a major who enjoyed the respect of all present. He mounted the stage and explained that we had met our goal, but he was not able to deliver the promise that he had made earlier. In fact, we were going to be delayed one day longer than our original departure date. The base was to be inspected by a general from Headquarters Training Command, and a formation fly-over was to be performed by the members of the graduating class so the general could judge the quality of the training we had received. He knew he had raised our expectations and was proud of our performance but now he was forced to renege. He hoped we would understand and accept his apologies and recognize that he was subject to orders just the same as we were.

Everyone was disappointed and groaning, but one individual could not contain himself and yelled "bull shit!" which rang out like a bomb going off. Well, this was a definite lack of taste on the part of the second lieutenant and it was too much for the major. He called us all to attention and told us we would remain that way until the guilty party identified himself. After about ten minutes at attention the major said he was prepared to keep us all night if necessary, but he did hate to punish everyone just to get at the guilty party.

In a matter of a few minutes a fellow lieutenant and good friend stepped forward and confessed that he was the one who uttered the profanity in the heat of the moment. He said he was sorry, but he didn't want to see anyone else punished for his indiscretions. "Besides," he said, "I only said out loud what everyone else was thinking," which was, in essence, the truth.

The major requested that all be seated, with the exception of the guilty lieutenant, and he proceeded to give him the lecture and tongue lashing he had coming. When it appeared that everything was going to be resolved by another public apology to the major as well as to all present, another major from out of the crowd came up on the stage and told the commander that he should court-martial the culprit. A lively argument ensued while we were all sitting there with our mouths agape wondering what was going to happen. It was bad enough to be embarrassed by a member of our own group, but to be subjected to this verbal exchange by our superiors was more than we anticipated or wanted to hear. It had never occurred to us that there could be dissension above the level of a lieutenant.

Finally the group commander had enough. He turned to the second and replied that he understood why we were upset; he had made a promise which he couldn't deliver and he was sorry too. But he had orders and we would fly the formation. This we thought would end the controversy but, as usual, we guessed wrong.

The second major started to bug him again and at this point the commander turned and said, "Look, this is my command and my problem. I will solve it in my own way. This man said B.S. to me and I say B.S. to you. Now court-martial me!"

There was a stunned silence. Then came the order "Dismissed."

As we were leaving the room there were several lieutenants muttering that we would fly since we were ordered to, but the formation probably wouldn't look too good. This must have been overheard by the staff because the day the flight orders were given we were told at briefing that instructors would be on board to fly the aircraft.

After briefing when I had completed the ground check and was in the cockpit in the left seat, the instructor showed up. We were to fly in the lead unit of the big formation in the #2 slot, flying somebody's right wing. I was glad because the #2 slot was easier to fly from the left seat than the #3. The instructor who came to my airplane was not my regular one but an individual I had flown with several times. He told me to get my tail end out of the pilot's seat and get in the right seat. Grudgingly I got up and moved, asking him if as well as he knew me, he really thought I would try to screw up the formation. He replied he didn't know and didn't care. He was going to fly the airplane and to keep my hands off the controls.

I was doing a slow burn, but my answer was a prompt "Yes, Sir."

We finally got off the ground and had the formation formed when we were notified that the general's plane was an hour late and that we should clear the area. The formation flew around for over two hours before the general arrived.

The instructor was getting fairly tired and said I could fly the plane while he took a break. I replied that if he couldn't trust me when we started out and since his orders were to fly the airplane, he could keep on flying. A little later the order came that everything was "go" and we should proceed with the fly-over.

It was a beautiful tight formation that crossed the field. The general was impressed with the training we had received. The instructors flew their best and I'm sure the general was never told who was in the pilot seats.

When we landed the instructor told me to thank the good Lord that our training had been completed before this last flight, and it would be better if this incident would just remain on the field. For me I was happy to go since all of us were caught in a situation where there were no winners. But I still knew my instructors were the best and they had taught me more than enough to compensate for one embittered day.

Unbeknownst to us the group commander, during our layover, had worked out a plan whereby we could depart Roswell in the early evening on the day of the flight. The announcement was made while we were turning in our flying gear. We were to proceed to the railroad station and travel to the Eighteenth Replacement Wing, Salt Lake City, Utah, reporting there no later than midnight on January 22. Wives of the married men could accompany them on the train for a fee. The officers with autos were allowed to travel on their own. There were 153 first pilots on the order, including those with cars.

It was a mad scramble as we all rushed to clear the base, at the same time calling our wives to pack everything, check out, and meet us at the railroad station. We loaded aboard several coach cars whose run-down condition was a disgrace to the American railroad industry. It was apparent that anything that could roll had been placed in service; round wheels were not a necessary requirement.

The comfort and beauty of the passenger trains of the late thirties had disappeared completely, along with the Pullman and dining cars with white linen tablecloths, fine silver service, and finger bowls. Having experienced this service on several coast-to-coast trips plus several shorter trips in the East, I can only say that I had seen racehorses transported in better accommodations than the army was accorded. As a farm boy I had seen sheep and cattle being loaded for the markets in Chicago and Portland in better rolling stock than was being provided, but this was "wartime," an expression which excused every flaw in our society.

The coaches were eventually hooked to a slow-moving freight train which stopped at all milk stops and pulled off on every siding to allow the express trains to pass. The engine emitted a constant stream of black coal smoke as it labored its way along the rough tracks to the sidings to pick up more coal and water and eventually into the stations to discharge and pick up more freight. Occasionally we sat on country sidings for over an hour waiting for express and other traffic to clear the lines before we could move again.

The couples joined together to play a war game called "Battleship" while others played cards to pass the time, but eventually even these diversions lost their appeal. We were tired, dirty, and hungry; no provisions had been made for eating. The wives would have prepared picnic baskets had we known ahead of time the conditions we would face, but, as usual, the only information given was to board the train.

Almost thirty hours had passed when we finally pulled onto a siding in the outskirts of Denver. We could see the lights of a grocery store about a hundred yards in the distance. Four of the lieutenants jumped off and ran for the store where they hoped to buy bread, the makings for sandwiches, candy bars, or anything that was ready to eat. The wives had pooled some ration stamps for meat in case wieners or cold cuts were available.

Just as they disappeared into the store Old Smokey started to pant and labor its way back onto the main line. In several minutes the lights of the store disappeared. It was our shortest wait on a siding, just a little under four minutes.

Of the four lieutenants who jumped off, three were married. Sherry and I were kept busy consoling the newly widowed. Their main concerns were what would happen to their husbands since they had jumped train, how would they get together in Salt Lake, and so on. I wasn't much help, but all I could tell them was if their husbands could reach the base at Salt Lake City before midnight on the twenty-second nothing would happen to them since we were not required to travel by train anyway.

About halfway between Denver and Cheyenne in the pitch black of night we were again shuttled onto a siding in the bleak country-side where we waited an hour and a half for several trains to go by. Once again back on the main line we huffed and puffed our way into the station at Cheyenne.

As we came to a stop near the station, in the dim light, I could see our lost lieutenants standing on the platform with their arms full of grocery bags. They scrambled aboard the coach with cheers of the occupants ringing in their ears. As they doled out the good-ies they explained that the stationmaster at Denver had placed them aboard an express train which passed us while we were on the siding and they had been waiting for us for over an hour and a half. We decided that the lieutenants had violated protocol by car-rying the bags of groceries in public, so in the future only the wives would be allowed to make foraging trips.

The train finally pulled into Salt Lake City and again the search for housing became the order of the day. Sherry and I were ex-tremely fortunate to find a room at the Milner Hotel within the hour.

Checking in at the Replacement Center we found that forming crews would be delayed briefly since there was a shortage of air crew members. The brouhaha at Roswell over the extra three days required for the fly-over faded into oblivion as this brief delay last-ed two months. Our only duty was to report to the center for four hours on weekdays.

With the pressure of the rapid pace of training etched in our minds it seemed strange to have absolutely nothing to do but visit for hours. However, as copilots, bombardiers, navigators, engi-neers, and gunners reported in, the process of forming bomber crews began.

The crews were formed on the basis of psychological tests which were given earlier. People were assigned in a manner de-signed to avoid personality clashes. One member of the crew must have Type O blood, a universal donor, and no more than two peo-ple from the same state could be on one crew.

The first to check in was the copilot, Second Lieutenant Myron D. Doxon (M.D. Doc) from Auburn, Washington. It was his first assignment after earning his wings at the twin-engine flying school at Douglas, Arizona. He was blessed with a fun loving, infectious personality and perpetual grin, and it was immediately obvious he was going to add humor and color to the life of the crew. Doc was also a licensed civilian pilot and railroad conductor before joining the cadet corps just two weeks short of his twenty-sixth birthday. Now twenty-eight, he had the distinction of being the oldest man on the crew. Doc and his wife Margaret had a two-year-old daughter, Kimmie.

The next crewman assigned was Staff Sergeant Edward W. Brown from Wier, Kansas, the flight engineer gunner. He was a very serious, sincere, dedicated young man who proposed to make the Army Air Force his lifetime career. Ed had been a staff sergeant since 1942 and was used to working with flying officers. He had crewed several different airplanes including the B-17. Ed was single with a rural background.

Then came the radio operator gunner, Corporal George W. Hinman from Pinckneyville, Illinois. George was small in stature, a feisty, talkative young man from the farm country. He was an expert in code and I knew he would make up for my own deficiencies in this area. With his expertise he was a welcome addition to the crew. He was also married. His wife Mary added a quiet, stable influence to his life.

Corporal Joseph J. Firszt from Chicago, Illinois, was assigned as waist gunner. Joe was single and in addition to being a gunner he was also qualified in radio code and trained as a flight engineer. Joe was very quiet and a dedicated crewman.

At the same time Private First Class Kenneth C. McQuitty from Ardmore, Oklahoma, was assigned as the ball turret gunner. Ken was single, light complexioned, and small enough to fit in the ball turret. He had a good education and an easy going personality. It was apparent from our first meeting that this would be the individual that in jest everybody would play tricks on.

Corporal Robert L. Lynch from Muldrow, Oklahoma, was assigned as the armorer and waist gunner. As armorer, he would aid the bombardier in the loading and fusing of the bombs. Bob was eighteen, single, from a rural environment, and very shy and quiet, but he knew his job. His pleasant personality and slow southern drawl counteracted the hyperactive personality of some of the men and made him a good crew member.

Private First Class Robert C. Larsen from Montana was assigned as the tail gunner. Unfortunately he was hospitalized at our first duty station and was not able to fly with the crew. He was replaced by Sergeant Martin J. Smith from Milwaukee, Wisconsin. Smitty was married but was more of a loner so we did not know much of his background.

The last two to be assigned were the bombardier and navigator. The bombardier was Second Lieutenant Frank S. Dimit from Steubenville, Ohio. Frank was single, nineteen years old, and just out of bombardier school. The navigator, Second Lieutenant Robert C. Work from Urbana, Ohio, had graduated from college with a degree in accounting and had also just received his commission. He and Frank were ordered to report to us at Ardmore, Oklahoma, after completion of a ten-day delay en route which all cadets were given at commissioning.

We were not disappointed when these two men arrived. Their personalities were as different as day and night. Frank was very outgoing and quick to see the humor in every situation. He was a crack bombardier, and his infectious grin and pleasing personality soon endeared him to the crew. Bob Work (Roco), also single, was more serious and given to hiding his emotions. He was somewhat aloof, but he knew his job and there was no question he would hold up his end.

These were the men who were assigned to me as my first command. These were the men whose lives and fortunes were joined with mine, and with them the lives and dreams of their wives and families.

As I evaluated the crew members, we ranged in age from eighteen to twenty-eight with at least four of us having our roots securely anchored on the farm. Brownie was the professional soldier. The rest of us had never served in the military except for our training. It was then I realized that I was going to need the ability to inspire and to teach because only the engineer and I had ever flown the B-17. The rest of the crew, including the copilot, had never been aboard a four-engine bomber. With a lot of help from some very dedicated instructors I had just nine weeks at our operational training base to train a combat crew.

We made a lot of mistakes in the beginning, some so bizarre they defied belief, others life threatening, and some just plain amusing. But we survived our mistakes and by our last few training missions I was extremely proud of my crew. I knew they could do the job, but could I rise to their level? I found out on our first mission as we battled for survival against the best that the Axis Powers had to offer.

I was flying formation by instinct when I heard the dreaded in-

The crew. (Bottom row, left to right) *Eugene Fletcher, Myron Doxon (with daughter Kimmie on his lap), Robert Work, Frank Dimit;* (top row) *Kenneth McQuitty, Robert Lynch, Martin Smith, Joseph Firszt, Edward Brown, George Hinman*

terphone transmission, "Tail gunner to pilot. I've just been hit." In spite of the chill that went up my spine, the sweat was pouring. I immediately ordered the waist gunner, Bob Lynch, to check on Smitty.

After what seemed to be an eternity, Lynch's Oklahoma drawl announced, "He's okay. He was hit in the chest and had the wind knocked out of him. He'll have a bruise, but it didn't break the skin. Thank God for the flak vest!"

The old ship was taking a beating when Frank called, "Bombs away." In the same instant the radio operator reported that only half of the load had dropped. Six bombs were still hanging in the left-hand racks. We started evasive action as the formation loosened up. Every ship was on its own until we reached the Rally Point.

"Gad, won't the bombardier ever close the bomb-bay doors?" The answer came promptly: "Bombardier to pilot, the bomb-bay doors won't close." Almost immediately the engineer reported the electric motor for the bomb-bay doors had shorted out and was smoking. The motor was located on the forward bulkhead in the bomb bay, approximately three feet down from the catwalk and close to the fuel transfer lines. A fire in this position could eventually burn through the fuel lines, setting the whole aircraft on fire or creating an explosion. The only way to prevent it was to unhook the hot lead to the motor.

I ordered the copilot to take charge of the emergency and directed the crew to help him in every way they could as I had my hands full trying to keep the ship under control and catch the formation. I was not aware of the drama that was being played out behind me as the bombardier and gunners attached the ropes that formed the safety support in the bomb bay onto the D-rings of Doc's parachute harness. The waist gunners snapped the other end of the ropes onto their parachute harness. Forming a human chain, anchored by the bombardier, the engineer grasped Doc's legs under his arms with his hands locked in an "Indian grip." Slowly they inched forward putting some slack in the safety ropes. With a fire axe in his hand, Doc was lowered head first into the open bomb bay. The roar of the engines and the noise of the wind rushing up through the bomb bay separated me from the action of the crew. When Doc knew he was in position he swung the axe, and after several blows was able to sever the hot line, disconnecting the motor. Our fire hazard was averted. Dimit inched his way along the bomb-bay catwalk, 15,000 feet above the English Channel, replacing the ropes, while the others returned to their positions. Doc had been given a view of the Channel which he was in no hurry to repeat.

The crew had solved their problem in a very dangerous but efficient manner. Now it was my turn to live up to their expectations. Could I land a B-17 still half loaded with bombs with the bomb-bay doors open? I knew that the open bomb-bay doors had plenty of clearance when the aircraft was at rest on the ground, but what would happen on the shock of landing? How much would the landing gear compress when it took the full weight of the aircraft? The dilemma was mine to solve as I ordered the crew to prepare for a crash landing.

The old queen of the skies, no stranger to adversity, filled the role of a protective mother hen as she gathered the young crew under her wings and clucked the sound of confidence inspiring a green pilot to use his capabilities to make the softest landing of his career. Filled with holes and groaning under the weight of the bombs, she responded to the controls as she settled onto the runway with her bomb-bay doors barely clearing the tarmac. Delivering her brood to safety she discharged her chicks, a group of scared young men who had beaten the odds.

The age of innocence was over. This was the first and last mission where we would leave the base in happy anticipation of a confrontation with the enemy. We had learned that the enemy played for keeps and this was a dangerous game. We were so naive we did not recognize that the actions of these crew members who saved our ship and our lives constituted "heroism," and they were not awarded the Distinguished Flying Cross. But we did know we had become that most admirable, complex, and proud entity: a unified heavy bomber crew.

How we forged ourselves into an efficient combat crew, and how we fulfilled our obligations to ourselves, to each other, and to our country is told in another book, *Fletcher's Gang*, which documents the experience of our thirty-five missions against the Third Reich.

Postscript

The first things in life are never forgotten. This is not confined to aviation but applies to all aspects of society which include the thrill or aversion of any significant event in life. The firsts always stay with you to become the measuring stick by which all subsequent activities are judged.

So it was with the wide-eyed, shaken crew that crawled out of the battered airplane on 6 July 1944. This was not our toughest mission by a long shot, nor was it our easiest.

All of the first pilots who reported into the Replacement Center at Salt Lake City eventually were assigned crews and reported to Operational Training Units in the United States for nine more weeks of training. Most eventually were transferred to England where they became a part of the many groups which made up the three Heavy Bombardment Divisions of the Eighth Air Force. These were replacement crews which were used as substitutes for lost crews. Some took the place of those being rotated back to the United States and others were used simply to expand the size of the group.

Most of the pilots from the Class of 43-J were never to see one another again. Not all survived, but those who did went their separate ways and it was only by chance that occasionally paths would cross.

A Boeing engineer once told me that over 60,000 pilots, including Army and Navy, received primary training in the Boeing Stearman biplane. This was just one model of the primary trainer. There was also the Fairchild and Aeronca PT-19 series, the Ryan,

Fleet, and DeHavilland PT-20 series, and several other manufacturers of trainers involved. But for me it was enough to record the personal, human side. Figures such as these I leave to the dedicated statistical historians.

Now to give an accounting of the few cadets and events which are known to me:

My first Primary roommate, who washed out and to whom I gave the name of Lester, eventually became a ball turret gunner and was assigned to a B-17 crew while I was at Salt Lake City.

After graduating from the Central Instructor School at Randolph Field, San Antonio, Texas, my brother-in-law, Cap, was assigned there to teach instrument flying to other instructor trainees. My sister was allowed to join him. He received two other assignments and at the war's end was flying B-24s.

Norment Foley completed a tour of duty with the Eighth Air Force and returned to a farm in Texas. Unfortunately not all of his crew survived as they flew some harrowing missions. In 1985 he told me that I did not know what work was until I had filled the gas tanks of a B-17 in an open field in France with a five-gallon Jerry can.

Cadet Gene Jones made the Air Force his career. He flew thirty-five combat missions in B-17s with the Ninety-sixth Bomb Group stationed in England, plus ninety-nine combat missions during the Korean Conflict. He gained nationwide recognition on August 18, 1960. While flying a specially modified Fairchild C-119 cargo airplane, he snagged the first data capsule recovered in flight from an orbiting *Discoverer 14* satellite. In fact, he personally flew the airplane that recovered two of the first three capsules. His unit was awarded the Mackay Trophy for the outstanding Air Force flights in 1960. Jones also was the aircraft commander of a C-130 that set a nonstop nonrefueling world's record of 3,800 miles in ten hours and fourteen minutes for turbine-powered aircraft.

Lieutenant Colonel Jones was assigned as Chief of the Air Force Flight Test Division at Lockheed-Georgia in Marietta. While there he personally flew every one of the C-141s that came off of the assembly line. With this experience he was assigned as Air Force Project Officer on the C-5A Galaxy and was also appointed Air Force Plant Representative. In this capacity he was chosen to be the military pilot for the first acceptance flight by the Air Force of the C-5A, the world's largest airplane. He retired from the service in 1969 with the rank of colonel.

At Santa Ana, after the war, a high-ranking officer and two master sergeants were court-martialed for charging the cadet corps for government issue physical training clothing.

From the countless thousands at the cessation of hostilities, a number of air crew members chose to remain on active duty with the Army Air Force, but the major portion of this huge manpower pool elected to return to civilian life—many to either start or finish a college education, some to establish a business, and others to return to jobs in the cities or on the farm. A minuscule number of the flying officers who received the temporary Army of the United States commissions received Regular Army commissions, but over a five-year period as the Air Force became a separate branch of the armed service, most were offered the opportunity to accept or reject a reserve commission. Those of us who accepted, along with others who joined the National Air Guard, combined to form a civilian pool of flyers available to the armed forces in the event of a national emergency.

On June 26, 1948, the first pilots from this reserve were accepted as volunteers to help man the Berlin Airlift as supplies were flown to the beleaguered city whose land access had been cut off by Russian troops. Then on June 25, 1950, the North Korean Forces crossed the Thirty-Eighth Parallel into South Korea. Many of us from the Reserve and Guard Forces responded to provide additional air crew members for a limited time for participation in the Korean Conflict. Some of this group chose to remain on active duty and saw service during the Vietnam War, but for me the call of the farm was overpowering and I elected to return to reserve status.

In 1941 the nation faced an emergency. The young men responded *en masse* by enlisting in the Aviation Cadet Corps. The reader will have to judge the success of this tremendous program since those of us who participated are too prejudiced to make an honest assessment.

Notes on Sources

The sources of the information contained in this book were many and varied. There were the letters that I wrote to Sherry along with my personal recollections. The chronology is kept intact within the framework of army orders contained in my personal 201 file, a compilation of every order affecting an individual officer of the U.S. military. The flying experiences are documented by each flight as listed in the military and civilian pilot log books.

As we progressed through the training schools our actions were recorded in classbooks. Some information came from handouts that were presented to us upon entering these schools, and the Douglas, Arizona, statistics were provided in 1943 by the Chamber of Commerce.

Relevant information was provided by Colonel Gene Jones USAFRet, Lorraine Littleton McNew, Catherine Rawlings, and Leonard Patton.

In addition to my personal photographs, pictures were furnished by Jack Nelson, senior engineer, Boeing Company, Wichita, Kansas, and my brother-in-law, Leonard Patton.